LOVE AND OTHER EMOTIONS

LOVE AND OTHER EMOTIONS
On the Process of Feeling

Jason W. Brown

KARNAC

First published in 2012 by
Karnac Books Ltd
118 Finchley Road
London NW3 5HT

British Library Cataloguing in Publication Data

A C.I.P. for this book is available from the British Library

ISBN-13: 978-1-78049-071-7

Typeset by Vikatan Publishing Solutions (P) Ltd., Chennai, India

www.karnacbooks.com

This book is dedicated to those whose love has given so much meaning to my life; my mother, Sylvia, who guided me to the very end; my wife, Carine, who continues this task with tender charm and deep wisdom; and my sons, Jonathan and Ilya, who make it all worthwhile.

CONTENTS

ABOUT THE AUTHOR

Jason W. Brown has for many years been clinical professor of neurology at New York University Medical Center, with academic appointments in behavioral neurology at Boston University, Albert Einstein College of Medicine, Columbia-Presbyterian Hospital, and Rockefeller University. He has been adjunct professor at the New York Psychoanalytic Institute. He is the recipient of the prestigious Copernicus Award in Poland and has received fellowships for research study in Bonn, Paris, Bucharest, and Moscow, in addition to laboratories in the US. Dr Brown has published ten books and over 200 articles in behavioural neurology and philosophy of mind, the most recent book being *Gourmet's Guide to the Mind* (2011).

His website is jwbrown.centerforcognition.org.

PREFACE

This work is an extended essay on a theory of emotion, with love as the paradigm that brings together the central phenomena in the psychology of feeling: drive, desire, belief, and valuation. The theory (microgenesis) derives from studies that began with clinical pathology and have since been applied to a variety of topics in normal psychology and philosophy of mind. I think it is fair to say that except for psychoanalysis (psa), the strengths and weakness of which are discussed in Chapter Seven and elsewhere, there is no comprehensive theory that deals in a responsible or penetrating manner with the varieties of emotion and their origins and relation to brain activity. There is, of course, an enormous literature on this topic both literary and scientific: specifically, on the chemistry and physiology of mood, evolutionary continuities in the expression of emotion from higher primates to man, attempts to categorize emotions as local or piecemeal phenomena, the interpretation of the higher emotions or affect-ideas as mixtures of basic ones like a color wheel, but there is no serious attempt to relate one emotion to another in the spectrum of feelings, nor to understand the micro-temporal process that leads from drive to desire to image, act, and object, nor the transition from non-intentional moods to intentional desires and attitudes nor a coherent account of these psychological phenomena in terms of brain process.

The fundamental questions addressed in this essay are:

1. What is the nature of feeling?
2. What is the relation of feeling to idea?
3. Do ideas generate feelings, and/or do feelings generate ideas, and if so, how?
4. Or, are feeling and idea—emotion and concept—part of the same complex?
5. How do raw feelings relate to complex emotions?
6. How do differences in the intensity of an emotion translate to qualitative change, or the relation of quantity to quality?
7. What is the relation of inner feeling to outer display, or the relation of feeling to its "embodiment"?
8. What is the relation of instinctual drive to desire and the partial or "cognitive" affects? How do hunger and sexual drive relate to desire and affect-ideas?
9. What role do judgment and reason play in emotion?
10. Is intentionality distinct from feeling or an expression of feeling?
11. Do non-intentional moods develop to intentional feelings, or the reverse? If so, how does this occur?
12. What is the relation of the emotions, or a theory of emotion, to brain process?

Any serious theory of emotion must address these questions, which are fully discussed in this monograph. The essay makes no attempt to confront the vast contemporary literature on the topic (Prinz, 2004; Singer, 1994), since the research tends to be motivated, and the data interpreted, in line with prevailing assumptions of a modularity that is incompatible with process thinking and microgenetic theory. Much of this literature, or the claims that are made on its behalf, can in my opinion simply be ignored, for the concept of modularity errs in so many ways that time given to its disputation would be time lost. Philosophical speculation and scientific psychology tend to rationalize feeling, or replace it with judgment without explaining the intrinsic (or extrinsic if you will) relations between reason and emotion. Specific emotions or affective states are detached from their diachronic history, treated as phenomena apart from this history and localized in the brain, which is conceived as a hypothetical circuit board. Reduction—to brain or gene—does not explain psychological phenomena but merely transfers them to another level of explanation.

The effort here is to propose a novel approach to love and other emotions with links to belief, value, brain process, and evolutionary concepts, and in so doing, hopefully, to demonstrate the novelty, coherence, and explanatory power of the theory. While the roots of microgenetic theory lie in earlier studies of neuropsychology from which the account of emotion develops, especially more recent writings on a process psychology of value (Brown, 2005), of which love is the strongest and most genuine (positive) experience, this work is meant to stand alone without reference to prior writings or theoretical underpinnings, though an acquaintance with those writings would be helpful.

When someone is asked, what is love, or when they ask themselves, am I in love, there is such a diversity of descriptions that one hardly knows where to begin. Some don't even believe there is a thing or state of love; others believe it is all that is worth living for. Some describe their lover, or the lover they desire, by a set of properties, as if there is nothing more to people than the properties they exhibit, or that someone exhibiting those properties would readily evoke a feeling of love. Some say it is essential to love one's self before others can be loved, while there are those—perhaps the wisest of all—who admit they know nothing of love until it should come along. We have all heard such remarks and many others, so much so that writing a book on love is a daunting prospect. Yet I not only believe in the feeling of romantic love, but have chosen to start with the ideal of true love and make it the centerpiece of this essay, for that is the love that, apart from parental love, matters most and for the most people, and to which all lesser or generalized forms of affection are compared, take their cue, or emulate.

The work begins with a chapter on falling in love that illustrates many of the themes taken up later in greater detail, such as the irrationality of passion, the totality of commitment, the idealization of the beloved, the subjectivity of all experience, and the oneness of psychic union. These topics are central to personal experience and the popular imagination, but because of their subjective basis, for the most part they have not been considered in most scientific or philosophical works. This chapter is meant to prepare the reader for the general theory that follows, as well as a discussion of the diverse forms of emotion that all circle about love as a point of fixation. Further, the chapter will introduce the reader to the author's way of thinking, and provide a guide to ensuing chapters on the relation of love to kindred feelings, such as mercy and compassion, self- and other-centered values, pathologies of emotion, the relation of love to sexuality and non-erotic forms of attachment, to varieties of affection, and to reason and judgment and other topics in the philosophy of love.

An account of the emotions would be incomplete without a description of the brain process that underlies the derivation of the emotions from drive through desire to object value. The microgenetic theory of the mind/brain state is briefly discussed since it has been explored in detail in prior studies. Suffice it to say that the account of the mental state entails a rapid actualization over growth planes in the evolution of the forebrain: anatomically, from ancient core to neocortical surface; psychologically, from memory to perception, from concept to object, from past to present and from mind to world. States recur in rapid succession (Brown, 2010a, 2010b) with the different emotions, or conceptual-feelings, referring to dominant segments in this transition of phases. The final thought or behavior reflects the segments in this process that are emphatic over a series of states, but every terminus incorporates all phases in the state.

CHAPTER ONE

Falling in love

A man who is "of sound mind" is one who keeps the inner madman under lock and key.

—Paul Valéry, *Mauvaises pensées et autres* (1943)

Introduction

We have all fallen in love or wanted to fall in love, and for those who have truly loved, when they look back, they often feel that falling in love was often the most wonderful part of being in love. There are so many reasons why people love each other, not only romantic love but also the love for family, children, pets, and possessions. One can fall in love quickly, at first sight as we say in English, in a *coup de foudre* (struck by lightning) in French, or love can grow slowly like a friendship that becomes romantic. The sexual can be a powerful bond or it can pull a couple apart. There are loves and longings that are stronger for being unconsummated. A couple can meet at a bar, a blind date, or on the internet. There is the wanting to fall in love, the fear of love or dependency, thoughts of past loves, inhibitions, biases, predispositions, loneliness, commitments to others, treasured memories, and painful disappointments.

There is the readiness, the timing and openness for a new love, issues of gender, age and social or educational inequality. There is the relation to hate, despair, rejection, humiliation and sacrifice, and to feelings of agency and helplessness. Given the complexity of the context behind every act of love, and the multitude of needs and predispositions, one can say that there are no wrong reasons for falling in love, just the wrong people to fall in love with. The topic is so difficult that it is unlikely any two people will agree on a given interpretation. Still, mindful of the warning above, I would like to offer some thoughts on this age-old subject from the standpoint of process (microgenetic) theory.

Psychology of love

Love is a form of value, and value takes many forms. It begins with drive in the unconscious (Ucs) core of the self. Core value is bound up with drive in relation to the self-preservative instincts, such as hunger. For microgenetic theory, the core category and the drive do not come together but are fused from the beginning in a single construct. Specifically, every affect has a conceptual frame and every concept has an affective tonality. The broader implications of this view are that feeling is the process of becoming and concepts (objects) are the substance of being (Brown, 2005).

The initial drive-representation is hunger, which is primary and unitary, replicating the self. Sexuality develops later as a secondary drive, replicating the species. First, the organism is replicated, then the population. Aggressive and defensive attitudes are vectors of drive expression. They take the drives outward in approach and avoidance, fight and flight, domination and submission. The category of the drive-representation develops to a concept and its affective tone, what I call conceptual-feeling, that aims to an object. The global pre-object (category) of drive narrows to the object (concept) of desire (fear, etc.), that is, the drive-category specifies an object-concept. Core self- and drive-category, say the unconscious self and the drive of hunger, partition to the conscious (Cs) self, concepts, images, and intentional feelings. Concept and feeling, though bound together, are now directed to objects that fulfill or satisfy feelings such as wishes, desires, or fears. A desire can be for an object in immediate perception or one thought about. It can be in the present, past, or future. The ability to think about an absent object is probably uniquely human. It is essential to loving, which develops so much in the imagination.

Instinctual feeling begins with a drive-category in the unconscious self and fractionates to conceptual feeling in the conscious self, where the object-concept is bound up with intentional feeling such as hope, fear, or wish (see Figure 2.1). The object-concept and its affective tone—the idea or memory of the person and the feeling for the person that expand in the imagination as part of the developing object—continue outward to become valued objects (others) in the world. This may be a difficult part of the theory to understand but to the extent such data are relevant to the theory, it is consistent with work on brain imaging. For example, the caudate nucleus is active in individuals who have just fallen in love. In those who have been in love a longer time, anterior cingulate and insula are activated (Fisher, 2004). The caudate and linked structures are associated with drive states, the latter regions are part of the wider limbic formation associated with subtler affects and experiential memory.

The debate in psychology whether love is volition or need, that is, intentional or involuntary, or what role decision plays in falling in love, reflects the proximity of the dominant segment to drive or to desire. The closer to drive, the more love is like unconscious need. The closer love is to desire, the more it is like wish, want, and intentional feeling. Volition does not precede and motivate action or emotion but is part of the same phase to which emotion develops. More precisely, the phase of desire is also one of volition, choice, and intentionality. One does not cause but accompanies the other. There is no sharp distinction since the dominance of one phase over another fluctuates. One moment an individual is madly in love, the next, there is indecision or uncertainty. This reflects the momentary accentuation of one or another phase in the actualization sequence. Love can begin with need and evolve to desire or it can begin with desire and descend to need, and find its complement in the needs of the beloved.

The conceptual-feeling—the feeling inside the developing object or object-concept of the beloved—externalizes with the beloved yet remains part of the pre-figuring concept. The feeling of desire that is part of the beloved in the object-development externalizes in the lover's mind as it moves outward into (as) the external world. We think the objects we see are the real physical entities that exist as we see them.

Actually, the world is the outer rim of the mind filled with perceptual images that appear outside and independent of the mind in which they develop. This does not imply the absence of a physical world, for unless a person is mentally ill or dreaming, the model is so accurate it might as well be the real-world.

We are usually unaware of the small quota of affect that inhabits all objects in the perceptual field. The trickle of feeling in the external field traces back to the drive-category. The perceptual field divides into innumerable objects like the tributaries of a great river, while the feeling that accompanies them narrows down to a partial affect. This feeling is the seed of object value. We know this occurs because in cases such as schizophrenia with depersonalization or derealization, feeling is withdrawn and objects seem unreal or mechanical. The change affects all objects, trees, dogs, people, who now appear as props, automata, or mannequins. The object also withdraws. It no longer exists as real and independent. The feeling that normally goes out with the object is felt within the mind from which it developed. When this occurs, the object becomes more thought-like and less independent. If the withdrawal is more extreme, or the world and its feeling-tone do not fully exteriorize, as in psychosis, the person may not know if he is awake or dreaming.

A similar process occurs in love, as the loved object withdraws to antecedent phases in the imagination where the real growth of love occurs. It is not without reason that one says, I am crazy about you, or I am madly in love with you, or to say one's "head is in the clouds"—in French, "septieme ciel"—for lovers are presumed irrational. To say one is "head over heels" in love does not mean postural disequilibrium but mental instability. By irrational is implied that love is not the result of a reasoned analysis or decision, not concerned with truth but reinforced by *post hoc* justifications. More importantly, true, passionate, or romantic love depends on layers in mind that are unconscious, pre-logical, and bound up with animistic and metaphoric thought (see below).

Interest

The initial sign of feeling in the world is the existence and reality of objects. We know this because it is altered in psychotic cases, when feeling is withdrawn and objects seem unreal. An affective tonality accompanies the object as it develops outward to the world. Ordinarily, this trickle of affect is evenly distributed over the field. Interest occurs when feeling is re-allocated from a uniform distribution in the field to one object or event (Figure 1.1).

Let us ask, what happens when you first see the person you will fall in love with? In the beginning, he or she is just another person in the world. Interest is the first sign of value, or value transmitted outward into the object as worth. It is located between desire in the mind and the trickle of feeling in the object, straddling inner and outer as an accentuation of the feeling that passes outward with the object. Interest can be weak or strong, and felt as personal or impersonal. We feel interest for someone or something, but we may also say that someone or something has interest for us. We say I am interested in that person or that person interests me, as if we are uncertain whether interest comes from

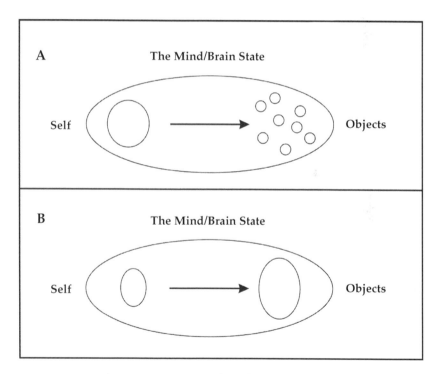

Figure 1.1. Feeling accompanies the object-development outward to perception. All objects have an affective tonality that is ordinarily evenly distributed over the field (A). With interest, affect becomes concentrated in one object or event as other objects fade into the background (B). This focal attention, or interest, is the initial stage of love.

the self or the other. Interest may start as a slight preference. Interest is perceived as value for an object (other) or the value the object has for itself. We say beauty is in the eye of the beholder, and we say love is in the heart, but it is the act of loving or beholding that transfers those qualities to what is perceived. According to an emphasis on the inner or outer pole in the trajectory of desire from the core self to external objects, value may be felt in the self as need, want or evaluation, or it can be assigned to the object, as worth or intrinsic value.

The composer Janáček asked, why do I pick this daisy in a field of daisies? Why did I notice this person in a room filled with other people? Often we cannot say what attracted our attention. The preference is derived from earlier unconscious segments, of which value in the other is a surface manifestation. The feeling that is normally distributed over the entire field is now enhanced in one object. Interest occurs when the feeling hidden inside all the objects of the field is sequestered in just one. It is a mode of attention to one object at the expense of others. We are speaking of love, but an object of interest can be anything, a flower, a rock, an idea, or a sunset.

With interest, a phase preceding objectification is activated so as to dominate the perception. Other people and events recede into the background. Put differently, feeling (and its object) undergo a retreat from externality—though the world remains external—and the phase of inner feeling is accentuated. At this point, the value of the other is not pronounced. Attention may be distracted or shift to someone else. You may never see the person again. But suppose there is an exchange of glances or smiles, and the interest is mutual. You talk to each other and discover after minutes, days, weeks, or months that interest has grown to curiosity, even affection. The person takes on greater value; his or her attributes are now special, unique, and admirable. You think about the other and want to be together. At some point, if feeling grows, you realize you are in love. This can happen even if you are not loved in return or with the same intensity, though usually the one who loves imagines or hopes to be loved, or thinks it is only a matter of time before the love of the other is received, or believes the more love that is given, the more love will be returned.

This scenario is familiar to all who have loved, or believed they were in love. The reason that falling in love for many is so intoxicating is that the value flowing into the beloved is, in reality, surging in the self. For interest or valuation, the dominant segment in the actualization of the other recedes from full objectification to an idea or ideal. The other is no longer another object in the world but a concept in the imagination. At this phase, feeling is magnified. As interest becomes more intense, other feelings are evoked, curiosity, intrigue, anxiety. The feeling that went out to the world calls up earlier segments in the actualization process, precursors associated with wish, hope, or desire. The object of interest no longer need be present. Feeling is linked to the concept, not the actual person, allowing it to fade or grow stronger in the imagination. The transition from interest or focal attention to affection and love recaptures segments—markers—of phases in the original perception as the dominant segment descends (is revived) to the Cs self.

Gradually, the other becomes the beloved. The fulfillment of desire creates a sense that the beloved complements an imagined emptiness before the beloved appeared. The union with the beloved gives the feeling of wholeness or completeness not present before. It is the basis of the oneness or the soul-mate that lovers are seeking. The intensity of feeling that goes into the beloved increases his or her worth, which in turn validates the love that is given and is often sufficient to overcome deficiencies—or idealize them—and offset setbacks, arguments, and rejection. The fights and reproaches establish the limits and test the bonds between lovers. After an argument, she wonders, will he call? He asks, will she return? A love that survives builds up trust, but over time disputes can lead to resentment.

The activation of feeling and the inward retreat have parallels in other spheres of object-concepts. In meditation, the focus begins with a single object or activity at the expense of others. All objects save one are unattended, and as that one grows, others recede. Eventually, attention is suspended from all objects except one. There is withdrawal to antecedent object-concepts, then deeper categories, finally it is claimed, to the ultimate ground of existence. Mystical regression is like love in that it leaves behind the world of objects in a descent to non-self, oneness, and total immersion. There is an absolute focus and faith in the object of feeling. The mystic will endure deprivations and mortifications to achieve god-union. The lover will go through rings of fire for his beloved. We do not without cause say all is fair in love and war. In Christian mysticism, Christ is the lover and the end of descent is union with god in love. Love for another person is like this in that the goal is selfless union with the beloved. David Bradford has written, with good reason, that love is mysticism for the ordinary man.

The flow of feeling and objects into (as) the world makes everything that is seen, touched or heard seem vibrant and alive. Feeling arising in the observer is felt *in* the object and *in* the observer. In primitive mentality, the awareness of mind in objects is the basis of animism, in which all nature—animals, trees, the wind, the tide—is penetrated by mind or spirit. The separation of internal and external is indistinct. Objects take on totemic or magical powers. The layer of animistic thought close to dream, just beneath the surface of rationality, comes to the fore in love when we say we have fallen under a spell or think of love as a kind of magic, an enchantment, as in fairy tales of witches brews and magical potions that make one fall in love.

If the beloved, and the feeling *for* the beloved and, I would add, the feeling perceived *in* the beloved, all flow out of the lover's mind, this transfer or ingress of feeling must be the basis for perceiving others as having feelings of their own. This concept is difficult to grasp. We see people and assume the feelings we recognize belong to them, not us. We have certain feelings about a person, but we do not believe the person's feelings come from us. We do not think we are the cause of that person's anger, pride, envy or depression. It seems strange to say that feelings in others are derived from our selves. But causing feeling in the other, and feeling the other's feeling, are different events. Everything happens in the observer's mind, including the feelings perceived in others, which trace back to the observer. This does not mean we create those feelings, no more than we create the person who feels them, even if the other is an image created in the observer's mind. Others and their feelings are self-realizations, models of what we think they are truly like. Because we see a model, not the real thing, we can easily be mistaken when our own thoughts and feelings are read into someone we love. This explains why we are often misled in thinking we are loved as much as we love. We see a smile or feel a hand on our arm, have warm conversation or exchange sex, and imagine those gestures are signs of the love we are seeking. For a long time we may deny we are deceived or unloved. If we acknowledge this fact for someone we love deeply, we feel foolish and betrayed. Unrequited love invalidates the love we feel and vitiates the worth we extend to others or attribute to what is truly in their hearts.

The "chemistry" of love

We often speak of the "chemistry" of love, not as a chemical reaction but as a sign that we do not really know what accounts for who we fall in love with. We can describe the qualities of the other and say this is the basis for our love, but the reasons are deeper and impossible to know. After all, to say the lover fulfills something the self needs or lacks, or that the person we love completes the self, assumes that people know themselves so well they can say what is lacking in their self-concept. Most people have no idea what their core self is like. It is unconscious, and thus unknowable. We are informed of who we are by the consciousness of our acts and thoughts, the patterns in our behavior, and the reactions of others. We know ourselves as little as we know the reasons why we have fallen in love with a particular individual. This is why we so often make mistakes when we fall in love. The choice of a partner can say more about who we are than all the analyses, self-justifications, and rationalizations that come with it.

This points to the fact that the idealization of attributes is not sufficient to account for love, for too often love is as much for imperfections, weaknesses, or vulnerabilities as for positive attributes. Here we see the influence of Ucs need over conscious desire. The inability to know the Ucs core and the shifting Cs self leads many to search for the true, genuine, or authentic self that is assumed to underlie its surface manifestations. The problem for the one who loves is that even greater knowledge of the true self, if there is such a "thing" as the true self—which is knowledge that comes to some naturally with aging and an acceptance by way of the reactions of others, or from successes and failures in life, that is, a pragmatism as to personal strengths and weaknesses—does not prevent the incomplete self from loving someone who fulfills or completes them in one way but mistreats or disappoints them in another, for others have needs of their own that may not be satisfied by the one who loves them.

This core Ucs self has the beliefs and values that make up character and the attitudes and behaviors of an individual personality. These determine who, how and what we will love. In passion, if not in platonic love, the choice may reflect a failure to accept shortcomings, or an excess of pride and contentment. A person who chooses someone to complement or fulfill what he or she is lacking achieves a degree of completeness that can provide a sense of a single self shared between lovers. Such love is symbiotic or parasitic. Opposites attract but they are often in conflict. There can be a build-up of tensions over lack of agreement on matters great and small, when and where to eat, where to go, spend vacations, enjoyments, religion, children, and so on.

The greater the difference, the less able is the individual to absorb the other in loving union.

Love for a person (or animal) and love for a thing

The philosopher Jacques Derrida spoke of *l'amour pour quelqu'un et l'amour pour quelque chose*, the love for someone and the love for something. We know there is a difference in the love for another person and the feeling for a coat, a house, or a diamond ring, but what exactly is this difference (Ch. 5)? How does the love for a person differ from that for a dog, a cat, a horse, a bird, even from a work of art, a jewel, a gown? We long for the love of a beloved, but in a pet we expect or imagine affection. The love for pets is instructive in that it is transitional from the love of people to the love of things. We attribute all sorts of human-like feelings to pets. We believe we are loved by a cat that rubs against our leg when all cats behave in this way. When a cat lies in our lap we take this as affection, not that it is the warmest place in the room. We believe in the love and loyalty of a dog even if these are instinctual responses. A dog is as loyal and subservient to its master as it would be to the leader of a pack.

The feelings attributed to a pet are an example of the process through which value grows to love for a person, and the process through which feelings from that person, real or imagined, are felt in the mind of the lover. In the beloved, as in a pet, we see a reflection of our own needs, who we think we are or want to be or what we are lacking. An elderly woman who lives alone with many cats may be lonely or have a need to care for a lost companion. A man with a ferocious dog may project in the pet some attribute of his personality—misanthropy, aggression, even timidity. The point is that feeling invested in others—people or animals—are outcomes of the self's own needs and desires.

If you love someone strongly, it is hard to be convinced to stop. This is especially so when the love is reinforced by the other. Reciprocity is usually needed if the love is to endure. One can feel feeling from a pet as well as a person. The flow of feeling from a lover or pet, even if imagined, is sufficient to sustain its value. The loyalty of a pet, its companionship, its mere presence, is often more than one receives from a lover. No wonder many prefer their dogs to people. Moreover, as with a lover, no one can persuade you not to love your dog no matter how badly it behaves. Even a dog that is ugly to others is beautiful to its master.

In contrast, non-living objects like jewelry or clothing, which do not return affection, tend to need vetting by others to justify their value or worth and the love you have for them. You love your diamond more if it is large, white, and flawless. You think your house, your furniture, your dishware, are more beautiful than those of your neighbor. With art, wine, or other fine things, the opinion of connoisseurs is important. For most inanimate objects it is important that others also find them valuable, whereas lovers and pets return affection and have less need of consensus. The essential difference between the *quelqu'un* and the *quelque chose* is that the latter tends to require approval as to worth, while the former is so invested with feeling, and reciprocates love or its simulacrum, that its value is relatively independent of opinion.

Fated to meet

Many couples invent a mythology about their first meeting. It may have been at a singles bar or on the internet, but they insist that had they not turned down another engagement, looked the other way at just that moment, stayed home or went to a movie, that is, decided to do anything other than what brought them together, they would never have met and this twist of circumstance leads them to think that some powerful force must have been at work in bringing them together, a force that for them is usually fate, destiny or the hand of god. This is not just acknowledging the role that luck plays in a happy life or the conjunction of two events. It is more than good fortune. There is a difference in saying, had she not laughed, I might never have noticed her, and had I stepped out of the car a moment sooner that brick would have fallen on my head. If I have the bad luck of a brick falling on my head or the good luck of winning the lottery this is not felt as fated or inevitable. It is merely a matter of good or bad luck. But in matters of the heart there are no accidents. How can we understand this difference?

Is contingency so colored by love that we strive for meaning in what is otherwise a chance encounter? We find no meaning in sheer randomness. The myriad possibilities of such events are perceived as independent of the agent. Yet people tend to think that the choice in a romantic meeting is largely binary, that is, doing one thing instead of another, in contrast to the accident of a brick falling on my head or the multitude of possibilities in a lottery, or even the millions of potential lovers one could meet. The multiplicity of chance is "out there" in the world, and so we would say are the odds of meeting someone you love. But once you meet that person, the chances seem binary, since they are now in the mind of the lover. The likelihood of meeting a particular person then reduces to a personal decision the individual has made, voluntary or not, that plays a central role in the encounter. In deciding to go for a walk instead of staying home, there are two options in which agency and intention have a part. The innumerable possibilities external to the decision collapse to the two or three possibilities internal to it, with the encounter perceived as the outcome of a lucky choice. Here we see the distinction of contingency and probability in the world and agency or agent-causation in the mind. For the lover, there is a tendency to look back to the reasons for the encounter or what events led up to a meeting. Not finding any that are persuasive, the person leaps to the conclusion that the decision was an outcome of fate, or an act of god, as when we speak of "a match made in heaven."

There is also the paradoxical fact that a match felt as fated to occur deprives the lovers of freedom, which may reflect the helplessness we feel to a love of great force. One does not decide to fall in love; it is something that happens to us. Fate is invoked in the felt absence of free will. Passivity or lack of agency can be interpreted as a state of possession, in which the lover has lost control or assigned it to the beloved. The suspension of agency points to the locus of love in the imagination. Some forms of imagery such as thought images are accompanied by volitional feeling; others such as memory images seem partly volitional, while still others, such as eidetic images, dream, and hallucination come unbidden.

There are, of course, other reasons why couples want to believe they were fated to meet. The idea adds romance and mystery to a meeting that would otherwise be commonplace. The notion that the couple is destined to meet creates an illusion of uniqueness in a sea of homogeneity by lifting the couple out of the great mass of ordinary humanity. The love affair becomes part of the narrative of a life and adds significance to the saga of an otherwise mundane individual history.

Cupid's arrow

Once in a while, perhaps once in a lifetime, but definitely not once a week, at least not for a desire that is more than sexual, you may fall in love all at once. You see someone and without knowing anything about the person, you know immediately you are in love. A love so intense and incendiary can make one question whether other loves in the past were genuine. There is a sudden overwhelming feeling this person is the one you have been waiting for, the one that fate had in store for you, the man or woman of your dreams, even if the person is not, as is often the case, exactly what you imagined. On reflection, you may wonder what it was about the person that attracted you, for he or she may not at all be your type, perhaps the very opposite of what you thought you wanted, certainly not the picture of a future lover in your conscious fantasies. If asked why you fell in love you might say it was because he was so handsome or she was so beautiful, or his eyes, or her smile, but the truth is, you really don't know.

One explanation is that such a love is like the imprinting of an instinctual gestalt in animals, when a sudden response is triggered by a particular form, such as ducks to their mother or pigeons to a hawk. Could a long-forgotten face of someone you have seen or known in early childhood, or some feature of that face, account for this reaction? Is it the movement, the manner, the voice, a gesture, some quality that is felt to be hypnotic and irresistible? It is not the character or personality that is assimilated and loved, or the reciprocity of the other that is needed, rather something inexplicable that activates Ucs feeling. We suspect this from the dissociation of the Cs perception of the person you fall in love with and the one you thought you would fall in love with. I am not even sure an individual must be predisposed to fall in love, for this can happen without seeking, or to someone who thinks they are already in love, in anyone at any time in their lives (see p. 177 for further discussion).

I do think many of us would agree that we can read a personality in the face. In some ways, the face is the fingerprint of the soul into which feelings and experiences are etched. Is it the face alone that arouses the love, or is it the person behind the face that is grasped in a sudden intuition? Do we have Ucs templates of the other that guide our choices, a kind of amalgam of our needs and wants, an archetypal image that underlies Cs knowledge? Is that person the only individual who could elicit such feelings, or are there thousands, millions, of others with whom one could suddenly fall in love? Is this image the construct of a need of which the individual is unaware or refuses to acknowledge? Is the force and suddenness of the feeling related to the desperation or loneliness of the person even if it is not consciously admitted? Does the need for the love trump the nature of the object? I suppose this is why we idealize those we love and describe them as gods or goddesses, as heaven-sent, for they realize near-mythic structures in the recesses of our most primitive longings.

Another difference between falling in love gradually and all at once invokes an analogy with the automatic expression of character in saving the life of someone drowning as opposed to the deliberation that precedes a moral choice. In the spontaneous act of saving a life, the life of the other is of all-consuming importance. One's own life no longer matters, only the one to be saved. This is comparable to falling in love all at once, when the other is suddenly of supreme importance and the self is "lost" in devotion. In moral deliberation, decision settles in as the self inclines to one line of thought. This is like gradually falling in love as other possible lovers are forfeited to one of infinite value. Moral deliberation entails a conflict of values and the coalescing of reasons to justify a choice. Similarly, the lover finds reasons to support the valuation bestowed on the beloved.

If this analogy holds, love at first sight would not reflect a purely sexual attraction—as many say—but would betray the character, the beliefs and values, of the individual in an immediacy that is ordinarily concealed in the derivation to consciousness. We think we know an individual by his actions over time—as we fall in love over time—but we also know a person by the immediacy of action. It may well be that the same person would elicit spontaneous and gradual love, just as the same moral decision would be reached whether action was immediate or delayed. A Cs decision in moral action may be too late, as a lack of confidence in sudden love can lose the love of one's life forever.

Submission and dominance

Perhaps more than we would like to admit, submission as the relinquishment of ego and self in service to the beloved, and dominance as its obligatory response, are part of loving. Submission in a shared love is not abject servitude but a reconciliation of complementary attitudes that ranges from acquiescence to surrender of will, even to death in love's service. There is no greater act of love than to die for the beloved, in sacrifice, protection, or in suicide when the partner is lost. We say one dies of a "broken heart" in grief or disappointment. Without the beloved, there is no wish to go on living. In literature, *Romeo and Juliet* are the great models, but we are all familiar with other examples.

What greater confession that the beloved has fully infiltrated your heart, that you are defined by the other, or that the other has so replaced the self, than to kill what is left of you when your lover is lost?

When we think of submission we do not think of selfless devotion but of the extremes of sadism and masochism, which have little to do with love. These are distortions of giving and receiving that become forms of psychopathology. Sadism is pleasure in pain inflicted on others, often linked to the sexual drive. Masochism may be the enjoyment of such pain, but it is also a way of offering one's self for reciprocity or engagement. One can love or need a person so much that you accept punishment for interest. Some people require abuse and put up with constant rejection, even brutality, to satisfy a need or in the hope of gaining love in return.

Sadism and its opposite are not fully sexual nor are they part of love but are related to aggression and defense as vectors for the drives (Ch. 2). In some respects they caricature the giving and receiving of lovers when the needs of the flesh conflict with the ideal of romantic love or, for that matter, with compassion or parental love, where giving is a kind of submission to the other's needs. When giving becomes sexualized, and reciprocity becomes punitive, the delicate balance of mutual surrender that love requires is exploited in carnality or enslavement.

Not all acts of submission are repaid by unkindness, and some such acts are the epitome of unselfish love. My favorite example is the love of the poet Friedrich Hölderlin (1969) and his beloved Susette Gontard. In his epistolary novel, *Hyperion*, Hölderlin chronicles love and longing in the letters of Diotima—who revealed to Socrates in the *Symposium* the secrets of love—for whom Susette was the model in life. What is fascinating about this couple is that Susette was said each day to read a portion of the novel to organize her day according to the events depicted, as if Hölderlin had written the script for her life (Linke, 2005; and in conversation). There are people who have a life plan according to which decisions are made, and there are those who surrender their freedom to the will of others who control them like puppets in every detail, but it is unusual to have your beloved live a life of such dedication that it conforms to a work of literature, with life imitating art in a story written by your lover without the knowledge it would one day be interpreted in relation to daily life. Possibly, Susette was so moved by the beauty of the writing that she assumed the *persona* modeled after her to imbibe in life the passion of this great epic poem.

The fact that Hölderlin became increasingly psychotic and was institutionalized in his thirties makes one wonder if a kind of *folie a deux* led Susette into a path of romantic pathology. Did she "stick to the script" of her brilliant young lover as mental illness undermined his judgment? I mentioned the need that many lovers have to create a narrative of the initial meeting, but it is astonishing that Susette's lover wrote the book according to which she lived her life. This story shows as well as any the depth to which lovers will go to exemplify their passion and how, as we all know, love begins, deepens, and remains in the imagination.

The soul-mate

Many believe a chief task of life is to find the soul-mate as a life-partner and spiritual half, a beloved that is not an attachment but one who fulfils, completes and fuses with the soul as a spiritual correlate of the core self. More than having interests in common, even sharing a heartfelt love, this is the merger of two into one without remainder, a fusion that is the key to understanding the true nature of love, and providing insight to other modes of value and profound emotion. This belief has undergone some revision in modern times. Indeed, Singer compares union and oneness to a joint bank account. The search for autonomy which is so prevalent in our times is in conflict with the surrender to the beloved, a tension between loss and assertion. One is reminded of Pascal's definition of man as "a being of dependence, longing for independence, and having needs." Progressive autonomy is the natural pattern but this leads to separation and alienation, thus the need for regression and return to earlier holistic phases of the core personality.

From a microgenetic standpoint, the other, the beloved, is an image in the lover's (self's) mind, not an adjunct. There are as many levels in the other as in the self that is its source. The lover realizes the beloved in part as fantasy by way of the inner segment of the process, and in part objectively by the outer segment that is modified and externalized by sensation. The combination of inner and outer in the mind appears in the lover's multi-layered representation of the beloved. Within the mind of the lover there is a depth and a surface *for* the beloved, and a depth and surface *of* the actual beloved in the lover's mind, that is, a self- and other-realization in the same mind. The subjective phase contributes the imagination, hopes, fantasies, and magical thinking that fill love with signification and make it so rapturous and intoxicating. The outer phase contributes an image of the objectively real to which the inner phase is forced to adapt.

Put differently, the self perceives the beloved as a valued object in the world. The micro-structure of this object in the self's perception traverses phases of experiential memory, meaning, and feeling, all of which are part of the final perception. When we look at our beloved, all of these antecedent phases are active. In addition to the stream of experience and feeling that lie behind and generate the beloved as an object, there is the participation of the beloved in the self's imagination. The love aroused in the self is a combination of feeling intrinsic to the self and patterns of experience in the unconscious, and the infusion of extrinsic feeling conveyed in the perception of the beloved. Two streams are at work, both within a single mind; one derived from past experience and present emotion, the other from the modification of that experience by an encounter with the beloved. The latter ingress of feeling taps and implements the endogenous constructs of the core to modify and grow in the creative imagination.

Thus, inner phases in the self's realization of the beloved, that is, antecedents in the perception of the beloved, contribute to the feelings that are, in reality, the product of the lover's fantasies. This is not to deny the mind-independence of feelings emanating from the beloved, but to stress that those feelings are filtered through the lover's mind, at times enhancing, at other times, discouraging, but at all times experienced in the self. In modern times, love is seen by many as an implicit negotiation or contract, with shared work, equality and alternating duties. The love I am writing about arises in the core of the psyche. It is not a surface contact occasioned by relations of social convenience. Two lovers or strangers do not come together like billiard balls, but issue out of their respective minds, each laden with differing intensities and qualities of feeling depending on the depth of feeling aroused in a given encounter. The ideal love is one in which the partners activate feelings in each other concordant with their own, and in which the depth of activation is adapted to the Cs surface where the partners must co-exist. When one truly finds the *Beschert*, the soul-mate, the realization of a beloved that is prefigured in the lover's Ucs and the satisfaction of self- and other-realization in a shared or collective Ucs, with depth and surface assimilated in lover and beloved, one can truly say an ideal love has been achieved.

Time and true love

Many who dream of true love ask themselves am I dreaming when I wish for true love, or am I dreaming when I find it? Can one say what true love is and how would we know were we to have it? What makes love true? It is not a statement that can be falsified or validated. Let me begin with the notion that true love refers to a feeling or state in an individual, not a couple. Many a lover who has loved in vain would say a certain love, even if unrequited, was the truest of all even if it was never shared. A true love must be unconditional, perhaps like the love of a parent for a child. In this respect, the not-fully reciprocated love for Diotima by Hyperion who divided his love for Diotima with that for Greece and Nature contrasts with the completeness, devotion, wisdom, and self-sacrifice of Diotima for her beloved (Silz, 1969).

Another clue to the nature of true love is when you hear someone say, sincerely, my love is eternal, or I will love you forever. I think this means, I will love you timelessly or for all time or duration, or that my love is everlasting. We may toss off such statements as the irrationality of the moment, but they go to the essence of true love in that for the moment, when such love is felt, the lover is out of time or rather, is totally in time but not the time of everyday life. The love is an eternity-in-a-moment that has shed all antecedent and consequent events. Love is like a dream. For those who do not feel it, or have been disappointed, it seems unreal or illusory, but as in a dream, the timeless self is on the crest of change without past or future, a self of the moment swept along by events in the feeling of continuously becoming now. To ignore the future and forget the past in the surge to immediacy is to have inex-pressible joy in the primal feeling of existence.

The gods are immortal. They cannot feel the eternal in a moment for each moment is an eternity, but temporal man feels the eternal when subjective time is suspended. When I say my love is forever I tran-scend the limitations of time and change. I mean my love is not eva-nescent like all other passing things, or life itself, but everlasting and in the realm of spirit. We try to capture in the mutability of feeling and the impermanence of word the eternal ideals to which they allude. Save nature's laws and life's ideals, all things erode and love is no exception. The closer a love to the ideal, the less it is a victim to change or decay.

In this way, as more than just duration, love enters the dimension of time. The fullness of true love is felt in the here and now. The mark of the unconditional is that love seeks nothing in return. This would be a benefit in the future. True love rejoices in the moment with all its richness and intensity when it is aligned with the process of nature and the lover feels most alive. To fall in love is to descend to the deep well of the subjective and the inner life, leaving behind the objects of the world, detaching from the many of the extra-personal to the one within the self, to go from feeling distributed over all things to a concentration in one, when the future dissolves and the past disappears. A lover who says I don't care what will happen or I don't care about the past gives voice to the feeling of being in the moment, in the becoming of things, which is the essence of life. I suspect it is the wish to feel each moment, to be in the moment without anticipation or reflection, without caution or hesitation, to plunge into the process of life regardless of consequence that is the aphrodisiac of love, and why seeking love one rarely finds it, for love comes most often to those prepared for surrender.

What is deeply felt is ineffable. To describe a love is not to feel it but to merge with the totality of the experience. The opposition of self to word and the distinction of word and object carry the self away from the core into the everyday world. Love survives in this renewal when a fully objective world is not achieved. The relation of love and sex is that physical intimacy and orgasm in the sphere of flesh are equivalent to intensity and oneness in the realm of spirit. To become one with becoming is to feel the generative process in the mental state, not outcomes or contents. This is not to watch, appraise, observe, scrutinize, but to be one with natural process, to become a tone in the rhythm of nature, to feel the oscillation and recursion, the vibrations of things that are the flux and melody of life. The metaphor of vibrations is reminiscent of Gorer's (1966) argument that the capacity to fall passionately in love is analogous to singing on key or falling in trance. This potential, it is claimed, may be universal to societies but uncommon to individuals. There are similarities to the withdrawal, self-abandon, total possession and oneness in trance as in creative inspiration, but love begins with the value of an individual. On this view, the expectation that one falls in love, stays in love, and marries the one who is passionately loved is analogous to all members of a society singing in tune or falling in a common trance.

Is love an illusion?

The idea that love is an *illusion*, that is, a distorted perception, or even a *delusion* or false belief, is ingrained in skeptical thought. This view owes to the irrationality of love, its fragility, loss, betrayal, and the disillusionment that often follows. For some, only facts are real, for others, only feelings. Emily Dickinson wrote that the deeper the love, the less the illusion. It is not love that is illusory, but the common illusion of being in love when a genuine fusion of the lovers has not occurred. A deep love is more real in the intensity of feeling, which is an outcome of the evolution of energy that is the life of all matter.

With another emotion such as intense fear, if one is about to be devoured by a crocodile we would not say fear is illusory or delusional. Fear becomes a delusion when there are no corresponding objects, as in paranoia. Love enjoys but does not require reciprocity. The beloved can be purely imaginary, absent, abusive, or dead. But even with the absence of an actual other, we can truly say we are in love and that the love is not delusion, but we can have the delusion we are loved in return. Even in cases of obsessive love or homicidal jealousy, when there are no grounds to believe in the other's love or infidelity, we cannot say the love one feels is unreal, or no less real than any other mental phenomenon? What makes love more real than anything else is that it pulses through the individual as a vivid reminder that we are alive and exist. For the philosopher, in the *cogito* to think is to exist, but for the rest of us in the *amo*, existence is most real in feeling, and feeling is most precious in love.

CHAPTER TWO

Theory of the emotions

All learning has an emotional base.

—Plato, *c.* 380 BC

Introduction

This chapter consists of two sections, one that describes a microgenetic theory of emotion, and a more speculative section on the nature of feeling and its evolution from energy in basic entities to the emotions and ideas of human thought. The sections are independent, one concerning observations on ordinary behavior, the other the metaphysics of feeling, though ultimately, for a comprehensive theory, an attempt must be made, as in the closing portions of this chapter, to combine the two sections in a unitary model.

The common practice of reducing emotion, and other functional systems, to discrete brain areas, chemical substrates or gene combinations avoids the question of what, exactly, is an emotion, treating emotion and its putative substrates, as encapsulated systems, with external relations to thought, perception, and memory. In contrast, microgenesis is a process theory of the mind/brain state, in which cognition and feeling are conceived in relation to transitional segments in the brain state.[1] The theory attempts to resolve the variety and richness of emotions and the derivation of feeling and idea in a unitary account of the mind/ brain state.

What is an emotion: James and Freud

One place to begin is with the theories of emotion advanced by William James and Sigmund Freud. One is an account based on extrinsic physiology, the other on psyche and unconscious process. To a large extent the theories forecast the debate as to whether emotion can be understood in relation to physiological or psychological factors, or ideally, both.

The James-Lange theory

The first question to ask is what is an emotion? We begin with the well-trod path of the *via negativa*, by saying what an emotion is not. Most importantly, it is not the perception of bodily changes postulated in the James-Lange (J-L) theory or in variations of the theory appropriated by others. James argued that an individual perceives a situation in the world and reacts with physiological changes in the body. These changes constitute the emotion. For example, to remove palpitations or sweating from anxiety eliminates the emotion. The implication is that the person apprehends, infers, or labels the emotion according to its bodily effects. For James (1884):

> "... the bodily changes follow directly the perception of the exciting fact, and that our feeling of the same changes as they occur is the emotion."

Bodily refers to the autonomic nervous system, not the brain, and the changes are in the periphery, not in direct brain activity. In J-L theory, the perception of such changes is equivalent to the emotion, but the account has been interpreted in relation to the "body image" or "body schema" as a means to revive memories in association with feelings aroused by the original perception.

According to this theory, an emotion *is* the perception of physiological change or its equivalent, or a judgment read off its bodily manifestations, while in some versions the reading is encoded in the retrieval of emotions and perceptions in memory. James was well aware his theory was counter-intuitive, though not as cognizant of the range of observations and research that failed to support—indeed, refuted—the theoretical argument. Indeed, the wide acceptance of the theory is surprising in view of the cautious arguments that James employed and in spite of—then or now—the absence of proof, the evidence of disconfirmation, and the failure of the account to explain many of the central problems in the theory of emotion.

In reducing emotion, for example, anxiety, to respiration and heartbeat, the account ignores the subjective context behind the emotion, which is taken to be its justification or rationale, not its correlate or cause. The account rationalizes emotion by turning it into a judgment or interpretation. The individual feels and interprets changes in the body that constitute the emotion. For the individual to designate anxiety by way of changes in the autonomic nervous system implies a judgment of the changes as descriptive of the emotion. The individual feels or reports the presence and degree of anxiety and its lifting or resolution as the situation changes, all of which are interpretations of physiological events. The changes have a label—anxiety, fear, panic—so that distinctions are supposedly made and named according to slight differences in peripheral physiology.

On this account, the inner experience of emotion is *consequent* to its manifestations. We do not have palpitations because we are anxious but feel anxiety when we experience palpitations. In a word, the subject reports and describes the emotion as an interpretation of its peripheral effects, which may be incited by, but are not directly based in, brain activity. Now, the occurrence of palpitations due, say, to cardiac disorder can give rise to anxiety. But if the condition is benign, and the person is reassured, the anxiety will not recur even if the peripheral changes do. I have had palpitations with anxiety due to an arrhythmia, but on learning that the arrhythmia is not serious, and noting that the changes soon pass, there is no longer a feeling of anxiety even though the physiologic changes are the same. This could be dismissed as habituation, but it does show that the bodily changes and the emotion can dissociate. Similarly, a pain in the foot may give anxiety if the person thinks it is the onset of a cancer, but if the person is reassured it is only a cramp, the anxiety melts away. We do not think the pain in the foot is equivalent to the anxiety but rather that anxiety is provoked by the meaning or interpretation of the pain. To attribute anxiety to peripheral changes assumes, as James pointed out, that in some sense the changes precede the emotion. This ignores an extensive literature on emotional changes secondary to brain stimulation or disorder (below).

We experience emotions in dream without bodily motion. A variety of emotions can occur without visible change in the dreamer. The range of emotions in dream is uncoupled from somatic activity, for there is motor inhibition during the dream. If nocturnal panic attacks or nightmares provoke agitation, could one conclude the agitation is the emotion if interpretation and judgment do not ordinarily occur in dream? Absent an interpretation of autonomic physiology, how does the dreamer know he is anxious?

There are cases in which the display of emotion occurs without inner feeling and there are cases with inner feeling that are unable to display it. Cases of sham rage or "pathological laughing and crying," which I reviewed many years ago (Brown, 1967), show that the physiological display can occur without the inner emotion. I have also seen a case of brainstem lesion in which the person felt inner emotion but could not display it; for example, feeling sad but unable to cry. This could be interpreted as a "disconnection," but sham displays occur in humans and animals on stimulation of the brain where there are no lesions to explain the dissociation. The individual who suddenly cries or laughs but denies inner sadness or joy presumably has the physiological changes without the subjective experience.

The theory does not account for the variety of subtle affect-states or the transition from states like anxiety to intentional feelings, for example, when anxiety transforms to fear as the object of the anxiety becomes evident. The major defect of the J-L theory is that it deals with moods such as anxiety, panic, happiness or depression, not with intentional feelings. In such emotions, an object or situation is not clearly perceived as an incitation. There may be no perceptual situation that induces anxiety or depression, which can occur without warning, and the subject searches for internal conflict or an unconscious source rather than a perceptual inducement.

The account of anxiety does not explain the transition through successive affect-states, for example, a morbid depression leading to agitation, or the transition from drive or need to want, wish, hope, and desire when the individual becomes aware of the object of the drive or mood. The theory does not explain the feeling of love or desire, the shift from attraction to affection, stages of greater or lesser intimacy, rejection, adoration, fascination, devotion, repulsion, hate, etc. It presumes the self can sort through all possible bodily effects and feel or diagnose the emotion based on a conscious or unconscious calculation of their relative strengths and distributions. Moreover, we observe people who have a strong reaction to the "same" emotional situation that another person deals with in a stoic manner, so the peripheral effects do not predict the inner experience, nor does the inner experience predict the behavior. If personal history and constitution are critical in determining why one individual feels extreme grief on the loss of a loved one while another does not, clearly the personal make-up of the individual plays a central role in having and experiencing the emotion and in the affective response.

In the J-L theory and its derivatives, the relation of feeling to idea has not been a topic for discussion. This is especially important for the variety of partial affects or "affect-ideas," such as pride, envy, shame, and so on. A central problem in emotion unsolved since the cathexis theory of Freud concerns the relation of feeling to idea (or object). What is the nature of this relation? Are feelings distinct from objects or ideas, as implied in the J-L account and, if so, how exactly do they combine (see below). Most of the feelings or emotions we experience are not anxiety or panic states, but such emotions as envy, pride, sadness, disappointment, humiliation, and so on. These affect-ideas are feelings that suffuse thoughts, or thoughts that suffuse feelings, and while they may devolve to intense moods they have not been the object of serious discussion in the J-L theory or in any other theory familiar to this author. Even with strong emotions, when we see or experience the transition of love to hate, or to grief, disappointment, or uncertainty, we do not suppose peripheral reactions are interpreted after the fact. Instead, these are subjective experiences that may or may not have peripheral manifestations.

The relation to memory is *ad hoc*. The transfer of bodily changes from the periphery to the brain merely underlines the basis of emotion in brain activity. This move postulates emotion as a somatic marker, leaving the relation of feeling to idea (memory) unexplained. Is this an extrinsic or intrinsic relation? The relation of a feeling to an idea, or an external object, is similar to the relation to memory, so that any theory of emotion requires a theory of memory, thought and perception, where the interpretation of feeling is consistent across these cognitive domains. Do feelings associate with memories or ideas? How do ideas find the appropriate feelings? Are memories lured to feelings or the reverse? The notion of a marker through which emotions are encoded in somatic or bodily change inserts a mechanism just when an explanation is required. The relation of feeling to memory, to idea, dream and object, is the pivotal problem in theory.

Freud's account of emotion

Freud tried to account for this relation by postulating the cathexis of memory traces by libidinal drive energy. He argued that memory traces were static entities deposited by perceptions. For Freud, one meaning of the timelessness of the Ucs concerned the identity of registration and retention (Leowald, 2000). The perception-memory trace was, in the metapsychology, transformed to a drive-representation or idea when it was activated—cathected—by libidinal drive energy, but how circulating energy locates the trace, or the trace attracts the energy was not discussed. The concept that sexual drive energy binds with a trace to form an idea is untenable. How among the innumerable memories, or potential neural configurations that correspond to memories, does drive energy find the proper trace? How does the trace attract the energy? Is there a physical "address" on the trace that lures the energy; is energy uniform or differentiated into distinct feelings that map to the specific ideas?

In spite of the many problems with a combinatorial theory, the notion survives to the present, for example in the view of the brain in terms of older limbic areas for emotion and the association to memory images, and neocortical zones for thought and "higher" cognition. For microgenetic theory, traces are not static entities but consist of the entire sequence from core to surface in the arousal of a mental content, while drive energy is derived to a succession of states of feeling. The "trace" and its feeling-tone develop through intermediate stages (Figure 2.1). On the microgenetic view, the "structure" of mind is temporal, not spatial.

Freud's theory was based on a synaptic model in which energy—or a neurotransmitter—activates or deactivates binding or receptor sites, but the static trace was never assimilated to energy as a dynamic flow. The model went through successive versions, but the core ideas of the metapsychology, especially cathexis and trace, remained unchanged and were vital to the concept of repression, which is the linchpin of psychoanalytic theory. For Freud, conflict, not peripheral physiology, was the basis of the emotions. The selective activation of memory traces by drive energy explained the arousal of feelings in relation to memories, while the withdrawal of energy from memories explained repression, or the failure of the memories to achieve consciousness. These matters have been discussed in some detail in Brown (1998, 2000).

Finally, approaches that reduce emotion to chemistry or anatomy are at best correlative, at worse, fabrications, but in any case they lack insight or explanatory power. The old idea of a limbic emotion that discharges upward for feeling and downward for display has no explanatory power. A change from one chemical substrate or brain area to another is a piecemeal approach that transfers the problem to a lower level of explanation. What may work for a mood like depression or anxiety does not work for an affective tonality like guilt or pride. There are no accounts that explain the transition from drive to desire, from one feeling to another, for example, from guilt to anger, or the resolution of a pathological emotion to one less disabling, that is, flux, deterioration, and recovery.

Finally, to focus on an emotion such as anxiety ignores the wider issues of drive, desire, and the partial affects, as well as the relation to belief, value, and character that determine the occurrence, quality, and intensity of an emotion on a given occasion. As for anxiety, a more compelling account, which was first suggested by Sander (1928) and explored by Smith et al. (2001), has shown that anxiety occurs with incomplete resolution of a perception. For example, in tachystoscopic studies, very brief exposures are associated with anxiety, which gives way to relief when the stimulus is identified. Descriptions by Goldstein (1948) of catastrophic reactions in aphasics unable to find words lend further support to this idea. The tension system set up by incomplete task solution described by Lewin and Zeigarnik (1948) or the affective tension associated with repression is another example. On this way of thinking, anxiety represents a failure of an affectively charged content to develop into consciousness.

A microgenetic approach

An outline of microgenetic theory is illustrated in Figure 2.1. The actualization of the mental state or of content in cognition recurs in a fraction of a second in a transit from an unconscious core to a conscious

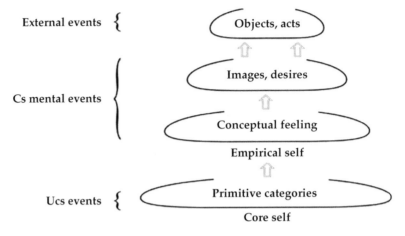

Figure 2.1. In the mature *human* brain, the mind/brain state arises in archaic formations bound up with the Ucs or core self, instinctual drive and drive-categories (drive-representations), passing to the Cs self and conceptual-feeling, finally to acts and objects in the world. Drive categories enlist the implicit values, beliefs and dispositions of character. Visual and verbal (inner speech) imagery is introspective content in the context of a full object-development, not a terminal addition but an accentuation of penultimate phases. Concepts in the Cs self become explicit values and intentional feelings. The trajectory from depth to surface is continuous. The final phase of world objects is the distal-most phase of mind. The transition is from archaic to recent in distributed brain systems, from self to object, from mind to world, from memory-like to perception-like events, from potential to actual, from past to present and from dream and fantasy to an adaptive resolution. Through a cascade of whole-part or context-item shifts, guided by sensory constraints at successive points, a fully subjective transition objectifies a perceptual world. The entire sequence—the absolute mental state—is an indivisible epoch that perishes on completion and is revived, in overlapping waves, in a fraction of a second (details in Brown, 2010b).

endpoint. The transition, in man, involves a continuing specification of explicit beliefs and values organized about drive-energy and categorical primitives, for example pre-objects in the satisfaction of hunger, to a conscious, intentional self-organized about conceptual-feelings that give rise to the images toward which the state is directed.

This chapter argues that an emotion is an inner or subjective feeling that is generated by the same process that deposits or actualizes an act or object, namely, the micro-temporal process that leads from the archaic core of the mind/brain state to its outcome at the neocortical surface. The development of an object, action or thought creates feeling within the micro-developmental process. This process and the feeling that is its manifestation constitute the *becoming* of the object, while the final object, idea or memory that envelops the process leading to it is its *being*, that is, the category that enfolds the feeling. The process that generates a mental content, including perception, creates an internal feeling that, when intense, spills over to external physiology.

The relation of feeling to the final object depends on the phase in the process that receives the major emphasis in the transition. Put differently, the quality and the intensity of an emotion are determined by the emphasis at a given phase in relation to context within the actualization sequence. According to the phase that is dominant for a given cognition, there is a different emotion and a different intensity. In general, enhancement at a deep or early phase gives strong emotions in relation to core needs, while enhancement at surface phases gives emotions referred to the object, such as value or worth. At intermediate phases, one has emotions within the category of desire (want, wish, like, dislike, hope, fear, etc.). At an early phase, emotion discharges in the body. At an intermediate phase the emotion, though internal, is directed to a pre-object or image. At a distal phase, the emotion is referred to, that is, *is ingredient in*, the external object.

The initial state

A first postulate is that drive arises through upper brainstem and diencephalon or hypothalamus to generate the initial manifestations of emotion and cognition. *The foundational drive is for self-replication*, not speciation, that is, to sustain the life of the organism. The drive is organized about the bodily needs for the organism to "reproduce" *itself*. Hunger (thirst) is the feeling tone of drive; food and water are the objects of the drive-category. *The sexual drive, derived secondarily from hunger, guarantees the replication (reproduction) of the species*, not the individual. The combination of drive as intense feeling with hunger as the drive expression and food as the (potential or virtual) drive-object, constitutes the drive-representation.[2] Hunger, feeding, and satiation are felt within the body. The drive representation is bound up with rhythms and feeding cycles, nursing, orality, and the older axial motor system. Drive states have the characteristic of an increasing pressure and the arousal of gestalt-like patterns that lead to consummation and satisfaction.

In the normal, waking human, the categorical primitives of drive either discharge in bodily space or, more typically, are derived to successive phases. The drive-representation, which is embedded early in the mind/brain state as well as in the full sequence, leads over a phase-transition to a mental object (image, thought) or an external object. Drive is the core of every cognitive act (Figure 2.2). The derivation of drive to successive phases mitigates its impact as the initial power or intensity distributes into and articulates pre-object concepts and individuated feelings. In extreme cases of need, such as severe hunger, thirst, starvation, or intense sexual need, aggression mediates the acquisition of objects to satisfy the urge.

A second postulate is that soon after birth, drive takes on a direction. Hunger, predation, and food selection are the active or aggressive vectors in drive-expression. The passive or defensive vectors are the

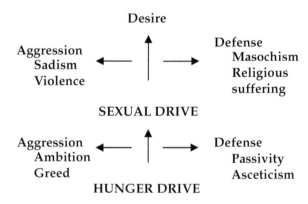

Figure 2.2. The core drive of hunger (thirst) replicates the organism. Hunger distributes into the opposing vectors of aggression and defense. These vectors underlie self-preservation in predation, escape, and avoidance. The hunger drive is derived to the sexual drive, which retains features of the antecedent complex. Some affective states relating to these drives and their vectors of expression are indicated in the figure. The constellation of hunger and sexual drive then give rise to the desires, which also have their implementations in acquisition and avoidance.

avoidance of predators, that is, not being food for other organisms. These two directions of behavior have been discussed extensively by other theorists, particularly Schneirla (1966), who claimed that approach and avoidance are the basic responses of all organisms. Even in paramecia, there is approach to a weak light and avoidance of a strong one. The concept was expanded by Denny-Brown (1963) in the interpretation of a spectrum of motor and cognitive responses; for example, he interpreted Parkinson's tremor as a rhythmic alternation of positive/negative, or approach/avoidance behaviors. This idea was the basis of his description of the flexor or extensor bias in pallidal and striatal syndromes. It was extended to psychological attitudes in the account of frontal and parietal lobes (and lesions) in relation to grasping (approach) and denial (withdrawal). The approach/avoidance dichotomy is thematic in the derivation of the emotions and plays out in complex ways in the pain/pleasure distinction and in a variety of other behaviors.

We are now in a position to examine more closely the nature of the instinctual drives that underlie thought and emotion. We can begin with the fundamental concept in microgenetic theory that things do not persist; they perish and recur. With recurrence there is an intuition of loss in every occasion of thought. Arising, perishing, and replacement are central features of the mind/brain state, as of all entities in physical nature. The surge of feeling from the instinctual core to value in the world, and the lapse of feeling as the state perishes or is incompletely revived in the ensuing state (Figures 1 & 2; reviewed in Brown, 2005, 2010a), account for all aspects of instinctual drive. The primary instincts, the so-called "four F's" of MacLean (1990), that is, fighting (aggression), fleeing (fear), feeding (hunger), and sexual behavior, can be interpreted on the same basis.

Drives and vectors of implementation

Feeding (hunger): The survival of the organism is its recurrence (arising) in each succeeding state; its death (perishing) is the failure of the state, that is, the organism, to recur. The primary instinct of hunger (and thirst) assures the arising, that is, recurrence, of the organism, and thus its survival. The organism survives each moment in its re-actualization. As the primary and most archaic instinct, hunger involves the oral, proximal and axial musculature, and the internal organs of digestion. Older regions of the brain regulate hunger and satiety. As with sexual drive, with which it is intertwined, hunger is progressively refined in a derivation through successive phases in the mind/brain. We see this in the delicacies of gourmet taste, pleasures of a sensual variety or the elaboration of primitive hunger, including cannibalism, into the complex and subtle rituals of table manners, richly documented by Lévi-Strauss (1968–1978).

Sexual drive: In the course of development, the sexual instinct develops out of the primary instinct of hunger.[3] The timing of this transition is controversial. For the psychoanalysts it is early, for others, later. The sexual drive is essential but not primary. Sexuality serves to replace the species, not the individual. First, a subject replaces itself in hunger and survival; then, in progeny, the species replaces the subject, though the subject (its genome) survives indirectly after death in the life of its offspring. As with hunger, the sexual appetite begins with arousal and leads to capture and satiation. The drive expression also involves the body axis in rhythmic cycles of need, pursuit and satisfaction and discharges in the midline motor system in the rhythmic movements of coitus.

The phase of the (hunger, sexual) drive-category: Drive is purposeful but non-intentional. There is no imaginary object, though the tracking of prey and pursuit of a mate appear to have proto-intentional features (Brown, 2005). The inner feeling of a drive is an intense urge for discharge. In human behavior this urge or need, though unconscious, is felt as a pressure for release. Animals are fully drive-oriented. At late stages in mammalian evolution, we see the first marks of individuality or personality expressed in shyness, aggression, tenderness, indifference, and other social behaviors. These marks of a rudimentary individuality signal the appearance in the mind/brain of the looming demarcation of the subjective field into a core or Ucs self.[4]

The transition from hunger to sexuality is marked by the extension of attributes of the initial drive state, such as olfaction, oral behavior and aggression, to sexual activity. In animals, elaborate mating rituals have the effect of channeling drive energy from immediate discharge into partial implementations that mitigate aggression. These behaviors are the distant ancesters of human desire and courtship. In human behavior, both orifices of the digestive tract are employed for sexual purposes. The breast serves as nutrient and attractant; there is pleasure in sucking, in being "devoured." Romantic courtship involves dinners, flowers, and candies. Flowers and perfumes excite by scent, as do the odors of food and the sex glands. In both, the sense of olfaction is prominent. We see an allusion to hunger in such metaphors as Shakespeare's, "if music be the food of love. ..." Hunger incorporates an object that literally perishes on internalization, while sexuality combines with the other in a brief fusion. The one is intra-personal, the other extra-personal, though the individuality of the extra-personal—the uniqueness of the other—only gains its true importance in human friendship and love. Hunger ingests, sexuality engages. In hunger, the other is devoured, in sex, it is penetrated.

Hunger and sexuality need extra-personal objects. In the latter, subject and object come together at the body surface. In the former, the other is ingested. In romantic love, the ingestion of the other is conceived as a fusion of two into one. We say, you are what you eat, but you become who you love. The metaphoric fusion of lovers is a refinement of the ingested objects of hunger. The other becomes part of the subject's psyche as food becomes part of the subject's body. Hunger is the life-sustaining force, grounded in organism. Sexuality depends on an extra-personal other. Hunger is more fundamental and derived to sexuality. The satisfaction of hunger is essential to survival, while sexuality can be postponed or diverted. The implementation of the sexual drive has an optional quality that hunger cannot afford.

Fight and flight (aggression and defense) are often considered as drives. Yet it is possible to interpret them as vectors or valences in the expression of hunger and sexuality. In hunger, approach and avoidance determine submission and dependency, capture, control, dominance, and acquisition. At the level of drive, hunger is at a pre-object phase. Sexual drive narrows the drive-category (normatively) to members of the other gender. Even in homo-erotic relations, the sexual organs are employed in ways similar to those in the conventional state. The range of satisfactions within the general category of sexual objects is more restricted than in hunger, which has a narrower scope, yet in the development of drive to conceptual feeling there is infinite variation in feeding and sexual activity as the drives individuate.

Fight (aggression): The drive to recurrence is the Will to realize a novel arising. The organism clings to or seeks to acquire objects of need and want. Aggression and its derivatives are the modes through which hunger and sexuality are implemented. Aggression is the forward motion in the arising of the state as it surges to the immediate present. It is a manifestation of the Will to survive and flourish. The ascending limb of the state satisfies hunger in the replication and protection of the organism and furthers the species in mate selection and the protection of offspring.

The aggressive impulse appears most strongly in rage and attack, but as with all the drives or instincts, it is derived to progressively more subdued manifestations. In animals, the aggressive drive accompanies the pursuit of a target in hunting and seizing food or in fight over territory, mating, and survival. Aggression is the core of what is derived to the self-assertiveness of want, including a variety of egocentric feelings—greed, arrogance, hate, pride, contumely—in which the satisfaction of the will at the expense of the other is centered primarily in the acquisition of goods or the protection of goods possessed. There is immediate discharge into pre-objects as drive-energy fills the act completely and unselfconsciously. Or, the drive is muted and transformed as it fractionates to diverse object-concepts. In partial expressions, such as criticism, sarcasm, ridicule or disdain, aggression distributes into a variety of lexical- and object-concepts. The subtlest display of feeling—a smirk, a joke, a sardonic grin—traces back to aggression as the vector of a drive.

In humans, all emotions, including aggression, arise in the values and beliefs of the core. The actualization of values and beliefs entails their reinforcement. The belief or value is implicit in the Ucs category of the drive. Anger or rage directed to a person derives from the belief the person has committed an injury or offense, or is dangerous. In criminal aggression, the other is a target of displaced hunger when it is transformed to material acquisition. A predator for food or goods exhibits the same drive as an animal, albeit with greater specificity and deliberation. The unlawful behavior of the sociopath does not conceal but is a derivative of Darwinian nature. Aggression in the sphere of value can exhibit selfish or unselfish valuations such as courage, defiance, sacrifice, and so on.

At the instinctual level, especially in animals, aggression is shaped by hunger and sexuality. In man, the savage expressions of drive crystallize to intentional feeling. Aggression transforms to anger or devolves from it. More often, aggression, especially in a sexual context, individuates to desire and pursuit, or it can transform to a ruthless or sadistic manipulation. The protection of goods or territory undergoes a transformation to acquisition, miserliness or greed. Aggression is distilled in competition, in business, sport, or through proxies in litigation or other commercial or criminal enterprises. The shift from core aggression to partial affects entails volitional feeling. The root of aggression in hunger and sexuality appears when we say a person has a *passion* for a career, a *lust* for power, a *hunger* for fame, or a *drive* to succeed.

The predominance of aggressive over defensive trends is assumed to be the outcome of experience in early childhood. That a genetic disposition is claimed for shyness indicates that fearfulness or timidity may be predetermined. There is evidence that a strong grip or grasp reflex in infancy signals an outgoing, assertive, more confident personality, while, hypotonic tone in infants signals passivity and acquiescence (Schilder, 1964). A tonic neck reflex to the right is a predictor of handedness. These genetic, motor and orientation biases develop together with the core drives as indicators of the dominance of one vector over another.

Flight (defense): Fear is the feeling that the objects of Will are under threat and may be lost, or that the Will to survive or protect is in danger, or the apprehension of loss or deprivation of those objects that aggression seeks to acquire or preserve. Fear is linked to the descending limb—the perishing—of the state, and the anxiety attached to loss. The greatest fear is loss of the self or the death of the organism. From this is derived the fear of loss of progeny and, by extension, the loss of others who are loved. Ultimately, fear is for the loss of valued objects, primarily the subject or self, secondarily its dependencies and possessions, just as the acquisition of valued objects inspires its contrast in aggression. The fear of a loss of organism, or self (death) is the other face of hunger, that is, fear of starvation. It is the fear of being devoured by a predator, that is, satisfying the hunger of another organism, or more abstractly, the fear of being destroyed by life's conditions, for example, divorce, poverty, shame. The fear of the loss or death of progeny is the other face of the sexual drive that transports the self to an after-life, on intuition or faith, or biologically in the replacement of the species.

Hunger, sexuality, aggression, and fear (defense)—life and death, creation and loss—can be understood in terms of the fountain-like arising and perishing each moment of the mind/brain state (Figure 2.1). The arising of the state is the recurrence of the organism and by extension, its offspring, supported by aggression in self-protection, predation, and protection of family. Fear is the apprehension of perishing, or the anxiety induced when the recurrence of self and family is in jeopardy. The arising of the mental state is the outgoing surge in the recurrence that underlies aggression and implements the drives of hunger and sexuality, while the perishing of the mental state underlies the dread that the self and what it values will be lost.

A supplementary perspective might take the position that aggression and defense are primary drive-processes, equivalent to hunger and sexuality, instead of being their instantiations. Pure aggression is an activity without content or goal unless it specifies what it is about. Undirected aggression is rage; undirected fear is panic. But even rage and panic have some object or some incitement. One could say aggression is an outcome of sexual drive but not the reverse, so that broadly construed, and in relation to hunger or sex, aggression seems to be an implementation. The primacy of hunger and sexual drive differs from the valences of aggression and defense, the latter being in service for the primary drives or their derivatives. Hunger and sexual drive are instinctual feelings that often occur without an external incitement, that is, arousal occurs spontaneously in the absence of a stimulus. They are also cyclical and/or periodic. In contrast, aggression and defense usually require objects as targets, either as lures or deterrents. Hunger as an urge exists without objects to satisfy it. Aggression in its different forms is the search and seizure of objects of drive-satisfaction. Hunger as a category of possible things to eat does not exist in the absence of objects or a pressure toward objects in the category that are fulfillments or satisfactions. One infers that hunger and sexual drive are categorical primes that generate an out-going search for objects, the targets of which become "containers" for the drive process. After satiation, hunger disappears. In what sense does the hunger-drive exist other than as future potentiality?

The transition from drive to desire

With learning in the course of maturation, drive-categories and the core self become the repositories of the implicit or unconscious beliefs and values that make up individual character. These serve as dispositions or presuppositions that, in man, guide the Ucs self of drive to partition to the Cs self of desire. The transition from instinctual drive to Cs desire is from category to concept in the resolution of objects and their affective tonalities. The pre-object categories of drive together with implicit beliefs and values form a subliminal construct that distributes into the conceptual-feelings of the explicit self. The core stands behind the drives, empowering them in Will, while the Cs self that issues out of this background is the agent of desire. The forward surge of Will passes from need to want. Agency is transitional from need and the cruder wants to the subtler proxies of desire in relation to pain and pleasure, such as like, dislike, taste, preference. The axis of the body is the somatic focus of drive; in desire, the psyche is the arena for a multiplicity of object-concepts and individuated feelings.

The feeling of desire weakens as it distributes over many objects or is indecisive for the one, and strengthens as it concentrates in a single object or image. Unlike a settled object in the world, desire grows in the private space of introspection and imagination. Drive has no inner space for pre-object (image) growth. The intensity of desire increases with a reduction in the range of potential objects. A failure of one image to resolve with clarity gives uncertainty and an inability to go forward. We all know people who think too much on possibility and fail to act with certainty, and others who go directly to action with little or no reflection. These extremes enclose a variety of subdued pleasures and aversions at intermediate phases when action on an object is postponed.

The core self of Will, drive and need goes out to objects without deliberation, while the conscious self of desire feels it can deliberate and choose which object to pursue or avoid. Desire (fear, wish, etc.) is the bridge of the intentional to the object (act, image, thought, etc.). With desire there is choice, including the possibility of inaction. Desire distills the force of drive into imaginative play. The optional character of its objects gives the feeling of intention or volition for the object that is chosen, except in passionate longing when an ideal category of one object is created (Brown, 2010a). Drive is felt in the body; desire is felt in the mind. The shift of desire from bodily to mental space is transitional to the ensuing phase when feeling, first as interest, then as worth or value, accompanies the object in its outward flow and detachment. Those models that locate emotion in the body depend on drive-like states or moods that are preliminary in the derivation. As the object resolves, feeling is felt in the mind, not the body, and when the object fully externalizes, feeling is observed or felt in an object that appears to be external to mind.

Affect-ideas

A central problem concerns the nature of an affect-idea, that is, a thought infused with feeling such as pride, humility, envy, trust, indeed, the whole inventory of distinctive feelings in the human repertoire. To what extent is envy a thought or a feeling? Is the unique quality of an affect-idea due to its thought-content or to the feeling, and how does one influence the other? Given the prominence of ideational content, an affect-idea is also like a judgment that carries a distinct affective tone. The feeling in envy is surely different from that in shame, but how different are the feelings stripped of thought? Is there such a thing as the feeling of envy without a thought or object on which the feeling depends? Can a person experience envy or shame without feeling it?

The confrontation of self and object—the drawing-out of the object (image) from the self—is essential to intentionality and is the basis of aboutness. The assumption that an affect-idea is a judgment or appraisal related to a state of affairs reflects the direction of self and conceptual-feeling into the object that the envy is about. The object moves outwards or becomes an image in relation to the self, whereas in drive there is no "separation" of core and pre-object. The distinction of the self, and the feeling it feels, or the object it imagines or observes, is derived from the immediacy and unity of categorical-primitives in drive.

An association of feeling to idea can be dismissed as untenable in favor of a unity *ab origo;* feeling and idea specify together out of a unified drive-representation. There is a partition of the drive-category and coarser emotions to concepts and refined feelings. With affect-ideas the concept has a strongly verbal component. Feeling distributes into linguistic acts or objects, that is, words as actions, or verbal images (inner speech) as action-surrogates. Immediacy of action involving the body midline gives way to postponement of action or gradual discharge into systems that involve the distal musculature, including vocalization and gesture. The lack of immediate bodily action prevents holistic discharge, allowing the feeling to undergo elaboration in the private space of introspection and imagery. Discharge also occurs into the part-actions of creative activity that realize an image incrementally over time. One supposes the "talking cure" works, if it does, by the intermittent discharge of conceptual-feeling into words as partial actions rather than directly and/or unconsciously into other more or less adaptive behaviors.

For example, a feeling may "occupy" a narrow sphere of value, as in the feeling of disappointment at a poor performance. This feeling may dissipate in a verbal medium of excuse and justification, or it may transform to anger or resolve or, if it replaces competing feelings so as to dominate emotion and thought, it may progress to sadness, even depression and hopelessness. Feeling grows and dies in the imagination, largely in relation to lexical concepts and linguistic imagery. Verbal images, or words as actualized images, are the action-equivalents of fight and flight, or aggression and defense. Feeling analyzed into words or verbal thought propagates internally instead of being depleted, as in drive, in the discharge to global motility.

The tree-like or fractal structure of the emotions leads from the root and trunk of core need, to desire and its innumerable branches, to the leaves of value that populate the world of perception. The shift from necessity to possibility, from the immediacy of need to imaginative choice, then to externality and independence, is replicated each moment as the mental state recurs. When the emphasis is on the proximal segment of the transition, need is foremost. If the distal segment is active, attention and interest inhabit objects in the world. Desire is intermediate, where the needs of the body adapt to the interests of the psyche and the exigencies of the world. There is a different feeling-tone at each phase. The force of drive-categories leads through the fluid concepts of desire and intentional feelings to impersonal objects of greater or lesser interest. The process goes from body to psyche to world, from generality through choice to definiteness.

Feeling in the world

The endpoint of the object-development is an object or action in the world. A drive-category is derived to an object-concept and, finally in action, thought or object, to an adaptive resolution. As the pre-object migrates outward, the *primitive categories of drive* and the *conceptual-feelings of desire* remain embedded in the object as part of its final structure. These phases contribute the meaning, recognition and identification of the object, and its value. In a word, an object is the surface appearance of a momentary epoch that includes all of its antecedent phases.

Object value is the final tributary of the affect-flow that begins with drive and accompanies the pre-object outward in its development. When a distal phase is emphatic, as in ordinary perception, the affective tonality is distributed evenly over the field. All objects are imbued with a similar affective tone. This gives the feeling that objects exist and are real. Specifically, the existence of the object, and its realness, are manifestations of the feeling that externalizes with (in) the object.

The conceptual-feeling that generates the psychic quality of intentional feeling is transformed to an object to which feeling seems to be attached, whereas what actually occurs is that a residue of the conceptual-feeling relinquished in the passage to an object remains ingredient, yet submerged, in the micro-temporal structure of the object as an attitude or judgment. An isolation of one object in the field with an accentuation of the feeling at the distal phase gives interest or selective attention. This grows to desire and value when earlier phases are recruited.

At most times, feeling sequesters in a single object, a tree, a house, a person, a work of art, and the object appears more beautiful, meaningful, or more valuable. When a proximal phase in perception is accentuated, we may be uncertain if the beauty, value, or meaning is applied to the object or is in the object itself. At other times when we gaze at nature and are touched by her beauty and plenitude, the immediate psychic precursors of the perception give the field a heightened signification. The value usually given to one object spreads over the object field. Occasionally, perhaps rarely, there is a feeling of the sublime. This is an experience of intense feeling in a simultaneity of the particular and the universal, the locality of the scene and the immensity and grandeur of its surround, and at the same time, an awareness of the transience of the moment in relation to the endless duration of which it is an instant, that is, an apprehension all at once of the local and the infinite in space, the ephemeral and the eternal in time.

Pain and pleasure

Some argue that the pleasure/pain principle is the driving force of life. If behavior is governed by pleasure and displeasure, as with approach and avoidance or desire and aversion, aggression and defense would be modes of pleasure seeking or pain avoidance, and value would be an appraisal of the sources of objects subsumed by this principle. The problem is that in seeking pleasure and avoiding pain, the richness of behavior is collapsed to a single positive/negative variable that is then used to explain the very richness it has eliminated.

The first exigency is survival, not pleasure, even if self-preservation can be broadly construed in accord with the principle. The selection of objects that promote survival is the seed of valuation. Some options are innately determined, others learned: foods, risks, dangers. The valuation of the object entails an aggressive or defensive strategy. The valuation inspires the response, and allows objects to be categorized into sources of pleasure and pain, but these are outcomes of implicit choices based on valuation, not the prior causes of those behaviors. Put differently, a positive or negative valuation induces an action, but since the incitement of the action is antecedent to the object, the resultant pleasure or pain cannot be the motivation but rather the conclusion of an action biased to an object that is consistent with its Ucs valuation.

For an organism to avoid a painful situation supposes an awareness of danger and/or the possibility of pain. The possibility of pain occasions flight, withdrawal, fear, immobility, or concealment. But bodily pain in non-human organisms, unless it is related to instinctual releasers or innate reactions, such as fleeing from intruders, noise, vibrations, or unfamiliar odors, would have to be first perceived and the response mimicked, or it would have to be directly experienced to be avoided by which time it may be too late for survival. This is why positive or negative attitudes, that is, implicit valuations, take precedence over the striving for pleasure and the aversion to displeasure. Pain, or the reaction to stimuli that appear painful, figures importantly in emotion as an aboriginal feeling with ancestral roots that precedes all other feelings. If we knew at what point in evolution an organism actually *felt* an occasion of pain, we would be at the threshold of subjectivity.

To this point, I have not discussed emotion or feeling directly, nor pain specifically, which is the prototypical feeling of animals. What exactly is a feeling? What is the "stuff" of an emotion, what is its nature and origin? To understand emotion we must trace its origins not only to lower organisms but even, I would argue, to physical matter. In this regard, pain or the reaction to stimuli deemed painful is a critical problem. We would not deny feeling to animals, perhaps even fish, but at some point we question whether the organism *feels* pain or merely reacts to it. There is no clear shift from a withdrawal from what we infer to be a painful stimulus and the presumption the organism *feels* the pain it withdraws from. A mollusk will retreat from an attack but does it *feel* anything? Do oysters "cry out" in silent pain when they are shredded by digestive juices?

A person in a vegetative state will grimace, withdraw or have decerebrate or decorticate rigidity on being pinched or lightly poked with a sharp instrument. We do not believe the "person," that is, the brainstem or sub-cortical regions, feels pain, that is, that the neural formations that mediate the response elicit painful feeling. If pain is Ucs or mediated by brain structures that do not elicit a Cs response, what sort of pain is this? If we deny consciousness to lower forms, should we deny pain as well? Is a fish squirming on a hook in pain? There are situations in human pathology—frontal lobotomy, pain asymbolia (Brown, 1986)—where pain is felt without its noxious quality. Is pain in a dream actual pain? Thus, a reaction to pain can occur without feeling pain and one can acknowledge pain without feeling it. In phantom pain one can even feel pain without painful stimulation. This is like seeing (hallucinating) objects in the absence of an external stimulus.

Some mammals show a difference in temperament, curiosity and a kind of bereavement on loss. A dog appears happy to see its master after a separation. These behaviors, and the presence of individual differences, imply the possibility of a subjectivity within which there could be painful feeling. In other organisms, pain is the sole barometer of inferred feeling when there is no evidence of inner or subjective experience. We attribute different feelings to withdrawal and approach. The withdrawal from pain is conceived to be due to a feeling of pain, as the withdrawal from danger is attributed to fear. In contrast, the approach to objects for mating or food is usually not conceived as a desire for pleasure. The inference of pain is prior to that of pleasure, since pain elicits a reaction while pleasure, to the extent it occurs, is largely internal.

As a perception, pain is grounded in the body as the most primitive mode of concrete feeling. There is no symmetry in the pain/pleasure principle. We would not say an organism that *feels* pain, as opposed to reacting to it, should also feel pleasure. Pleasure, if not the absence of pain, depends on a complex of perceptions that differ from the substrates of pain. Pain has a source but not an object. Unlike vision, audition or olfaction, it is taken as pure sensation or feeling, while pleasure usually has an object, such as sex, food, or shelter.

In lower organisms, pain is less a perception than a state of existence or being. A perception requires a perceiver or a subject that feels, whereas pain in lower organisms cannot be distinguished from the organism that feels it. Pain is not one feeling among others but an intensification of a common feeling that pervades and animates all organism. Arguably, pain is an occasion of intensity in the baseline feeling that generates organism. Put differently, pain is a concentration of the process through which the organism actualizes. One moment, feeling takes the form of motion, another of digestion, and another of a pain-like reaction. The same feeling that creates the organism is molded to a manifestation in behavior. It is not that the organism feels; rather, feeling makes the organism what it is. Intense pain completely consumes an organism in that it sequesters the momentary creation of the organism in a given mode of being. An intense pain that signals the loss or impending death of organism receives the full force of the life urge or its becoming into existence. In physical matter, feeling is the internal dynamic or energic pattern of the entity. In vegetative and primitive life, feeling is tropism, motion, activity. Approach and avoidance are vectors. They are constitutive, and do not point to subjective feeling, which is an event within a subjective field or in relation to a subject.

When an organism is not in pain or aroused by a painful stimulus, feeling is continuously revived each moment of existence. Feeling *is* the existence of organism, without which it is an aggregate of elements, each of which has its own feeling-quality. As organisms evolve, so too does feeling. The totality of feeling in the pain of lower organisms becomes the locality of pain in organisms with subjectivity, and the perception of pain in higher mammals with a subject-object relation. In humans, a self feels pain as a perception. Pain, pleasure, drive, value, desire, and all the affect-ideas are diverse manifestations of feeling in relation to the evolutionary development of the organism and the dominant microgenetic phase, but they are all derived from, and exemplify, the common *Feeling* that creates the organism.

Thus one can say that feeling as the central phenomenon of existence is not sporadic pain or pleasure, but the essence of the life of every living thing and, by implication, as energy, underlies the generation and recurrence of inanimate entities as well. Feeling is equivalent to the process of actualization through which things come into existence and recur. In evolution and in the actualization (microgeny) of the mental state, feeling, concepts, and self appear as separable entities, but all diversity in mind and the perceptible world evolves out of feeling as process. Thus, we can say that feeling is not something an organism *has*, it is what the organism *is*.

Metapsychology of emotion: panpsychism and emergence

An account of the transition from matter to mind—whether continuous, episodic or saltatory, whether graduated or emergent—is a first step to a theory of human feeling. Such an account informs an interpretation of subtle emotional states and their relation to ideas. The normal tendency of mind to analysis, to contrasts and distinctions, is overcome by a retreat to the forms or constructs that generate the partitions. A distinction is a first step to an understanding, but a fictitious rupture can obscure a continuity that is essential to what one is trying to understand, namely, the diachronic process through which the mind/brain develops and through which its objects actualize. The most important of these is the mind/matter (brain) divide, which is resolved in a proper account of the role of feeling in the evolution of the mental life.

The microgenetic approach to the Cartesian duality of mind and matter, or of brain and consciousness, entails that the proto-psychic is ingredient in physical entities, as in the metaphysics of Spinoza. A form of panpsychism is the only intelligible response to the evolutionary origins of human mind, of consciousness and value. Otherwise, the appearance of mind will, at some point, demand emergence and an artificial coupling to brain. In postulating an identity of matter and the proto-psychic early and throughout evolution, panpsychism avoids the need for later resolution. The gap in causal passage from brain to consciousness is resolved in the conjoint evolution of physical matter to material brain, and in the evolution of the proto-psychic to human mind.

The alternative to panpsychism is a Rubicon theory in which emergence only adds mystery to gradualism and continuity. Speculation has to consider the evolutionary stage where emergence occurs, the neural events and psychic phenomena involved, how it is linked to the assumption of identity, the recurrence of emergence at successively "higher" levels, how emergents differ from resultants, the progression of emergent phenomena to more complex states, and whether emergent phenomena have causal efficacy, for example, whether consciousness as an emergent is causal or epi-phenomenal. Emergence intersects with complexity at successive stages of evolution. Emergence is essential to complexity theory in presuming that consciousness arises, that is, emerges, when a system is sufficiently complex. However, the emergence of consciousness cannot be explained by invoking complexity. Pattern is a factor. So is temporal extensibility (below). An increase in the complexity of acoustic noise does not give Beethoven.

A critique of panpsychism that presumes primitive consciousness or psychic experience in physical entities sets up a straw man for

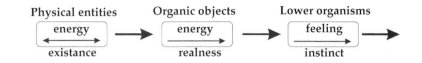

Figure 2.3. The isotropy or bi-directionality of physical feeling in physical entities leads to the assumption of a direction or anisotropy in organic entities. Energy takes on direction and transforms to feeling, which subsequently transforms to drive. The combination in a subjective space of drive and categorical primitives undergoes a derivation to a self and conceptual-feelings. These further individuate to objects (objectified concepts) and their affective-tonalities (value, worth).

refutation. What mind and matter have in common, in animate and inanimate matter, in proto-organism and proto-mind, is their pattern of foundational process. A cell or a bacterium is a physical system with pre-psychic properties that forecasts the development of a brain. The cell approaches, withdraws, feeds, reproduces. Primitive feeling in the cell inherited from energic patterns of inorganic matter elaborates some kind of urge to survive. The *progression of energy to feeling* is the key to the commonalty of the mental and the material, a relation that is subtler than one might suppose. It is an axiom that only the obvious is evident, while the ubiquitous often escapes detection (Figure 2.3). Panpsychism requires a novel approach to both mind and physics.

Temporal extensibility

The fundamental operation in the evolution and actualization of the mind/brain is a whole-to-part shift over the temporal extensibility of an entity. The model for higher organism entails an entity as a waveform of energy that exists momentarily before it is replaced. In the wave of such shifts that conveys a becoming from potential to actual, causation is in the generation and replacement of entities, not the impact of one actuality on another. Bosanquet put it, "all causation is holistic, that is, the control of the parts by some whole." But in what respect is the "control" causal? If a virtual oscillator can emerge out of independent sub-systems (Dewan, 1976), might the reverse transition, sub-systems "emerging" out of wholes, be a qualitative process that does not have causal predictability?

The shift from whole to part *within* an entity recurs in the evolution of mind out of non-sentience. In a given actualization, the *initial* whole is a potential for completion that stands behind the parts (phases). The *final* whole is an epoch of phases that exist when the entity actualizes. An initial whole as potential generates parts as phases, but a final whole as entity has parts as constituents. The simple, fundamental and power-ful law that is the governing principle of existence in mind and nature is that entities become what they are through whole-part shifts over the temporal extensibility of epochs (Brown, 2005).

The proto-psychic begins with isotropic energy over the temporal extensibility of elementary particles. This can be conceived as a wave-form that completes one cycle, which is then reinstated. The epoch can be as brief as a chronon (Whitrow, 1972) or have the duration of a mental state. Consider the orbit of an electron in a hypothetical atom. The atom cannot be bisected and the electron frozen in mid-orbit. The orbit is not a sum of the electron's positions. A complete revolution of the electron is necessary for a minimal epoch of existence. Things do not just exist, they *become what they are*. To exist is to complete one cycle of becoming. Half a thing, half the minimal duration of a thing, half a mental state, a phase in the transition laying down the mind/brain state, does not have existence independent of a complete cycle.

Basic entities materialize as epochal packets of energy; perceptual objects actualize as categories of feeling. The surge of energy takes on direction as feeling. Once direction stabilizes over a significant dura-tion (and complexity), feeling is no longer uniform. Variation in feel-ing is variation in behavior. Eventually, successive phases become loci of feeling in formative process. The energy that creates physical enti-ties transforms to the feeling that arouses animate nature. Energy is not experiential, not a primitive mode of consciousness, but is proto-psychic as the basic source of feeling in organism. Energy that is theo-retically isotropic or time-reversible takes on direction as it transforms to the anisotropy of primitive feeling. Vegetative life is an example. We may be reluctant to attribute feeling to plants but the constituent cells show tropisms, such as a differing response to weak and noxious stimuli. These responses are mirrored in the larger system in growth, orientation, and decay. In tropism, energy shifts to a time-directional process. The forward direction of feeling in primitive life is the origin of the subjective aim in human thought. In animals, it is the seed of purposefulness. When a flower turns to the sun we do not interpret this as purposeful, nor do we usually attribute purposefulness to instinctual activity in organisms such as insects, but these primitive reactions are the leading edge of feeling in the material world.

The apparent aim of tropism becomes the ostensible goal of drive. Action in the organism that hunts is directional or goal-oriented. Though not voluntary, action seems purposeful or *proto-intentional* (Figure 2.4). In behavior motivated by drive, potential options are buried in the act. The animal makes implicit choices, such as prey selection, wind direction, whether to pursue and how far, when to capture or give up the hunt. Proto-intentional behaviors such as hunting, nest-building or digging up a grub or a bone, seem directed

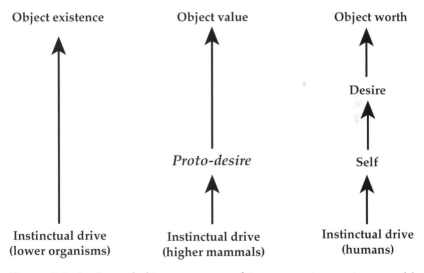

Figure 2.4. Instinctual drive generates objects as existents in a world not fully independent from the organism. In higher mammals, drive partitions to proto-desire. As the self arises out of the core, conceptual-feeling underlies the variety of human desires. Implicit value at the core develops through drive, to desire, and into objects as value or worth.

to a goal. However, behavior is rigidly constrained by stimuli in the immediate surround. The organism is unlikely to be conscious of the goal pursued, only responsive to the sensory conditions (sight, sound, odor, etc.) in its *Umwelt* at each moment of the pursuit. The proto-intentional forecasts a class of desires in which implicit choices that are potential in drive become explicit and conscious. Automatic or drive-oriented behavior leading to adaptive action becomes deliberate when it becomes Cs. Consciousness of mental content arises in the transition to perception as an explicit image of choices that are implicit in spontaneous acts. The accentuation of a penultimate phase creates consciousness of self, choice, and decision. Feeling in relation to concepts in the human mind reaches its apex in introspection and intentionality (Brown, 2005).

The pattern of evolutionary advance is from energy over brief durations that lays down momentary entities to feeling in increasingly more complex life forms, to drive in pre-human or proto-intentional organisms, to intentional feeling in human thought. The shift from energy to feeling to drive to desire accompanies a growth from primitive categories to abstract concepts. Epochs that enclose the categorical primes of instinctual drive are derived to the affect-laden concepts (conceptual feelings) of human cognition.

Feeling (emotion) and idea (concept)

Every concept has an affective tone; every feeling is enfolded by a concept. This statement seems refuted by common sense when we observe intense feelings—love, rage, fear—that seem to have little or no conceptual content, or when we have abstract concepts, say mathematical ones, that seem devoid of emotional tone. We reach such a conclusion when we ignore the categorical nature of intense emotions and the affective process beneath the surface of abstract concepts and treat the affect or idea as content, avoiding the temporal or diachronic process through which it develops.

Feeling coalesces to a variety of affects in its brief journey to actuality. In an ordinary state, drive-categories are first activated. The potential for strong emotion is subdued by the derivation to conceptual feeling. Emotion is further mitigated as it settles in the world. Attention to one object (idea, memory) shifts the affective tonality to desire (fear, etc.). Concurrently, the object becomes more like an image or thought. No longer fixed in the world, it undergoes elaboration in the mind. Memories and other linguistic, conceptual and experiential relations are evoked. The object, still in the world, is now active in the imagination.

The distribution of feeling over the axis of its development, an accentuation or relaxation at a given phase, the degree to which it is usurped by the main line of development or shared among potential paths in conflict or contemplation, whether it goes outward into many tributaries or fills segments prior to externalization, determines the quality of feeling in a momentary state. The flux of emotion from the pre-object of drive to the image of desire to object-value is like a river in which the rumble of a waterfall passes through a stage of turbulence to the still waters of a lagoon. If we observe at which stretch in the river our fragile raft settles, we get some idea of the true nature of emotional experience.

Notes

1. The microgenetic theory on which this chapter is based has been discussed in many books and articles. The reader is referred to a recent book (Brown, 2010a) and papers that range from Brown (1967) to Brown (1998, 2003 *inter alia*). The history of the theory is reviewed in Pachalska, MacQueen, and Brown (2012).

2. Freud used this term for the activation of a trace to an idea by libidinal drive energy. Here, the drive and the category (feeling and pre-object) are a unitary entity.

3. Bradford (2011) writes that for early Christian mystics, sexual drive developed out of excessive hunger. He cites Evagrius Ponticus (ca 370) as writing, "fornication is a conception of gluttony."

4. For a discussion of the evolution and organization of the self, see Brown, (1999, 2010a).

CHAPTER THREE

Love and desire

.

If one does not hope, he will not find the unhoped-for.

—Heraclitus

Introduction

Contemporary accounts of love tend to describe what passes *between* a subject and an object, a lover, and a beloved, each "bringing to the table" some attributes, emotions, and values in a relationship that is like a negotiation in that it rests on the cooperative interaction of separate individuals. For some this negotiation is a contestation of power, the completion of an inventory or a resolution of complimentary obligations, Others see it as pathology, a neurotic alliance, a projection of the subject's needs onto the other or, on a more rational plane, a bestowal, a judgment, or appraisal of what is desirable or undesirable. On this view, value is transferred to the other, much like to any other object, and a judgment is made as to whether the value is justified by the qualities. This entails that the subject encounters the other as a mirror of the self or as a supplement for what is lacking, as if *adding* the other will harmonize with, magnify or compensate for what is

51

present or lacking in the self. Subject and object are autonomous units that combine with greater or lesser success. The romantic ideal of oneness gives way to shared interests, mutual benefits and equality of labor, more like a partnership or contractual relation than a unity of souls. This way of thinking, which can be occasioned by hard work and the pressure to survive, is now the outcome of an analytic materialism in which couples are conceived as the interlocking parts of a machine, a collection of autonomous units that interact through surface contacts, while the romantic ideal of the soul-mate is treated with contempt or cynicism.

Another way to look at the nature of passionate and true love begins with subjectivity and attempts to go from the inner life of the lover to an intra-psychic absorption of the beloved. It *accepts* the other as an *entity* independent of the subject but *apprehends* the other as *intra-psychic* yet *extra-personal*, a creation of the self's imagination. Love and allied states such as affection, interest, desire, compassion, or for that matter rejection and disappointment can be interpreted in relation to their psychic infra-structure. The subjectivities of lover and beloved are not interactive but assimilative. The authenticity of the love depends on the degree of coherence across corresponding yet inaccessible psyches as well as the mutuality of need, desire, and genuine giving that each offers and receives. On this view, the beloved is infused with the subjectivity of the lover, truly possessed, and created in the conceptual imagination as the center of a cognized world. The stronger is the imagination, the greater the fantasy, the more facile the formation of an ideal, the deeper, that is, the more subjective, the love and the less the objectivity. Conversely, the more objective the love, the less love there is. To see one's beloved in an objective manner—"warts and all" as we say—is to accept, to approve, to judge, and appraise, but not to truly love. This follows if idealization is essential to loving. The unmitigated fact is that love has to be unreal to be true or, rather, the unreal has to be the heart's only reality. Regardless of whether one agrees with this assertion, to interpret love as an intra-psychic ideal rather than an inter-personal bond leads to insights inaccessible to conventional theory.

For some, the love for a person differs from the love for an animal or inanimate things and possessions (Ch. 5). Others argue that the passion brought to love is the same as that for art, revolutionary fervor, and other things and ideas. Kant gave a concrete example of the incompatibility of reason with romantic love when he declared that philosophy was his mistress. Others ignore the universality of libidinal drive and displace the sexual impulse to non-sexual erotic enjoyment (e.g., Singer, 1994). This has relevance to the difference between falling in love all-at-once and a love that develops gradually, the former often but not necessarily sexual and dependent on physical attraction, the latter often but not necessarily an intimacy based on compatibility, friendship, and shared knowledge.

Love is not static; it has its fits and starts. There is jealousy, disenchantment, accommodation acquiescence, despair, anticipation, boredom, disappointment, and a host of other attitudes and emotions. It is one thing to distinguish the manifestations and forms of loving and another to unify them in a coherent psychology. For this, the continuities are truer guides than the distinctions. The challenge is not to carve out different forms or intensities and explain them by different theories or reduce them to brain localizations and chemistry, but to arrive at an account of the psychic structure and the transitions across states of loving (as well as resenting, exploiting, etc.). This must include how the world and the self are never again the same after the beloved is encountered, how love grows and decays, how it is sustained and, finally, how it continues or dies when love is betrayed or the beloved is lost.

Since Plato's description in the *Symposium*, there has been a tendency to speak of one or another form of love in relation to its distance from sexual, selfish or egocentric attitudes, or in relation to the refinement of its objects. This rationalization of love is incongruent with the realness of physical feeling that is the whole point and value of passionate love in human experience. There is a sense in which reason is antithetical to passion, one centered in objectivity and detachment—"dispassionate reason"—the other in irrational subjectivity. One can go by degrees from one to the other but differences of intensity or quantity are differences of kind or quality. Love is not merely an intensification of affection, for the transition to love engages one's beliefs, values, one's entire personality, indeed, one's very existence.

More generally, a "philosophy of emotion" is seen as a contradiction. There can be a science of love and there are many sciences of knowledge, but knowledge is one thing, emotion another. One can love doing science or gaining knowledge but not love its objects; one loves the pursuit of knowledge, not the knowledge gained from the pursuit. In brain disorders, knowledge and feeling (or action) can dissociate (Isaacson & Spear, 1982). Frontal lobe patients may describe what is right and do what is wrong. To know a thing is not to feel it. To believe the self is an illusion does not lead to insanity unless the belief is invested with feeling. Ironically, true beliefs often carry less conviction than false ones. A suicidal terrorist will kill and die for a belief that is patently untrue, as a jealous or disappointed lover may seek revenge over a trivial slight. This is the difference between the intense emotion of core values and beliefs and the verbal jousts of superficial ones. The passion in philosophical argumentation is usually not over the conviction in a belief but is an egoist effort at persuasion and a sign of competitive zeal. Indeed, there is no place for passionate conviction if philosophy is impersonal truth-seeking, since the passion for an idea is often detrimental to a determination of its truth.

Belief is part of semantic knowledge as the repeated exposure to episodes distills to the concepts that forecast them. In this process, experiential memory and personal feeling, in which specific objects or encounters (episodes) are recalled, shift to conceptual knowledge where the episodic "tag" is lost in the object- or lexical-concept. In semantic knowledge, concepts embedded in relational networks are drained of affective tonality. Episodic knowledge presumes the uniqueness of its object and the serial order of its occurrence. Love undergoes this transformation as episodes coalesce to categories of belief that nourish the ideal. With a parting of lovers, or when love transforms to appraisal, the episodic recurs where, as a distinct event, it can be kindly or unkindly judged. One recalls the joy of a first meeting, or the sorrow of the last.

This shift is at work in transforming love to an intentional act in relation to reason and judgment and so cleaving the feeling from the concept. In judgment, the selection of a beloved is like choosing a new suit, how it looks, feels, fits, what it costs, and so on. It turns unconscious need into a truth-judgment that leaves unexplained the passion and devotion, the sacrifice and surrender, that is, the totality of involvement, and the scope of behavior from puppy love to perversity. Feeling comes from drive based on need, which is individual and perspectival, and rational only from the point of view of the actor, not based on what is good or true. The role of feeling diminishes as the properties of its objects supervene. The intensity of the One is unpacked in the affective tone of the many. When love is transformed to volition, to choice or decision, the attributes of the other are primary, and the whole and the needs it embodies recede into the background. This move accompanies the shift of desire to an intentional attitude centered in aims, ideas and objects;

the object dominates the feeling in the mode of loving. The outcome of this finesse, as Socrates argued, is a loved object rarified to a hermetic conceptuality that finds in philosophy its natural home.

Some convert love to desire in relation to its objects rather than its source and trajectory. The emphasis on desire in love is legitimate, but a focus on the content of what is desired distances outer from inner and assures that desire will differ according to its object, or that every object will elicit a different desire (or aversion). The objectification of the other entails a *representation* of desire as a doorway to its "reification" as a substance-like entity. The first step is to transform desire from a process to a state. With this, desire becomes a logical solid in relation to the perceptual solid of its aim. The further tendency is to claim a propositional content that can be submitted to a truth-determination. Can one truly love for golden hair or is this a poetic device, a fetish or an instance of *pars pro toto*? The other as a packet of object-qualities for appraisal perverts the actual process of conceptual-feeling in which antecedents and consequents—phases in a continuum—are inseparable.

Along with this focus on the distal phase, the use of a "because" or "that" clause, for example, "I desire that *p*," or "I desire *p* because," takes the process of desiring (wanting, fearing, etc.) as an effect of the thing desired. While this conforms to common sense, which assumes the object (lover, assailant) provokes the desire (love, fear) or that desire is secondary to its incitation, not a subjective realization, the same object that excites love or fear in one person leaves another unfazed. The individuality of desire and the diversity of its objects, along with its affective quality, complicate explanation and, on these grounds alone, appear to justify the reduction to other phenomena no less complex. This step, once taken and legitimized, displaces the object from a subjective ideal to a shared topic—a belief, a proposition—the truth or rationality of which can be judged. In this move, there is also a transfer of intentionality from the self to the object-content (Brown, 2010a).

Regardless of the aim, intentionality obtains in a desire that implements a drive as its object specifies. To explain drive in terms of its object, or to account for desire in terms of its concept or image, ignores formative process, disconnects the spatial or synchronic content from the temporal or diachronic context, and reverses the direction of actualization. Desire gathers its force as feeling sequesters in the imagination. If desire is explicable in terms of objects, why is it emptied for those objects when it is replaced by them? Desires are intentional feelings that anticipate but do not actualize intentions. The various strategies that seek to explain desire in terms of cognition rather than emotion share the attempt to eliminate the inner relation of self to desire and the thread of subjectivity from the self through desire to its extra-personal manifestations. A byproduct of this static account is the attempt at correlation with brain area, for example, locating love in some part of the brain, but this only further cleaves apart phenomena that are segments in a continuum.

Desire has been studied as having a "functional role" in disposing a person to an action or bringing about some state of affairs (discussion in Schroeder, 2004). It has also been equated with incomplete, diverted or blocked action, as a motive for an action (see below) or a wish that is otherwise not obtainable, or as an alternative or substitute for acting. This supposes that desire causes or incites an action, and is not a phase in the action-development. To feel desire is to experience an actuality, not an imminent precursor. A state of desire may precede a state of action, but the action replaces the desire, it is preceded but not driven by it. Specifically, the substrate of the desire that leads to action is non-actual, embedded in the action-development. Usually, desire is not discussed with reference to the self as its source, nor as an implementation of core drive. The emphasis is on affective overlap or reaction, or as a motivation for action, or in relation to belief, or with regard to the distal external phase in the transition of will to action, not the proximal phase of arising or the transition from unconscious drive to conscious goal.

To objectify desire is to turn it into a quantity that can be described in terms of intensity. In English, we speak of strong or weak desire, but this is not the case for some languages, where one does not ordinarily speak of *intensity* but of qualitatively different states. The variation in strength refers to distinct feelings, say, obsession and passion at one extreme, attraction and interest at the other. A weak desire, whatever else it may be, is not desire. Intensity is less a sign of strength or weakness than the quality and/or degree of resolution. Desire in some respects is the reciprocal of anxiety, the one abating as the object resolves, the other increasing as alternatives are eliminated. When the choice that is *implicit* in the actualization of a desire becomes explicit, that is, when an object of desire individuates an unformulated background, feeling shifts from uncertainty to conviction. The "intensity" of desire is reduced in the coming-to-the-fore of opposing desires that are ordinarily unnoticed or bypassed, for example, when indifference or interest precedes or replaces love. Incomplete specification is not a mark of lowered intensity. In anxiety, the intensity is greater but the feeling is not that of desire, nor is it intentional. Anxiety occurs when other feelings, conscious or not, compete for priority.

Take the transition from interest to love. We do not speak of interest as a weak desire, for interest may never evolve to desire, and it can occur when desire is absent, for example, in curiosity. Interest occurs with focal attention, or when feeling is uncertain or when there are other options. Romantic interest may not progress to desire if the individual is unsure it is reciprocated or is reluctant to give up other opportunities or expectations. Sexual interest may not proceed to affection if it is for sex only, or mitigated by selfishness, conflict, competition, fear of commitment, preference for solitude, and so on. This is not a weakness of desire so much as hesitation in one line of development or a suppression of the potential of other paths to rise into prominence. For desire to become intense there is a "dropping out" of alternatives with a "carving in relief" of the one path that remains. Other states of weakness or opposition have the same basis, for example, desiring without trying. Conscious or unconscious tension implies that one path has not emerged with clarity. The situation is reminiscent of the young man who asked which girl he should marry and was told, if you have to ask, the answer is neither. One could say the love is not strong enough, but in truth, the feeling for the girl is not love.

Regarding the relation of desire to motivation, the latter is an activity at the inception of willing or the activation of the mind/brain state, closer to unconscious drive and animal behavior. Motivation is ordinarily less specific. When its object resolves, and is anticipated or thought about, it is replaced by want or desire. The terms are often interchangeable but there are important differences. One can have a general *motivation* to work and a *desire* to work in a specific capacity. One can feel desire but lack motivation. The reverse is less common, that is, motivation without desire, but there are states such as the will to succeed without a specific goal, or a motivation for action under duress or the threat of reprisal, say a motivation to pay back taxes to avoid a fine or prison. In such instances, the motivation is for one thing and the desire for another. Generally, the earlier phase of motivation specifies in a desire where, if concentrated, it accentuates a direction to the object, or dissipates even as the desire remains. A person may continue to love and desire someone but know there is little chance of success. It seems likely that desire without motivation reflects various checks or competing emotions, such as lack of courage or confidence, opposing beliefs, etc.

Willing as a forward surge, and motivation as activation without a distinct object, are accompaniments or forerunners of drive-categories that lead to intentional states. They mark off categories of feeling that include wishes, wants, fears, hopes and so on, any of which can dominate cognition at any moment. For microgenetic theory, desire is a segment in the mental state midway from its onset in unconscious will to its termination in conscious acts or objects, with the entire state an epochal whole. This means that an antecedent phase is neither causal to the next nor separable from the ones that follow. The transit is like a wave that hurtles to the shore, each segment of which can be given a separate designation though it is unbroken and continuous and the segments are categories that shift with each recurrence.

Desire and belief

The interpretation of desire in terms of belief, for example, I desire a vacation (person, thing) because I believe it is good, is an attempt to consign desire to cognition, that is, thought, and drain it of feeling, that is, eliminate emotion as a confound of rationality. This strategy justifies an explanation in terms of a judgment, say of goodness or truth, even as it sacrifices the meaning or psychological reality of its topic. What is the value of an explanation that does not address what it purports to explain? Belief accompanies, underlies or is transitional to desire but cannot replace it, just as an image is transitional to an object, or meaning to phonology, yet one cannot thoughtfully explain a thing by substituting another that is equally in need of explanation. Still, this maneuver is widespread, and probably owes to the pressure for a scientific explanation that reduces psychic contents to brain or genome. In philosophy, however, it is a sham to distort and trivialize psychological phenomena as problems of logic or rational thought. The fact that explanation engages reason does not require a rational entity for an object.

What is the relation of belief to desire? Implicit beliefs in the core are unconscious biases or tendencies, valuations, presuppositions that guide the organism in its relation to the world. These beliefs specify in the relation of subject and object, later, self and other. Pleasure-seeking and approach/avoidance derive from instinctual aggression and defense. The unconscious primitives or drive-categories that guide feeling and sexual behavior in animals evolve in humans to distinctions in consciousness, such as those of mind and world. Implicit beliefs in the core constrain the wants and aversions of conscious choice. Unconscious beliefs foreshadow conscious desires but do not motivate or cause them; rather, they are inferred from desire as proclivities to action.

The unconscious belief lays down a bias or trend that, in human experience, is refined in the drive-category. In human thought, instinctual categories adapt to become unconscious presuppositions, for example, an implicit belief in a real outer world. An *explicit* belief is the conscious derivative of an unconscious one. This derivation involves a qualitative change, not a copy of the ancestral form. Implicit beliefs are not plucked out of the unconscious and deposited in consciousness, or illuminated by a conscious searchlight, but specify as they transform into conscious phenomena. The specification, *inter alia*, makes the belief intentional, delays action and permits the intra-personal image to propagate in thought as a forerunner that is embedded in an extra-personal object. The dominant segment of the mental state can vary each moment over phases in the actualization from drive-like, to desire-like, to object-like segments, accounting for the frequent confusion of drive with desire, or desire with its object.

For example, desire in love develops from implicit attractions that conscious belief serves to justify, that is, inherited repertoires that bias mate selection. This transition is displayed in the confusion as to the extent to which sexual attraction figures in love, or the role of thought and imagination in judgments relating to the loved object. Similarly, in the transition from hunger as a drive, to desire in the choice of nourishment, a vegetarian may justify a preference by ecological or religious belief, but the preference—belief, object—develops out of generic categories related to primitive feeding. Instinctual trends or animal preferences in food selection are constrained by experience to novel sub-categories. Even table manners, which could as well be considered little acts of kindness, even if they serve for class distinctions, derive from primitive modes of feeding and digestion, including restraints on cannibalism (Lévi-Strauss, 1968/1978). Conscious belief accompanies desire not as a cause but as an explanation, for example, I desire x because I believe it is good, or I believe x is good and therefore I desire it.

At best, implicit and explicit beliefs are causal as constraints, that is, to the extent they define an act by eliminating alternatives.

From instinct to ideal

Carnal love, or romantic love as *eros*, is aligned with appetitive behavior, while value, volition and the union of souls in loving friendship (*philia*) were, for Plato, transitional to the love of wisdom. The major themes of writings on this topic since the *Symposium* are the debasement of sexual attraction, the adornment of sexual drive to the love of friendship and of non-sexualized objects or ideals, love as an attachment among diverse genders, and the replacement of spiritual union by intellectual compatibility. The fusion of lover and beloved in a completion of the whole has, for the most part, remained the myth it was in the discourse of Aristophanes. Schopenhauer went so far as to write that sexual attraction is proportionate to its moral and physical properties, which depend on the degree to which virtue and deficiencies are balanced in union. Conversely, some modern scholars reduce love to a biological drive in which the mating of opposites widens the gene pool to facilitate survival.

When the object of love is not an individual but reason, truth or the good, or when it is distilled to compassion or the love of humanity, the meaning of love and the feeling of being in love, are distorted beyond relevance to everyday life. For many people, cynicism only takes one disappointment. They acknowledge the reality, indeed, the indispensability, of desire but dismiss lovers as moony. Since love comes and goes while reason and truth prevail, there is a mismatch of the particular and evanescent with the timeless and universal. When love "detaches" from the particular and spreads to the category, its object is an idea that entails intentional feeling, agency, and choice. While the passion for an idea can be as powerful as that for a person, is it still love when the romance, obsession, and sensuality for a concrete individual is replaced by an ideal that is uncoupled from, though still illustrated by, a particular? In love, the other is a unique particular from which the ideal is generated. The instance is the paragon of the category. Her intelligence, his beauty, is beyond compare! Stendhal wrote that the lover sees perfection in the beloved.

To idealize the perfection of the beloved is not the same as the idealization of perfection. As an ideal, perfection can encompass a variety of particulars, especially mathematic ones, whereas the ideal in love is related to the attributes of the beloved. Any or every quality can be perceived to be perfect, and the perfection of a beloved is believed by no-one save the lover. The idealization retains the individuality of its object, with the category enfolding a set of attributes in the beloved that are not readily transferred to another person with similar qualities, in contrast to other ideals—courage, truth—in which the particulars are illustrations.

What is the relation of individual love to a love directed to the most abstract, or least particular, of all ideas, that of god? In the giving and receiving of god's love (*agape*), some attributes of the erotic recur in fantasies of wedded bliss, celibacy, fidelity, and obedience to god the father and, in mystical descent, the search for oneness with god's love (Leuba, 1925). Here we see a continuity of the passion for a concept or ideal with that for a loved object internalized to an image or category. With love of god, there is no object that can be perceived, known or grasped except for its ideal properties, such as eternal, all-knowing or all-powerful. On the other hand, primitive feelings, instincts, and drives in animals seem devoid of ideational content though appetites enfold instances, say edible and non-edible objects, or potential and inappropriate mates. Could one say the love of god is a mode of erotic or non-erotic desire in which the dominant object recedes to—or begins with—an ideal category in the imagination that grows independent of its source? Some forms of pathological love such as erotomania are like this, but so is the love of god that is unrequited.[1]

To the extent that the love for concrete or abstract concepts that are categories of unique particulars is identical to that for ideas and beliefs that are not, the feeling of love would be invariant across its differing manifestations. This might suggest that the feeling of love is attached to, or liberated by, the object or idea, and that feeling and object attach or detach *at will*. This approach, which is still prevalent in spite of a dearth of evidence in its favor, splits the idea from the feeling and equates love with knowledge and choice rather than emotion or intuition, a trend accentuated by the energic quality of feeling that leaves little ground for rational discourse.

The ideal and the particular

Consider the process through which a love that is directed to an object—abstract or concrete, animate or inanimate—withdraws and so accentuates a phase in the imagination (conceptual-feeling) where external features revive underlying categories excluding those which might nullify otherwise ideal individualities. The loved object finds its source in the mind of the lover, in this respect leaving the objective world and external interest for a sphere of subjective ideation. The object is still in the world but earlier segments (concepts, categories) are enhanced prior to objectification. An object in the world or in the mind will no longer have an apportioned quota of affect, but swells with feeling in the arousal of antecedent phases, especially those brought to life by artistic creativity. Love and desire have their substrates in the normal underpinnings of everyday objects. More precisely, the retreat to pre-object categories replaces the interest in a perceptual object as the first step in idealization.

The enhancement at early phases in object-formation drowns out attributes that are undesirable or extrinsic to the category. A limp, a large nose, an odd personality, cultural or religious differences, quirky political beliefs, are "swept under the rug," justified or dismissed as inessential. The ideal is prior to an objective locus, so what would otherwise be an ordinary object is prefigured by a valued category. The rough spots are smoothed over as other attributes take on appeal or an attractiveness that often mystifies the judgments of others. Almost any object or idea can undergo expansion and idealization in the imagination. Indeed, when the ideal erodes with experience, latent incompatibilities, no longer marginalized by the romantic ideals that justified union, rise into prominence as a kind of negative ideal that justifies separation. The beloved who was most wonderful and brought magic to life is now a monster who makes life a living hell.

As the concept within the object comes to the fore, the existence of the object—its minimal affective investment—heightened to interest, is replaced by the more intense feeling associated with pre-object phases in the affect-development. The interest that isolated the other in the perceptual field becomes a desire to have and possess. Interest in an objectified concept becomes desire for a subjective pre-object. As love grows in the imagination, the precursors of the object become its idealized categories. Phases in normal object and affect development uncovered in the inward regress are shown in Figure 3.1.

The phase of category-formation in the transition from drive to desire or from the instinctual to the intentional carries the developing configuration from need to wish, or from necessity to possibility. The ingress of the beloved to its conceptual antecedents creates a dominant

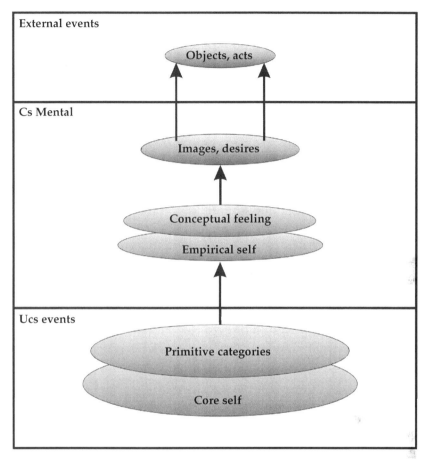

Figure 3.1. The object withdraws—is revived—with an emphasis at an out-going phase of conceptual-feeling (idea, image, desire) where it undergoes idealization and growth in the imagination. The conscious self of wish or desire is derived from the core self of drive or need. Identification or fusion occurs as the qualities of the beloved assimilate to earlier phases of self and conceptual-feeling.

focus at an earlier segment in this transition. The closer the segment to *unconscious drive*, the more the beloved must satisfy the lover's *needs*. The closer to *conscious desire*, the more the *wish* must be fulfilled. Need implements the mentality of the core, informing the wish as it ramifies to diverse mental and external events.

According to this way of thinking, certain properties are idealized as endowments of the beloved. Ordinary features become objects of adoration. The part replaces the whole, the whole is colored by the part, and the feeling formerly directed to the whole, of which the properties are parts, is channeled into the property itself as a kind of disembodied concept. In the *Symposium* and elsewhere, Plato has part-whole relations going from lower to higher, for example, from the sexual and corporeal to the refined, from body to soul. The progression is to qualities with good effects on the lover, to good qualities in general, then to deserving or loving the good as a category independent of its instances, then to the wisdom of seeking the good and, finally, to the love of wisdom (philosophy).

Consider someone who likes the taste of ripe grapes. Ripeness as a property of the grape becomes an object of interest, then the seeds and season that give that ripeness, then the fruition of which the grape is an instance, then fruition generally, then the fertility and plenitude of the earth. Each of these attributes or concepts can propagate from the simple pleasure of eating a grape, as from Proust's madeleine. While the propagations are not necessarily aims or reasons for enjoyment, underlying the love of grapes may well be an aesthetic of nature, just as the capacity to love can manifest a deeper love for what is good. The genius of Plato was to know that every particular, itself a category, can be traced to categories of wider scope.

In love, the ideal is a perfection of the abstract, but the concept of the ideal develops when object-properties split off as categories to which the objects belong. To say a painting is beautiful is to say that beauty is a property of the painting, but when the property is idealized, as the category of the beautiful, the painting becomes an exemplar. In art, taste may change and cultural values may differ, but the artwork as an instance of perceived beauty remains much the same. In love, the needs and wants of the lover change, as well as the features of the beloved that fulfilled them. One speaks of the ideal or category as eternal and unchanging, but the idealization of traits in the beloved, unlike the storied hero and castled princess of myth and literature, requires an effort to survive the natural growth and decay of organism.

One does not want to say love is for properties and not the person who exhibits them. A person is not perceived piecemeal, as a bundle of properties, but as a whole in which those properties are subsumed or from which they are extracted. The properties may be initial attractants but their importation is not ordinarily what permeates the subjectivity of the lover; rather, love is for the individual as a whole from which the properties, attributes or qualities are selected. One can admire beauty and intelligence, or respond to physical attributes, but genuine love is for the beloved, not the properties. Love is an assimilation of selves, not a fixation on attributes, though idealization is for those attributes that distinguish the beloved from others. In a word, the self of the beloved is inculcated in relation to need, with the qualities idealized to reinforce and justify that love. Were this not true, love could not survive aging or illness, in which some attributes are lost or altered. Conversely, we know that the attributes of a childhood sweetheart, frozen in time, grow ever fonder in recollection, as do those of a loved one after death. This follows if true love is an intra-psychic assimilation, not an interpersonal association.

It may well be that love changes when the beloved changes in the decay of personality when one can no longer say this is the person I loved. I have seen loving care go on in Alzheimer's disease or other brain disorder with an erosion of the original ideal, at least until the healthy partner is no longer recognized. Love endures in the imagination even as the former self of the beloved is transformed, though institutionalization usually occurs when there is no glimmer of reciprocity. Still, there are occasions in which a healthy partner or parent is devoted for years to a loved one in severe illness, brain injury, coma. Clearly, this reflects the need to care or give love more than the need to receive it. The feeling is likely encouraged by a loving memory of earlier times or a shift to empathy or compassion. The belief in a life-union of souls is very much a reality, even if it is rarely evident in behavior. The beauty of true love is not the foolishness of a false belief, for it is no less false than any belief that cannot be verified.

On the other hand, the explosion of cosmetic surgery to enhance body parts as sexual attractants and obscure the effects of aging shows that many are fearful of being unloved—or desire love—for physical features. The subjectivity of desire is secondary to the physical accoutrements of its object. While there is no denying that initial attraction is often sexual, stimulated by instinctual drive, and that deception and trickery are well-worn tactics in mate-selection, in animals as well as humans, the use of such deception, even to a caricature, indicates the extent to which sexuality replaces love, love becomes mechanical, and the love-object becomes a commodity. Physical attractants have a primacy over interior values and impede the depth to which love descends. We say, in truth, that such a love—if it is so called—is superficial, which means that it rests at the objective surface of the mental state. This is another measure of the shipwreck of materialism, externalism, and object-property distinctions, a consequence of which is the high rate of divorce in Western societies. The quest for love goes on, but in the modern world the subjectivity of the beloved and the belief in a union of souls are exchanged for qualities that no longer serve as lures to attachment but are ends in themselves. Romantic love is still the dream of many but it no longer makes the world go round; indeed, nowadays it is a rare occurrence given the valuation of accidental features and the assumption of interchangeable parts.

Reason and the ideal[2]

The idea that love involves a judgment suggests that volition is involved, even if implicit. Hamlyn (1978) argues that only a being with beliefs and judgments has the capacity to love. This does not mean that love requires a judgment in the sense of a conscious decision, nor the reverse, that judgment implies love, though it can impel valuation. When the choice of the beloved is driven by unconscious need, the beloved is selected over other possibilities, just as any judgment, however well-reasoned, entails a greater valuation of the option chosen. Unlike judgment, love is played out in the conceptual imagination. It is likely that only a person *capable* of reason could love deeply, not that reason is a guide to the choice of a beloved but because it is adaptive and narrows the range of possible others. Reason also contrasts with unreason or irrationality, that is, not the manic or psychotic but the pre-rational or paralogical that is a precursor to the rational. The possibility of reason must exist for it to be relinquished. Otherwise, the person is irrational, immature, or mentally defective. Both reason and madness—in love or other matters—depend on the capacity for an inner life of imaginative thought.

A central observation on the relation of feeling to reason is that feeling comes first and judgment follows. We do not think that reason gives feeling, that is, that love ensues on a clear-headed analysis of the virtues and failings of another person. Instead, deliberation reinforces an emotional bias with justifications for a decision. A judgment that conflicts with a feeling has force only when feeling relents. The judgment exploits the "weak spot" in the feeling, a zone of ambiguity, vulnerability or uncertainty. Justifications provide grounds to dilute or reinforce an emotion that lacks rational support. Deliberation can supplement or replace feeling, reinforced by reflection on the qualities of the beloved, or imperiled, as in jealousy, whether justified or not, by the gossip, critiques or mendacity of others. The prototype is *Othello*, where reason is not pitted against emotion but occluded when emotions are intemperate. This play illustrates that deliberation is not necessarily more rational than feeling. Rather, it accentuates ideational content not apparent in the emotion; indeed, it is the affective tonality latent in a concept that gives impetus to deliberation when it is finally a precursor to action.

Desire is an intentional attitude. The pursuit of the beloved is purposeful, even voluntary. Yet from a psychological point of view (Brown, 2010a), the intentional is not the cause or source of the pursuit but a description of its character. One could argue that all intentionality is desire (fear, etc.), or that there are no non-intentional desires, or that one cannot have an intentional act in which a desire does not aim to be realized. The intentional is a defining characteristic of desire. In the same way, one cannot have "free" will without consciousness, but one is not the cause or condition of the other; they are co-dependent phenomena when the mental state takes on a certain configuration. The same applies to reason. There is irony in the observation that love is an escape from a rationality that is a product of the same evolutionary advance on which it and love depend.

Reasons can be given for love, but love does not flow from them. The reasons are justifications or explanations of the feeling of love, but the love is something other than the reasons given for it. Reasons may express feelings but do not lead to them. This is even more striking in falling out of love, which is often painful but hardly a rational decision. We do not decide to stop loving. We stop loving and try to explain why[3]. We may decide the choice of the other was mistaken but then love has already been lost and the "decision" is just an acknowledgement of this fact. This may be a rational conclusion but the failure is not the result of rational thinking. When there is a loss of reciprocity, reason may conclude that all hope is lost, but this may not mitigate suffering, which can persist despite the rational decision.

In some respects, to derive feeling from reason, or to account for desire based on the properties of the beloved, is like tasting a meal from reading a list of its ingredients as Brahms heard music from a score. This possibility, indeed this way of thinking, illustrates the poverty of a love based on an inventory of attributes. Were I to list the qualities of my beloved, and if those qualities were the basis of my love, it follows, and some philosophers have so argued, that I could love anyone with the same qualities. Yet common intuition, if not logic, tells us this is unlikely, for it is not just the qualities that are incentives to loving, but the imperfections that add to the humanity of the beloved and at the same time satisfy unconscious need. The failings and inadequacies of a beloved are no less important than the virtues, for while the latter may be provocations of conscious desire, the former are fulfillments of unconscious need.

When the idealization of attributes is not sufficient for love or when love is as much for imperfections, weaknesses or vulnerabilities as for positive attributes, we see the influence of unconscious need over conscious desire. A telling illustration of this is in the film, *Belle de Jour* by Bunuel. A woman in a sexless marriage to a man who seems ideal in every respect, who she loves, becomes a prostitute in the afternoon. When she is asked why she does this, she merely replies "I don't know," though the film suggests childhood abuse. The unconscious need that appears in dream is acted out with erotic pleasure in the day though in a state of incomprehension. It is, in fact, the very perfection of the husband, a handsome and loving doctor, who is incapable of the brutality she needs, that forces her to other satisfactions. Unlike the categories of conscious wish and the intentional self that are the basis of her love for her husband as a romantic ideal, the unconscious self of primal need does not form ideals but seeks occasions of satisfaction in primitive categories derived from instinctual drive. One supposes that in the deepest love, unconscious need and conscious desire are equally fulfilled. For many, the deficiencies are most endearing, idealized one could say, making true love a harmonious web of ideals and imperfections.

Conscious ideals and unconscious needs

The tendency to transform the feeling of one person for another into an ideal such as goodness, truth or the absolute, entails that love achieves ideality and purity in the sphere of perfection, or that only perfection—as in the love of god—deserves absolute love. When ideal reason attains perfection, ideal love consents to be reasonable, and perfection loves or reciprocates itself. The ideal perfection of truth or beauty gives love as rational volition. While it may be possible to will the self to fall in love, and many do, repeatedly, we tend to think such love is forced, desperate, artificial or disingenuous. True love neither consents nor is volitional. Reason is the enemy of love as rationality is its antidote. We say one is madly in love to emphasize the lack of control and helplessness of a person overcome with emotion. Nor is true love perfect or reasonable. Perfection is closer to perfect fitness. A bacterium that is perfectly adapted to its host has a perfection that is analogous to the perfect fit of two lovers. There is a beauty in fitness but this is not perfection. First, because it is a local phenomenon; second, because all things defy stasis. Organisms are constantly adapting, becoming more or less perfect in this sense. Process theory is incompatible with perfection. Even the god of process is in change.

We seek perfection as a personal and philosophical ideal. The object of love is conceived as perfect when everyday attributes are replaced by ideals. However, perfection requires stability and the unchanging. The inter-relatedness of all things is such that everything is dependent on some other thing with all things in some sense necessary for any one thing to exist. An object is a contrast in a spatial and temporal surround. An organism is no less dependent on this surround than the food it eats or the air it breathes. With inter-dependence there is lack of self-subsistence and absence of perfection. Nature is a continuous evolution to fitness. The organism adapts to its environment as one individual adapts to another. The adaptation involves the couple as well as the individual, for lovers adapt to each other as couples adjust to changing appearances, attitudes, and circumstances.

The tendency to idealize the beloved places him or her on a pedestal as incomparable. She is a princess, an angel; he is a lord, a king. It is not surprising therefore, that another source of romantic distress is the discovery that the individual cannot accommodate the ideal. If one sees the beloved as perfect, even if perfection is confined to what is perfect for the lover, there is bound to be disappointment. The truth is that only illusion—"living in a dream"—can sustain the idealized version of any man or woman. Since the beloved participates in an ideal category of admirable qualities and realizes an ideal that can mystify the judgment of disinterested observers, it is inevitable that "true" love must, in some sense, be false to be the love that it is. This means that lovers must be in a state of denial to hold on to the fiction of the ideal. This is similar to faith in which a believer must deny all contradictory evidence. Reality chips away at the imagination; every moment of togetherness puts the ideal at risk. This is why love is often best preserved by intermittent contact when the imagination is no longer under siege and the ache of longing is a palliative to the malignancy of incessant contact.

The tendency to idealize the beloved explains how one or several features can enlarge and take on primacy while those less favorable are ignored. A person can be loved for their eyes, a smile, a voice—in the poem of Yeats, for golden hair—even as the lover acknowledges the other's shortcomings or failures. One hears, I am in love in spite of sexual difficulty, lack of humor or generosity, excessive drinking, physical ailments, and so on. Clearly, the positive qualities assume an importance that overwhelms the disagreeable ones. In every love, only a few properties of the individual undergo categorical expansion, while those outside the ideal—excluded from the "reasons" why one falls in love—persist, dormant, and unattended, as seeds of despair for future harvest. This is painting in broad strokes what happens in every act of perception, where objects are categories that stabilize the changing particulars within events. Every object is an event-series or a category over instances of appearance that achieves stability by virtue of self-similar replications. Similarly, the beloved is a category of like-appearances in which the potential dissonance of appearances dissolves as the idealization of a few particulars appropriates the identity of the whole.

Reason and intuition

We can love the wrong person and know we are unreasonable, and we can reject a person that reason tells us is right. The match may be "perfect" but the timing may be off, and even then, it is a feeling felt now and then that subsides into the compatibility on which it is premised. Romantic love is not a combining but an assimilating. The self absorbs that which is lacking and transforms to a novel unity. The effort to reconcile discriminations in unity, for which love (for god, truth) is the highest goal—"highest" in a shift from "lower" objects, or from things to concepts—transfers love from feeling to reason and in so doing loses it. The priest will sermonize on god's love for his children, and their love of god, but only in mystical descent is god's love felt.

The chemistry or intuition of love is not in the satisfaction of conscious desire but the fulfillment of what is complementary in the core. The conscious self knows what it wants but not always what it needs. A wish or a want is an implementation of a need that is more fundamental. The unconscious need, which directs reason to its outcome, can also lead to painful misadventures. The need that is the target of psychoanalytic therapy cannot be reached by reason alone, not only because the unconscious is antecedent to reason or underlies and gives rise to rational thought, but because reason is an outcome, perhaps a veto, but not a search engine. Ideas are final actualities, not starting points, and a succession of ideas is a succession of endpoints. Even if the preparatory bases of thought in the unconscious could be accessed, they would have a structure incompatible with conscious reason. To paraphrase Wittgenstein, if the unconscious could speak we would not, or not fully, understand it.

Pascal's famous epigram, which refers to the intuition of god not romantic love, that the heart has its reasons that reason cannot know (*Le cœur a ses raisons, que la raison ne connaît point*) implies that reason fails to understand what love "knows" directly. Intuition in the romantic sense is immediate, holistic, probably based on subtle perceptual cues such as gesture, facial expression, prosody, and the pragmatics of language and behavior. To act on intuition in love is an act of faith as in religious belief. For many, the love of god depends on the apprehension of order, symmetry, grandeur, and complexity as well as an awareness of constancies, laws, or regularities. Such laws can be grasped by reason but this alone does not lead to faith, just as the qualities of the beloved in themselves do not account for loving. Indeed, the most profound and unconditional love may occur for someone who is scarcely known to the lover. Conceivably, this intuition is grounded in the connection some people establish with horses, pets, or other animals when, it could be argued, the deep unconscious of human instinct is in synch with the world of animal mind.

Intuition is a necessary leap of faith when reason fails to give certainty. Truth can be obscured by language when conscious desire conflicts with unconscious need. The transition from need to want, from unconscious to conscious, is not a mere conveyance; it is a gradual translation from one language to another, from symbol to fact, from fantasy to reality. In this qualitative transform, the self and its contents actualize as one of many possible routes to implementation. The conscious self and its desires are mutable, not necessarily in conformance with unconscious drive. Desire can be for the many as well as the one.

Its targets may be exchanged. One may profess desire but be hesitant or tentative. One may feign disinterest to mask desire or feign desire for covert ends. Is a bouquet a gift or a bribe? Is the other pursued for love or mischief? Is sex a consummation or a lure? In such instances, unconscious ends precede conscious means, which are instrumental in achieving the tacit goals toward which they are directed. Since the "disconnect" of need and want is occasioned by lack of access to the unconscious, and the transition is uni-directional, the deceptions and strategies of desire must be "decoded" by intuition to disambiguate the possibility of insincerity.

The conscious wish is in play in the individual who, seeking a likeness, finds a companion. The gaze of the self at its replica—a Rorschach in a mirror—is a resemblance not a complement. Does similarity lead to passion or to friendship? Is opposition necessary for completion? The myth of Narcissus is not an example of passion for likeness but a satire of its futility. Regardless of the degree to which lovers are a match in likeness or in difference, the self absorbs the other to supplement its own infrastructure, seeking wholeness in completion or absorption in acquiescence. A lover becomes whole in receiving the qualities of the beloved in the imagination or, in giving, in the assimilation to a novel totality.

The blending of opposites begs the question why the coming together of contrasts leads to completion, not conflict. Opposing qualities are received as virtues, not repudiations, and fusion is based, one hopes, not on neurosis but on need and mutual fulfillment. The striving of the unconscious can lead to discord or harmony. Since the core and its needs are unconscious, and one cannot know at the beginning if the love is real or will last, contrasts between lovers are sources of attachment as well as later disillusion and unhappiness. The initial sources of attraction and the satisfactions of erotic need give way to disputes and alienation when passion does not evolve to companionship. Contrasting personalities make for stimulating partners but the overlap of commonalties makes the union endure. Even in couples that on the surface seem mismatched, a deeper union must be present. The similarities that insure friendship and companionability must be sufficient to offset conflicts after passion subsides. The predicament lies in the mutability of emotion in relation to changing occasions and the incompleteness inherent in growth and decay, thus the imperfection of organisms that constantly adapt to survive.

What we know about the other may influence how we feel, but love is only alive when we accept feeling, not knowledge, as the core of loving and the ultimate nature of things. Love is not rightly the "highest" emotion but it is the one mode of feeling in which we are bound together in a living dynamic of relatedness. The relation of self to non-self (object) that is the foundation on which self-consciousness develops is not a bridge to the other but a penetration to a common ground. There is incomplete revival to the conceptual sources of the other in the core with both lover and beloved, self and other, arising in the same plane of primitive mentality. True love uncovers the original home of the beloved. To find a true love is to remove the accretions that obscure a vision of the one who has always been there waiting to be discovered.

Love and the object

Is the feeling or meaning of love imperiled by the many objects and uses of the term or does the object, in its development, generate feelings of love or other emotions unique to that object? When one says, "I love my new hat" or "I loved that film," is there a dilution or over-inclusion of the romantic meaning? Certainly, we admit the vast difference between loving a hat or film and loving a person, but could the broadening of reference account for the ease with which some people say they are in love or seem to routinely fall in and out of love? This is not to imply that saying "I love you" cannot correspond to a feeling of love, just that the wide scope of employment of the term has some relation to the concentration of affect in the speaker when that term is used. Indeed, to say one is in love does not signify, at that moment, that one is in a state of loving. To report one's feelings is not to feel them; the feeling or experience of love is prior to language. To repeat the words *I love you*, may be a sincere expression of love, or it can be a meaningless mantra. Indeed, even when the vocabulary of love is most eloquent, a self-conscious speaker or writer can be remote from lived feeling. The poetry of love is composed in privacy—emotion recollected in tranquility[4]—as an image that embodies a feeling compressed in a phrase. The actual experience of love, for a beloved, a child or for god, is ineffable.[5]

Thus the question, does the application of the term to so many objects weaken the force of feeling as it widens its scope? Does the widening of the category dull the sentiment conveyed in saying "I love you"? Does the generality in the use of the term influence its application in specific contexts? Once at a dinner, a woman said her husband was passionate about his wines. I asked him if this was the same passion he had for his wife, and he begged the issue with charm, saying that at least he was the master of his vineyard. The incident, however, points to the difficulty in using the same word to describe the feeling for a variety of objects and how it differs, if it does, according to the object to which love is applied.

One can say the feeling of want is closer to need, urge, and drive, while desire is elaborated further in the process and is closer to wish, to hope and expectation. These terms capture subtle differences in feeling-tone in relation to the experiential and situational context and dominant phase of process at which they arise. So one answer to the questions raised above is that the quality and intensity of love (or any feeling) for a thing or a beloved, depends on an attunement of the microgeny in relation to unconscious dispositions and conceptual-feelings in the passage from drive to desire. Terms influence meanings because they actualize concepts that constrain and deliver them to consciousness, not because the concepts are built of the terms they realize.

In romantic love, the object—the beloved—seems in opposition to the subject (self) as the thing that is loved, an opposition thought to depend on an interaction of self and other. We all want to hear an affirmation of love (approval, value, desire, etc.), but this actualizes the oneness of lovers into a subject-object relation, turning a feeling that inheres in a concept into a statement that implies agency. The self that declares, "I love you"—more precisely, the set of phenomena that includes the speaker, the listener, feeling, statement and their relative "positions," distinguished by what is earlier, later, prior or consequent in the mental state—does not so much describe the feeling of love as it motivates the declaration. "We are love" or "the love that fills us" are more apt descriptions. Desire, pursuit, and acquisition fill the mind of a lover as the self wills the choice of the beloved. But far from *conscious* willing, once love and the ideal fill the imagination, passion, and volition are almost reciprocals since it is often the case that the greater the passion, the more powerless the lover, a passivity incorporated in phrases such as falling, madly, overcome, helpless, and so on.

When thought is centered at a phase of imagery and choice, the self seems to plan and strategize. How can I be with my beloved? How can I make her/him love me? Is my love hopeless? Am I loved in return? The volitional or intentional is co-temporal with conceptual feeling.

When one leaves the highway of drive and passion for the byways of refined feelings, choices *implicit* in the conviction of love—the certainty one loves and is loved in return—become *explicit*. At every phase there is a covert sculpting of possibility as feelings, acts, and objects carve out potential. With a prominence of the intentional, as in desire, the individual is conscious of options and uncertainties. The voluntary in love is the feeling of choice when passion is no longer dominant. What happens is that the self becomes conscious of an implicit decision that would otherwise have been embedded in the transformation to an ensuing phase.

The notion that love involves judgment conforms to common-sense as a widely accepted way of describing *inter alia* the state of loving. It implies that an attribution of love is optional, which in passionate or true love it is, but *implicitly*. The elicitation of acts and objects as sets of contrasts out of potential by way of constraints at successive phases entails possibility at every phase, such that the final configuration is the final choice, even if the individual is unaware of choosing and perceives the actual endpoint as a spontaneous finality.

Love may be rational or irrational, mature or juvenile, healthy or neurotic, according to the needs that underlie it. It can be shaped by unconscious need or conscious desire, but the proximity to need determines its authenticity. The earlier in process the sources of love, the closer to need and drive, to primitive cognition, compulsion, and unreason. The irrational is less voluntary. The intentional entails a judgment, which can be independent of rationality, though reason is associated with consciousness and volition. The idea of love as a defiance of reason agrees with the view of passion as a destructive force and the usual incompatibility of passionate courtship with domestic tedium. It is not the destiny of passion to guarantee recurrence. Union in love is a wholeness of spirit or self that lasts as long as love lasts.

One way to think about love and its object is to distinguish the varieties of emotions—passion and ecstasy at one extreme, interest, fondness, and affection at the other—or the sexual and non-sexual, the concrete and abstract, living and non-living objects, love for an individual or for an idea, and consider each a unique state of affairs determined by extrinsic relations. On this view, the intensity or quantity of feeling differs with its object, and this change in feeling accounts for what appear to be qualitative differences. I think the correct interpretation is that an object is an extension of the subject's mind, *an objectification of the internal relations in a wholly subjective field* with the consequence that a shift from interest to desire, from drive to affection, or from passion to boredom, points to the dominant segment over phases in the actualization process and from one moment to the next.

Autonomy and wholeness

The regression of the beloved to an imaginative phase in the mental life of the lover has the effect of a revival prior to full analysis. The oneness with the beloved actualizes a locus in the mental state before full individuation. In most people, individuation leads to progressive autonomy (Brown, 2005). This process is arrested in love as incomplete individuation and organic wholeness replace final detachment. The magnification of the antecedent or juvenile is an example of neoteny (Brown, 1996), with growth at phases ordinarily submerged in a transition to endpoint cognition. The retardation of the juvenile in morphogenesis as a means of evolutionary advance, for example, post-partum brain growth with open cranial sutures, is repeated in dependency and fusion.

There is good reason why we speak of lovers as childish or foolish, relating to the psychoanalytic concept that love depends on transference from an incestuous to non-incestuous object, and the likely derivation of romantic love and the wish for intimacy from the experience of parental love and the ancestral cognition of childhood. The life-course from fusion with the mother to separation and death is replayed each moment in lived experience. Objects, like individuals, strive for independence, only to perish and be replaced. The world develops in the mind and vanishes as a novel world appears. The natural outcome of incessant perishing is autonomy and final detachment. The world disappears, the self decomposes, all replaced in the minds and memories of others.

Ultimately, loving is a form of valuation, in which attributes of the beloved are valued above all others, and in which those valuations become part of the value system of the core. In the assimilation of value, the self is transformed. Self-centered or egocentric values are moderated by those that are other-directed or unselfish, to the point where the self identifies with the needs of others, shares their wishes, now part of the lover's core, even to self-sacrifice for the sake of others. Philosophical theories also equate love with value, for example, Velleman (1999),

Kolodny (2003) but as appraisal, evaluation or bestowal (Singer, 1994), namely, projections onto the other of judgments of worth (Helm, 2005).

Instead, the implicit or unconscious values that, with implicit beliefs, are the engines of behavior come to be infiltrated by the beloved. An implicit value is a deep category of thought and action that drives the mental state to outcomes that are self- or other-directed, thus to behaviors that can be judged as good or bad. Values and beliefs are the primary constructs of character, instilled in maturation by experience and adaptation. The idea of love as judgment or appraisal, or as a valuation of the worth of the beloved, even if this is more characteristic of friendship than true love, along with the unselfishness, even altruism of love, the tendency to admire the good in the beloved and ignore or rationalize the bad, the progression from the carnal to the spiritual, the seeking of union with god or the good, all bring love into relation with moral concepts (Brown, 2005).

Notes

1. The goal of mystical union is to bathe in god's love but many claim that a perfect god could not be expected to love individuals with all their imperfections.
2. The reference to the irrational in relation to emotion implies an absence of rational judgment, volition or deliberation, not illogic or lunacy. The irrational may or may not be adaptive but that is independent of its (lack of) rationality.
3. In the novel, *The Alchemy of Desire,* by Tarun Tejpal, a man suddenly becomes aware he is no longer in love and attempts to understand why.
4. Wordsworth, *Preface to Lyrical Ballads.*
5. Imaging studies on those who say they are in love are clearly measuring something other than love.

CHAPTER FOUR

The reconciliation of the emotions: love, envy, and hate

Odi et amo. Quare id faciam, fortasse requiris.
Nescio. Sed fieri sentio et excrucior.
I hate and I love. Perhaps you ask me why I am doing this,
I do not know; I only feel it happening, and I am crucified.

—Catullus, *Carmen 85* (*c.* 60BC)

Love and hate

In a play by Pirandello, a man on his knees pleads for the love of a woman who rejects him. His pleas continue and she becomes contemptuous. Finally realizing that his entreaties are useless, he rises to his feet screaming, I hate you. This very plausible scenario, in which love suddenly transforms to hate, actually rage, implies a closeness or opposition of love and hate. Many a love is punctuated by fits of anger and bouts of remorse. It is likely that the lover in Pirandello's play would soon forget his hatred if he were embraced and reassured he is loved after all. Is the opposition in the domain of emotions like that, in the realm of meaning or perceptual experience, of life and death, night and day, black and white, or hot and cold? With drive-like behaviors one has oppositions such as hunger and satiety or fight and flight, but in the sphere of human emotion, why do we think oppositions are closer than neighboring items? Why does the mind attend to oppositions rather than gradations?

In most instances there is a gradual transition from one extreme to another, not a sudden replacement as in love, and most transitions are reversible. Love may be replaced by hate but the reverse also occurs. We are usually not sated or starving but somewhere in-between. Is the abandon of love a passion that spills into other feelings? If intensity of feeling is a characteristic of the individual regardless of what feeling is felt, say in the distinction of passionate and phlegmatic personalities, the quality of the feeling would be independent of its intensity. "Still water runs deep," the saying goes, to capture this intuition, that a feeling can be strongly felt but not apparent to the observer, which by the way is another argument against the James-Lange theory. The other side of this observation, for example, "shallow brooks are noisy," refers to those who are demonstrative with feelings that come and go quickly.

In the example from Pirandello the reaction is to the rejection but also to the humiliation when a declaration of love is ignored or ridiculed. The rejection is not merely for a statement, but is dismissive of the intent for sacrifice and devotion. The response depends, on the one hand, on the interplay of rejection, humiliation and ridicule, and on the other, on the degree to which the love is invested in the beloved. Humiliation and/or ridicule invite hatred more than rejection, for the way a love is rejected, together with the beliefs—expectations, etc.—of the lover, influence the reaction. A rejected lover can become aggressive, even homicidal. That we understand such reactions is seen in the lesser punishment in many countries for "crimes of passion." Among the emotions that occur with rejection are a feeling of impotence in which the disapproval of the beloved is taken as a tacit aggression, that is, if she doesn't love me, she hates me so my hate is what she deserves. There is also the feeling of loss or theft of a precious object, jealousy, the feeling "if I don't have him or her, no-one else will," and/or rage at a person who, in their indifference, has shattered all hopes for the future. And of course, violence can turn inward as depression or suicide.

Unrequited passion can lead to anger but so can other provocations. Some people fly into a homicidal rage if they are accidentally bumped on the street, or if a car pulls in front of them. Intensity of feeling is not a sign of kinship to the circumstances of its occurrence but signals proximity to drive. Generally, the more superficial (objective) the dominant phase, the more distributed, external and weaker the affective tonality. The relation of love and hate points to an equivalent cognitive depth of an involuntary focus of intense feeling in one object of consuming interest.

The primary instigators of hatred in love are rejection, lack of reciprocity and betrayal, which are taken as evidence that love is not returned in kind or degree. With rejection, the self is not merely deprived of the values of the beloved; its intrinsic valuations are diminished. Ridicule is a means to humiliate. Rejection or humiliation is not just for the interests and advances of the lover but is a repudiation of the lover's values, character, and personality. The lover can sacrifice the valuations of the beloved but when the lover's worth is rejected or ridiculed, the feeling of unworthiness exposes the beloved's appraisal of the lover as valueless. It is not the withdrawal of the supplemental value of the beloved that incites hatred, but the threat to the core self when all it has to give is treated as an object of disdain. The extent to which the beloved is incorporated in the unconscious self determines the intensity of the reaction; the deeper the ingression, the more devastating the loss.

The response can range from justification to criticism to re-appraisal and greater self-knowledge but also to rage and revenge. The effort to avoid dissolution is *self*-preservation. The indifference of the beloved is usually less threatening than the mocking and scorn that undermine the self-image. When values that account for self-identity are ridiculed, the self clings to its former identity and directs anger at whoever attacks its core structure. The self can forego the assimilated beloved on realizing a lack of reciprocity, but it cannot easily ignore the repudiation of the values and beliefs by which it is constituted. Not all rejected lovers are enraged or suicidal, no doubt owing to pre-existing differences in self-esteem, "ego-strength" or autonomy. However, if one handles rejection in love indifferently or with detachment, it is likely the love was not intense or genuine.

The encroachment by the beloved on the lover's core is conditional on trust, since the assimilation of the other is a potential threat. The individual who is fearful of commitment may not fully trust the other to assimilate values that can be a prelude to betrayal and loss. Sexual relations can be a source of pain or pleasure depending on whether the individual is fulfilled or violated. The innermost chamber of the lover is penetrated, psychically in love, physically in sex, each with the potential for immeasurable joy or profound sorrow. The other is accepted in the oneness of loving, but a withdrawal of valuations and an attack on the core are threats to identity and personhood. Thus hate appears as a self-protective act of aggression to sever the bond by which the self can be destroyed.

Hate is anger *at* the object; love is desire *for* the object. Hate divides, love unites, though unremitting hatred can become a perverse motivation for continuous attachment. Ordinarily, the imagination in love and hate leaves the sphere of perceptual imagery and discharges in action. In love, the desire for proximity is the ground of sharing. In hate, the desire is to vent anger, to hurt or to be rid of the other by separation or destruction. If the survival of the core is at stake, as it is in the betrayal of a passionate and genuine love, the self must either collapse or be protected and the threat must be removed or eliminated. Individuals with a strong sense of self may be less vulnerable to the humiliation that is the basis of hate in unrequited love but most likely, as noted, they are less capable of passionate loving.

There are many reasons for rejection and many ways to manage it, some pro-active, others after the fact. To describe the modes, means, and methods of rejection is to recount a history of human experience. An individual may approach the other too forcefully or not forcefully enough. A personal trait may be unappealing. The disparity in attractiveness, culture, or intelligence may be too great. Whatever the reasons, the loss of love or the discovery it is not genuine, owing to acts or revelations of self or other, including the transfer of feeling to another lover, decant to a mutual lack of intuitive knowledge of self and beloved. The conscious expectations that guide each lover are out of synch with core needs and proclivities. We may be told who we should love, or have a list of attributes we are seeking, but most traits sought in a *partner* or those instructed to a novice, are found in all cultures (Buss, 1994). Mate selection has a utilitarian quality but this is not necessary for falling in love. The current joke, that the economy is so bad that women are now marrying for love, embodies this sentiment. Historically, passion and marriage were believed incompatible. "For better or worse," as the marital oath goes, a person guided to the beloved by unconscious beliefs and values is, if love is reciprocated, more likely to find emotional release, even if conditions are not suitable for lasting union.

We think of hate as bound to love even if reason tells us that the proper emotion in rejection is sorrow, not anger. To some, sorrow or melancholia is anger directed at the self, while hate transports anger outward to the source of the injury. Love and hate are blind to reason. Their similarity suggests that, with rare exceptions, lacking a passion for either emotion, a person who is incapable of hating is incapable of loving. Love and hate can be—often are—obsessions. The individual is absorbed with the other who fills all thoughts and desires, in love or in anger, to the exclusion of others, even other activities. Revenge is the satisfaction of hate as union is of love. The one destroys, the other creates: life and death; value in organic wholes, the energy of atomic parts; synthesis and analysis; integration and decomposition. The Hindus well understood the foundation in a single entity—*Shiva, Kali*—of the power to create and to destroy. The power to harm, even an injurious wish, though unfulfilled, replaces the helplessness in abandonment, especially the disempowerment that accompanies rejection.

There is grief when a beloved, who has become part of the self, is lost in betrayal or death. In some respects it does not matter whether or not the parting is deliberate. A beloved lost to death is, from the perspective of the lover, no less lost than one who decides to leave, except that death does not provoke guilt or feelings of responsibility and animosity, and removes the fantasy of reunion save that in the after-life. When the beloved dies or abandons the lover, mourning may reach the point of suicidal depression (for some, the ultimate in emptiness or self-anger). The death of the beloved leaves an objectless void for ideals that persist, but if the lover is willfully deserted by choice, not happenstance, that is, by the capriciousness of the beloved, there is someone to blame for the loss, for example, the beloved or a competitor. In death, one may blame the doctors but usually one can only shake a fist at a merciless god and feel doubly abandoned, while in rejection, hatred fills the emptiness that in death remains a void.

In the sense that hatred for the beloved is hatred for his or her values and beliefs that are installed in the lover's core, hatred can be interpreted as anger at those configural patterns in the self that the beloved represents. When mourning is replaced by anger, the anger arises from an injury to that aspect of the lover's self the beloved has altered or infiltrated. In the absence of anger, when the defensive vectors prevail over the aggressive ones, or when self-protection is achieved by intra-personal growth and renewal rather than extra-personal action, grieving is a mode of self-recovery, a period of healing (reconstitution) of a self that formerly was a composite of the beloved.

Hate, imagery, and idealization

Love is bound up with the assimilation and idealization of values of the beloved. Hate entails a negative valuation, and a belief—true or false—the other has gravely wounded the self or some person or thing the self loves. How does an ideal of the beloved evaporate in hateful thoughts or impulses? What in hate corresponds to the ideal in love? We think of ideals as positive values. We would say goodness or truth is an ideal, but not evil or falsehood. A negative value is an idea that seems to gather affect in conflict with its opposite. We can imagine that love is the opposite of hate even in the midst of hating, but less often do we think in the act of loving, that its opposite could be hate. Yet when love dies, hate may fill the vacuum as unspent passion is channeled to anger by disdain.

Positive or exocentric values or ideals tend to realize the forerunners of the *percept*-development, while negative or egocentric values tend to be realized in the *action*-development. The object-development under-lies the formation of categories and affective tonalities that are biased to a morally *positive* direction while bias to the action-development tends to acquisition and the enactment of selfish needs. The natural course of the negative is through the precursors of action, that of the positive, the antecedents of objects. Put otherwise, action tends to survival and self-affirmation, perception to the affirmation of others in need and dependency. Thoughts arise in the delay of action as imagery takes on a positive or negative aim, yet the negative is biased to action by instinc-tual aggression. Naturally, contrasting responses may—often do—occur, action serving to implement positive values, perceptual imagery taking a negative turn with violent thoughts leading to aggression. Yet, plans driven by aggression are probably less common than plans gov-erned by pleasure (Freud's principle). Since self-pleasure is not neces-sarily at the other's expense, especially in love and sexual desire, and since many people will endure suffering for desirable ends but are not sadistic,[1] imagery tends to dwell on the agreeable, even if it is for the benefit of the self. Imagery can represent a range of possibilities and conflicts denied to action that action must resolve. There is ordinarily a definiteness and finality to aggression that contrasts with the flexibility and openness of pleasure, as in the contrast of bodily pain and physical delight.

As I have pointed out in the past, there is evidence in neuropsychol-ogy that action generates a feeling of agency, while perception generates a feeling of passivity. That is, agency does not initiate or guide an action but is generated as part of the action-development, as an incipient or overt phenomenon, whereas the objects of perception are felt to be received by the person, not because sensory data come to us from "outside," but because the object-development elaborates an attitude of passivity to objects that are actively produced. This insight, that the feeling of activity or passivity inheres in conscious action or perception, such that agency is felt to precede action and passivity to underlie the independence of objects from the observer, reinforces the idea that activity implements aggressive or self-centered values and passivity implements the defensive or other-centered ones. However, although these vectors are in opposition, they are not restricted to one or another value set but are biases with considerable overlap in their implementations (Figure 4.1).

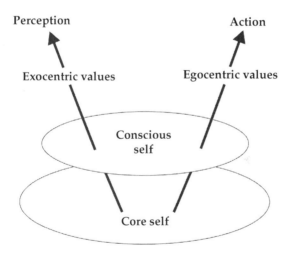

Figure 4.1. The unitary core fractionates to the main limbs of action and perception. Language production and perception are grafted onto this development. The action-development carries the self and body outward to the world to implement drives and desires. The percept-development deposits objects as aims. Generally, the action-development actualizes egocentric values, or values that realize self-interest. The percept-development actualizes objects as targets of self-interest but in its passive or receptive attitude conveys a feeling of self-denial in which the interests of the object (other) have priority over those of the self. This division is a bias that can shift in either direction.

Thought arises in the abeyance of perceptual realization as visual or verbal (inner speech) imagery comes to the fore. Thinking can be rational or irrational; it can be recurrent and obsessive, creative, and idiosyncratic, and it can appear in wish, daydream, reverie or fantasy. For the most part, the imagination is self-indulgent. Desires are sometimes clear, at other times disguised, but at all times seeking pleasure (or avoiding displeasure). Only rarely does the pain of others give self-pleasure. When it does, and when infiltrated by personal grudge, it can be a breeding ground for hate, along with images of violence. The other is ordinarily a means to self-pleasure. It is unusual that a wish consists of tormenting someone, and the pleasures others offer the self may be pleasurable for them. The pleasure of love and the beloved in the imagination contrasts with the relative poverty in the imagination of inflicting pain.

Polarities and transitions

It is the case that the human mind seeks dualities where there are mainly gradations. We concentrate on extremes because gradations are invisible, impalpable and inaudible. The mind settles on (creates) an object, an idea or emotional state, that is, a category, as a perceptual or logical solid. We see objects in motion, not a succession of snapshots constituting an event, or an event carved into objects. We speak of an emotion as a state, yet it is a fleeting experience that is never exactly the same. We revive events in memory with greater facility than the feelings that accompanied them. The categorical nature of the object contrasts with the dynamic or processual nature of the feeling. Ideas, objects, inner and outer stabilities, are artificial demarcations. Unaware that flux is constitutive, or of the transitions in and out of states, we still do not have the experience of objects as contrasts, or that what exists is in relation to what does not. The *via negativa* in religious or philosophical thought—the elimination of what the object is not—is critical to the microgenetic process though it is not accessible to ordinary mentation. The poet Mark Strand captured this reality when he wrote, "in a field I am the absence of field ... wherever I am, I am what is missing." We are defined by what we are and what we are not. From this realization, and from the blindness to gradations, the idea of opposing states comes into mind.

The process leading from one object or feeling to another, as well as the process that creates the object or feeling, is opaque to thought, while the relative stabilities that arise in process are perceived as sources of the attachments between them. We isolate a feeling and give it a label. We perceive the feeling—love, hate, affection, etc.—even if we cannot say how and from what state it develops or why it varies from one moment or thought to the next. Generally, the account of feeling follows the state of feeling, especially with strong feelings, for the ability to describe a mental state is, itself, a mental state and to some extent antithetical to having the state being described.

The rapid turn of love to hate has been taken as a sign of great love, though one psychoanalytic interpretation (Bergmann, 1987) is that passionate love is merely an interlude in a transition from melancholia to suicide. But a love that ends in hate need not eventuate in depression. And suicide or self-hate is not necessarily a consequence of hating someone, losing someone, or blaming one's self for the loss. The psychoanalytic concept of hate in relation to depression may owe to the parallel observation that depression tends to be prevented by narcissism or self-love. This illustrates a problem for explanations of emotion in terms of contrasting states when the micro-structure and transitions between them are obscure.

The path of *gradually* falling in love is from interest to passion. Hate would not seem to involve a series of states that is the reverse of falling in love. If such a series occurs, it could go from passion, to affection, to interest, to displeasure, to anger, and then to hate. This would be an odd transition, though it is possible. Hate is not one pole in a spectrum with love at the other. Falling out of love more often leads to friendship or indifference than hate, which occurs with an adventitious event, a betrayal, a nasty divorce or, as in the opening illustration, a humiliating rejection. Pirandello shows how abrupt the contrast can be. The phenomenon can be compared to instinctual displacement (Lorenz, 1971; and the ethologists), in which an impediment in the expression of one instinct results in the substitution of another, such as hunger displacing anger. I have treated soldiers in the midst of battle who suddenly fell asleep. Some argue that love is a human instinct, or derived from instinctual attachments, for example, the elaboration in the imagination of a (?self-sacrificial) instinctual need for the other, for example, maternal love and dependence, that serves to sustain affection over time. Hate would then be a similar elaboration in the imagination of a (self-protective) need to maintain over time a state of insistent aggression.

The direction of all feelings and the path through which they develop is from drive to desire. To speak of a scaling or staging of emotions is to mechanize this transition, while to link emotion to brain area or chemistry is to make claims as to the machinery. The transition is the same for all emotions with the differing forms determined by the dominant phase (e.g., depth), context (e.g., concept, experience), vector (e.g., approach, avoidance), and conceptual content. On this view, the emotions follow a parallel path, with the contrasts between them either slight, for example, shame and humiliation, or profound, for example, mania and depression. In the former, we recognize a subtle continuum from one state to the other. In the latter, the disparity is so great we concede opposition and take it as explanatory. But oppositional thinking occurs for emotions or concepts other than love and hate. For example, in depression the opposing state could be happiness or equanimity as well as mania.

What exactly does it mean to say one emotion, love, is the opposite of another, hate? Why is love not an opposite to disinterest or the absence of love or, as Freud thought, to indifference, which in the elimination of affection merely opens the door for hateful feelings? In addition, there is the contrast of giving and receiving love. Certain emotions tend to impede the arousal of love, for example, anger, pride, or apathy; other emotions such as interest or affection prepare the way for it. If one feels hate, it is difficult to love, but so is it difficult if one feels envy or fear. A person who hates is probably unhappy, but we do not contrast the two states. We can go from joy to grief as rapidly as from love to hate, say on hearing of a personal tragedy, but a rapid shift in state is not evidence of opposition. Indeed, the intensity of grief on the loss of someone who is loved suggests that it, rather than hate, has greater validity as an emotion in opposition.

What in the imagination could tie love to hate? Emotions such as fear or envy that can replace affection are not in opposition to love. Fear can be as intense as any emotion. It is bound to an object, can develop rapidly and contrasts with anger or aggression, not love. Hate as extreme anger, or anger that persists (is revived) over time in the absence of an actual object, would be in opposition to fear, just as aggression is opposed to defense. The humiliation one endures for the sake of love can lead to spite or hate when the offense is unjustified. Aggression and defense, the outgoing and ingoing vectors of primal hunger, that is, eat or be eaten, extend to sexuality in pursuit and acquiescence, or domination and submission. The upshot is that the very concept of emotions in opposition, or even triangulated, is without foundation.

Hate usually lacks an erotic character. I can hate the policies of a president but the opposite of such hate is not to love the policies but to approve of them. If hate is a strong form of disapproval, love is not a strong form of approval, for a strong approval of a policy would not be construed as love. I can strongly approve of certain people, teachers, acquaintances, without loving them. Approval in this sense is closer to respect. As with love, hate can be interpreted as an intentional attitude in relation to desire for an absent object. Unlike love, where reasons are invented even if the lovers admit the attraction is a mystery, justifications for hating are conscious and clear. If John loves Joan, he cannot say exactly why other than reciting her qualities, but if Joan hates John, it is because he has done something dreadful or refused to do something helpful.

The reasons for hating may be senseless, say, in racial or religious hatred, but since hate, like love or other emotions, is usually not rational, that is, adaptive, deliberative, it can be directed to almost any object. One says, I hate broccoli or shuffleboard, or I love squash or tennis, but this is just an emphatic way of saying that certain things or activities give pleasure or displeasure. The extension of meaning to such objects diverts attention from genuine love and gives the impression that feeling is intentional. But to say I love squash or hate shuffleboard does not answer the question, why is one food or sport, *inter alia*, preferred over another. To declare a preference is to announce a feeling, not to feel it. Saying grass is green may "intentionalize" object and color awareness but does not explain how we perceive them. Similarly, in romantic love, we may ask if this is the right person, is the reciprocity genuine, what does the future hold in store, but these hesitations are not signs that the love is intentional. To question a love is to doubt one truly loves.

Hate and love are not instincts but instinct-derivatives and distinctively human emotions. Animals show anger and the higher mammals exhibit something like affection, but for animals to hate or love implies the growth of conceptual feeling in the imagination and a judgment of outcomes, not merely choosing the most adaptive path. Hate is for some object or thing that need not be present; in this respect it is intentional. It differs from rage, which is usually spontaneous and involuntary. Hate is conceptualized anger. We choose to hate, and may relish hateful feelings of revenge. But if mental states are determined, we should forgive those who hate us for they do not act freely. We should contemplate our own anger with the view that it may mitigate or postpone action. Animal behavior may be purposeful, like attachment, but it is instinctual, not intentional. To love someone entails the wish to possess, to share or become one with that person. In hate, the wish is to destroy or see harm come to that person. Hate eradicates, love assimilates. Yet ironically, both dissolve the object, one by absorption, the other by annihilation.

If we choose to hate, do we choose to love? We can wish for love, or meet someone we hope to fall in love with, and though some writers have ascribed choice or judgment to love, I think true and passionate love is involuntary. The attempt to treat love as a judgment is valid when passion has faded and what remains is like friendship where conscious choice is present. In true love we ignore or are oblivious to faults. Friendship is affection in spite of them. The attributes of a friend are valued; those of the beloved are idealized. The passion of love—a sudden flash or gradual onset—will fade over time as it becomes intentional, though within the volition of sustained loving there remains, in devoted couples, a nucleus of feeling that draws on unconscious need, resists analysis and is not the outcome of conscious decision.

When love dies

The Italian writer, Giuseppe Lampedusa wrote of his marriage, fire and flames for one year, ashes for thirty (*fuoco e flamme per un anno, cenere per tranta*). As passion fades, incompatibilities are adumbrated that were previously obscured. A scrutiny of the objective replaces an immersion in the ideal. We all see unloving couples who treat each other with scorn and abuse. Such couples may no longer be in love but they would not fight with a stranger so terribly, and over such trivia, so there must be some residual feeling even if little more than dependency, emptiness, or the sadness of a love gone sour. We might say the union persists though the ideals that were its basis have long since dissipated. The erosion of conscious desire that attracted the lovers in the first place finds compensation in the bedrock of unconscious need. The bonds that keep loveless couples together are diverse—habit, loneliness, economic—and may have little to do with love. I once read of a British couple, married for thirty years, who played the lottery each week hoping to win enough money for a divorce! Love can go the way of disinterest, even contempt, but it best survives when it negotiates limitations that, if successful, evolve to a kind of intimate friendship. The weakening (objectification) of the ideal may even lead to a dependency on the habitual, a trust in its mutuality, a tolerant complacency and shared memories even with disaffection and a longing for the days of passionate feeling.

The manner of separation determines if the lover is friendly, despondent, or consumed by anger or grief. With greater detachment of self and object, the beloved is no longer a categorical ideal in the imagination, that is, no longer a subjective pre-object, but objectifies like other objects at the endpoint of the mental state. When the beloved is fully external, the intensity of a locus in the imagination shifts to a relatively affect-free locus in the world. The feeling that was concentrated in one object of value and its internalization to an intense emotion is now diluted in externalities. To be rejected is to be discarded. In the outward shift from a dominant locus in the psyche to one in object space, the beloved is drained of feeling and "thrown out of the mind."

Time, Yeats writes, "drips to decay like a candle burnt out." The loss of a loved one is a forceful reminder of the fragility of life and the tenuousness and brevity of pleasure. A lingering reminder of this sensibility is a nostalgia tinged with sadness, an eagerness to grasp the moment as it passes, helpless to the loss of youth, beauty, innocence, spontaneity. The loss of the beloved, and not just the loss but the recollection of moments of pleasure, brings an intense focus on privation, isolation, and disunion. In love the beloved evokes joy, in mourning, sorrow, whether in the remembrance of a smile, a gesture, the hope of return, or the despair of parting. Some sorts of suffering are best tolerated as a doorway to salvation, others, in the romantic spirit of Shelley, who wrote, "... come then sorrow, sweetest sorrow ... of all the world, I love thee best."

The process involved in arousing libido is similar to its detachment. The psychoanalyst, Greenson (1978) once remarked, wittily, in a discussion of the resemblance of weddings and funerals that, in the former, one laughs on the outside, cries on the inside, while in the latter it is the reverse. This goes to the ambivalence of partial attitudes. Grief can be affected in gestures of propriety as it purges ideals that have become oppressive. Some consequences of death are beneficial, such as freedom or inheritance. The "dark side" of marriage looms before a couple on the threshold of "wedded bliss." To fall in love for one set of "reasons" and marry for another is the death knell of desire if the marriage becomes a protracted mourning or penitence for a hasty bargain or transient pleasure. Yet, it is easy to be cynical of innocence and irrationality in love. The romantic fool is the foil of the cynic, but the cynic will never know the lover's joy.

The intensity of mourning is often taken as a sign of sincerity, like the odalisques of the Inca who competed in shrieks and breast-beating for the most worthy of the consorts. One might prolong or simulate grief to fulfill the expectations of others or their commendation. Mourning can become a moral obligation like satisfying a dying wish. Surely it is a rite of passage in every culture. In the natural mourning of a beloved, when love is deep and heartfelt, the lover feels as if he or she has in some sense died as well, but there is mourning for friends and acquaintances, not just the beloved. Some mourn the loss of pets, indeed, any loss of objects that are important to the self, a business, a possession. There is even a kind of mourning for the younger, happier, more agile self that has aged and transformed to that of the present. I recall the tears of a friend, a concert pianist, lamenting the loss of youthful technique on listening to a concerto recorded years before. In contrast, the lack of mourning for a beloved, a wife, husband, close friend or relation, implies an absence of sensitivity, insularity or self-absorption and vitiates the authenticity of whatever feelings may have existed. Still one can ask, what precisely is the relation of love to loss? What happens in the fracture of genuine union or on the pain of final separation?

The moral dimension extends to the extremes of sacrifice for the beloved. How deep and persistent is grieving before it is considered excessive or abnormal? Morbid grief is said to be pathological. For some, love is necessarily neurotic. Others cannot fathom what they do not personally experience. Is prolonged grief, like depression, a sign of suffering or slow recovery? To die when the beloved is lost, or compound death in suicide—the Romeo and Juliet syndrome—is the ultimate test of love. The lack of a will to go on or the wish to die is obligated if one is deprived of a love so powerful as to split the self in two and guarantee a life of loneliness and despondency. A lover might die for the beloved as a parent for a child. If the willingness to die to save a life is the proof the love is real, or that life without that person is worthless, what prevents the lover or parent from suicide if a beloved or child dies? That one dies to save a life—even that of a stranger—but does not commit suicide on the death of one who is deeply loved is an asymmetry worth exploring. A suicide that saves a life forestalls a death, but one after a death compounds it.

What of occasions when a person dives into a river to save a stranger? Near my village in southern France, a child fell into the rapids and three strangers dove after her. All drowned. Such acts are signs of character and courage, not love. Reminiscent of an episode in the Decalogue of Kieslowski, a Polish friend told me of a man who watched in horror as his little boy sank on a sled into a hole in the ice. To dive into the water was almost certain death and would have left a wife and several children destitute. Where is the moral responsibility in such cases? Reason dictates caution. The act is foolhardy and the odds of success or survival are slim. Should the love of a father for a son have led him to risk his life in the attempt? It was not love but courage that was lacking. The father mourned his dead son and no doubt grieved his failure to act, though if it would have been irrational, indeed fatal. If courage leads a stranger to risk his life, should not love give courage grounds for action? In a suicide, or when the risk of death is great, there is a balance among several inclinations: love and exocentric feeling; prudence and egocentric feeling; and courage, with the dominance of one possible course of action facilitated or blocked by others.

Loss or death affects us according to the degree to which the idealization of the beloved infiltrates or encumbers the self. In deep love, when mourning is genuine and prolonged, there is a gradual extraction of the beloved from the self-concept. To the extent the beloved has become part of the self of the lover (parent, friend), the death of the loved one is a loss of what has grown into the self and become part of its nature. In true love, when the beloved is so much a part of the self that the boundary of self and other dissolves, the loss of the beloved is a dismemberment of the self.

There is a wide breadth of opinion on mourning. Some say prolonged mourning is self-pity, or that a brief period of mourning is a sign of a healthy ego, or that the life force presses to the future or that new mate selection is an evolutionary imperative. Were we to quantify the embodiment of the other in the self, would we say the ideal is a self in which the other accounts for fifty percent of qualities—the perfect match in the myth of Aristophanes—or that eighty percent points to a weak, dependent self, or that twenty percent suggests too much autonomy or a superficial contact? Is it morbid and against the grain of life to think too much on the past? Some savor the memories of a past love, others press on to the next encounter. Mourning is similar to the micro-temporal loss of objects in every renewal. The object mourned recurs to the limits of remembrance. Restitution occurs with adaptation to loss, replacement as a mode of denial or healthy attachment to image. The feeling of loss and tears of separation in every farewell anticipate the irretrievable loss of the other in death or abandonment and the final loss of what, for most people, is the most precious of all, the self.

One might suppose the inability or unwillingness to move ahead arises as much from fear or lack of confidence or opportunity as obsession with the past. Personalities differ, one more inward than the other; uniqueness and diversity are essential to a lover's belief. Normally, as one ages the past looms larger in the imagination. One recalls occasions of pleasure, but also remorse, regret over an errant life, the self one might have been, adventures missed, opportunities lost, a life of compromise.

There is the phenomenon of mourning a dead leader or celebrity who might only be known through the remote contact of radio or television. The world-wide mourning of Princess Diana, Michael Jackson, or Jack Kennedy are examples. Such people are idealized as beautiful, brilliant, inspiring, or creative. They would not be so mourned if they died of old age, but a premature death deprives their admirers of further "contact" and raises the specter of their own vulnerability and the possibility of early death. In mourning a celebrity, we see the idealization of the other who, in death, assumes a greater share in those who grieve than in life. The attributes of the person—the charm, talent, leadership, accomplishments—replace the individual as idealization shifts an object to a categorical type.

Grieving can take many forms, and merges with depression where the loss may not be a person but a home or a job, where it is not so much the loss of human valuations derived from others but an erosion of confidence and self-respect, a sense of failure, a loss of hope for success or a setback to striving and ambition. In all instances, it is a response to loss that depends on the identification or dependence of the individual with the lost objects. Mourning is a form of depression, but the loss is for a loved object not the object world. In ordinary depression, the world is lost or has no interest for the individual. There is no fulcrum on which the depression turns. A person may seek to fix or locate a depression in life events, but unless there is a specific loss, an accident or other event, that is, a *reactive* depression, no one occurrence or combination of events incites the mood. In *endogenous* depression, with loss of interest in the world, apathy or anhedonia, the incitation is not apparent and the mood is attributed to neurochemistry. Loss of interest is a withdrawal of feeling from the world as a whole. Sadness in mourning decants to the loss of one person or thing as its source. That some people grieve for pets more than family or friends introduces another dimension to mourning, namely, the strength or autonomy of the self, or its dependence on the other, even an animal, and the loneliness that ensues when a companion is lost. To some extent, the pet is also idealized or it could be replaced by another animal.

Mourning in most instances requires an adaptation to a novel self in which idealized attributes, the beauty, generosity, love or attentiveness of the other, that have grown into categorical ideals in the core self, are held on to in the absence of their source. The assimilation of the other to the self erodes in the return of self-valuation and autonomy. Often enough, however, with no grounds for invalidation, the ideal of the other—lover, parent, friend—continues to flourish, indeed grows stronger. Ideals that cannot objectify into lost objects remain behind in the imagination as qualities of perfection. The persistence of the ideal in memory when the object or event is no longer available for a reality check may explain why experience is often recalled as happier than it was in actuality.

Jealousy

From an evolutionary standpoint, jealousy is part of the instinctual repertoire that helps to safeguard paternity for males and, for females, serves to ensure protection and assistance in child-rearing (Buss, 1994). Whether jealousy is an instinctual reaction that is forecast in the genome or a derivation of egocentric feeling influenced by culture and personal experience is an open question. The problem with simple correlations based on evolution is that the absence of jealousy could be explained on the same basis, namely as liberating the male for wider copulation and the female for wider mate selection. If exclusivity and infidelity can be interpreted by contrasting interpretations of the same adaptive pressures, both interpretations are unsatisfactory. For animals there is competition among males for access to females, which works for the selection of advantageous features. If this were readily transferred to humans, strength and intelligence would be favored in selection, males would be polygamous and females would accept, not contest, the evolutionary pattern. There is no evolutionary benefit to the male to remain with one female after reproductive success unless access to other females is limited. Similarly, one could argue an advantage to the female of multiple encounters with competitive males that outweighs the benefits of protection or support. A problem for the standard account are findings in primitive cultures, such as Aborigine, that insemination is not linked to maternity when the quickening begins several months after copulation.

Regardless of its utility or adaptive value, the psychic structure of jealousy is similar in men and women, with slight though not unimportant biases. These include the tendency, in men, for greater discomfort over sexual infidelity, while for women an infidelity that involves a transfer of affection tends to trump distress over casual sex. If men are less faithful than women, it may reflect a difference in libido, opportunity, egocentricity, or risk-taking. The greater ability of men to limit infidelity to a purely sexual encounter without emotional engagement allows them to encapsulate the activity in states of objectified action that is relatively affect-free. Perhaps for this reason, men tend to be more vindictive for sexual indiscretion than emotional reallocation, and women more forgiving for sexual dalliance but not an affair of the heart.

Jealousy is both simple and complex. Simple in that it is common and near universal, often interpreted as a sign of love, and complex in that it entails a mix of feelings alien to the spirit of love, such as selfishness, possessiveness, anger, and resentment. Since jealousy can be a source of rage, it touches on the category of hate. In the broader sense, a person might be jealous of a partner's enthusiasm for a hobby, travel, a career, all of which can deprive the partner of intimacy and threaten the stability of the union.

There is also a relation to envy, which is the feeling that one should have what others have or be in their place. It is often tinged with anger at privation when objects that belong to others are thought to be undeserved or that a person has greater merit for what others possess. In some instances, the terms are interchangeable, for example, I am jealous (envious) of their good luck or happiness. When used in this sense, jealousy is not related to the union of lovers. Nor do I think jealousy is so closely related to the fear of losing the other since it occurs in people who have just met as well as those who are tightly bonded. Jealousy can flair up with an innocent flirtation, a casual encounter, or an imagined preference, even a character in a film or novel, when an implicit comparison is felt to be unflattering.

This implies that jealousy should be interpreted along the lines of rejection, as an attack on the beloved's self, instead of a fear of loss. The intrusion into a couple of a real or potential threat or the pursuit of another, is taken as disinterest in the beloved, lack of valuation, an injury to self-esteem or a repudiation of the beloved's giving and commitment. In true love, the beloved fills the lover's thoughts and attention. When attention is diverted, questions arise as to the authenticity of the lover's feeling. On the other hand, the person who is jealous displays a narcissism or egocentricity that is contrary to the spirit of love, when the *demand* for union and exclusivity replace the *desire* for it. To insist on fidelity is like insisting on love, which once freely given must now be enforced.

Envy

Envy is the over-valuation of an object in the possession of someone for whom there is some affinity and relative equality of means. Like jealousy, which is usually for a person, envy tends to be specific to objects or attributes belonging to the person. One does not envy a museum for its wealth or collections, but rather, an acquaintance whose goods are such that they are desired by the self. One is jealous of a person who threatens the interests or affections of a partner and envies the goods of that person. Both are directed to the other, or his or her goods, and both refer to a self that is found wanting in affection or in goods. Either emotion can consume a person and lead to anger, which can be directed outward at the other as a source of distress, or inward to the self in suffering and/or privation.

Envy and jealousy manifest and further erode a lack of self-confidence. They do not create the lack but accentuate it. The individual feels inadequate or of insufficient value. These emotions are interpreted in relation to the constitution of the self and the goods of others. They are variations on desire, in one for a beloved in danger of loss, in the other for the goods of another that cannot be possessed. These are not so much different emotions, but different relations of self, other (object) and desire that color feelings to appear as distinct affects. More precisely, envy and jealousy are biases in the desire for a beloved or for goods in danger of loss or unable to be satisfied in a self that is incomplete or unfulfilled.

Jealousy for a competitor can become envy at his or her gifts. Envy turns to jealousy when the self fears the loss of a beloved or when objects of envy for the lover become objects of desire for the one who is loved. If the self desires the goods of the other, this is not love but acquisitiveness or betrayal. The qualities of personality or character that are objects of desire are inseparable from the person with those qualities that are the basis of love; they are not "properties" that can be cleaved from the other, such as wealth. In this way, love can be infected by cupidity, when the individual desires a person not for the properties of character, but for the character of the properties. The state is shaped by the self (strong, weak) that desires an object (person, goods) and impediments (others, self-limitations) in its satisfaction. According to the mix of these factors, we designate the emotion as envy, jealousy, acquisitiveness, greed, frustration, or anger.

Hesitation, procreation, and self-protection

The instincts for procreation and self-preservation are often in conflict, and their derivations guide the lover in the bias to surrender or autonomy. The biological justification of sexual attraction is physical union leading to reproduction. Love requires a spiritual or psychic union in which procreation is as often accidental as inevitable. True love excludes others, children as well, for they shatter the intimacy of lovers even as they fortify the union of family. A child diverts love from the parents and entails responsibilities that collide with those for the beloved. The child becomes the object of sacrifice and affection at the expense of romantic love, as if passion were the lure of the unborn to find a path to realization.

The hesitation to give one's self to the beloved—the uncertainty, the failure to commit—though it can be a sign the love is not genuine, can also represent the tacit pull of autonomy against the forces of procreation that underlie the implicit contract that draws couples together, for which sexual pleasure is the seal. Lovers echo the call of the child-to-be as the wisdom of age-old passage. The insolubility of romantic love and parenting that lies dormant in the unconscious summons a couple to decide how love is to be sustained. The lovers mull over what is to be lost and what to be gained. It is a good thing that lovers are irrational or they would foresee that the passion in which they are immersed must subside if some remainder is to endure, perhaps for the greater part of a lifetime. Lovers offer the beloved their one and only life and then, for a child, forsake the ardor, the romance and oneness, for true love cannot be triangulated. Conscious decision is antithetical to passion, but hesitation is the stirring of reason in its self-protective role against impulse.

The drive to individuation is opposed to that for community, which is manifest in the security that family affords, not only for the child but in the shared labor and mutual aid essential to marriage or its equivalent. Community reaches its limit in abdication, individuation in alienation. Love resolves these competing pressures, one to an extreme of independence, the other to possible loss of self. We see these pressures at work at many social levels: autonomy of self and oneness with the other; individuality and dependency; solitude and companionship; and the claims of the individual versus those of the community that are central to so many legal and moral issues. We should also examine anger, jealousy, and rejection in this light, that is, in the tension of self-giving and self-protection. But then one asks, what is the self that gives and what is there to protect? If to be complete is to incorporate the other, what can the self point to as truly its own? The self is an outcome of an individual and social history, an amalgam of inherited traits, parents, friends, teachers, a stew of assimilated beliefs and values that achieve a relative coherence or constant identity. Each of us, as the descendent of others, as of our own former selves, is already a community of more or less harmonious attributes.

The union of lovers is absorption not addition. When a couple sees itself as a sum of separate individuals, assimilation is incomplete. In this connection, some mention of parental love and the attachment of mother and infant is warranted, especially since infantile attachment is deemed the archetype of subsequent modes of loving. However, the concept of attachment, indeed the very term, implies an external relation between individuals. This might be appropriate for animal and much of human bonding, but not for the account of the child's love of the parent as the foundation for romantic love. The irony is that infantile attachment conceived as the source of romantic love is, in fact, responsible for its demise, as the death of a flower is the seed for its renewal. The infant is a kind of parasite to the mother as a host, then to the couple as support.

In some ways, love is also parasitic, the lover assimilating the beloved who, then, in need and desire, assumes a share of the lover's mind. A difference between love and exploitation is that parasitism becomes a symbiosis of mutual benefit.

Often, an infant only hastens or solidifies the natural adjustment of passion into friendship or co-existence, but if the love is unwilling or too strong to change, the child must be unattended or the passion of the couple is doomed. Cupid's arrow can kill as well as enflame. Yet there are compensations for the demise of *eros* in parenting. Most mothers and many fathers feel a devotion to their infant that defies rational explanation. Apart from the instinctual bonds and rhythms of mother-baby interaction, the infant has no language, little communication, scant personality, and scarce reciprocity, all of which are important to romantic love. There are no beliefs or values to absorb, the child does not become the mother, yet the mother is entrusted with the child as a precious object. The mother may choose to have a child but not choose the child she has. The child is the outcome of a sexual act that may have been pleasurable but not necessarily loving, while the mother's love for the child and the child for the mother is, *pace* Freud, non-sexual. The pleasures of parenting are muted and intermittent. An infant is barely distinguishable from others of its general type and gender. As with a beloved, it undergoes idealization and inspires such adoration as, for the mother, to be more precious than the father, even for her own life, which is surrendered in large part for a total dependency whose smile and gurgle are the sum reward for her efforts.

What is striking about parental love in its optimal state is its asymmetry, and the contrast with the mutuality of romantic love. In this respect, the love of an infant is closer to the love for a pet. If one asks parents why they love their baby they would probably say, to the effect, it is so cute, adorable, clever—as if they had won the baby-jackpot—but the truth is, like the chemistry of true love, they have no clear idea why the baby is loved, other than that the baby is theirs. Every reason serves to justify all others, except the innate feeling of attachment that itself is inexplicable, an attachment that even in primates who lack a self-concept is purely instinctual. Such attachment is found in primitive organisms like fish or birds. In most animals it is brief; infants mature rapidly and pairings do not endure. In the wild, infants are born of necessity not desire, and the female is seized, not loved. Human attachment is, on the one hand, clearly derived from patterns of mother-infant behavior in animals, but it is an unlikely precursor of romantic love. The need for companionship may be instinctual—man is a social animal—but this can occur without love, certainly without romantic love. Evolutionary pressures induce couplings through the drives, social and sexual, but do not explain the quality of loving, especially its imaginative growth and relation to artistic inspiration, creativity and religious feeling, which defy a simple reduction to instinct.

Note

1. I am reminded of the remark that the main problem in life is that there are too many masochists and not enough sadists to go around.

CHAPTER FIVE

Desire for things

To whom he may entrust his complete self, Lay bare his mind and speak his perfect will Showing the secret places of the heart.

—Guillaume de Lorris, *Roman de la Rose, c.* 1230

Introduction

This chapter explores in greater detail the desire for material things. For many, the love for others and the love for things are symmetrical, sometimes complementary and sometimes competitive. However, the "love" for things is desire, not love, whereas the love for others incorporates desire or, put differently, one desires to possess or accomplish something, but does not truly love the thing possessed—or one loves possessing the thing rather than the thing itself—while the desire for the beloved is a preliminary to love or its implementation.

While the love for a beloved differs from that for children, family, or friends, and even romantic love has its ups and downs, the quality of feeling for others—hate as well as love—differs from that for things, with pets and art occupying intermediate or transitional positions. One says, I love my car, my home or my fur coat, and such goods are often desired and chosen over objects of romantic love, yet it is doubtful that the *feeling of love* is identical for animate and inanimate objects. More likely, the diversity of love-objects reflects an over-inclusiveness of the term, that is, the dilution of reference for the word "love," but there is also confusion of love with desire. Even if the desire for goods is stronger than the desire for love, it is the beloved that is loved, not the goods, which, once possessed, are not loved but enjoyed.

In the popular sense, "materialism" is the desire for things or possessions in opposition to the genuine love of others. We might ask, what is the essential difference, even in true love, between the idealization of properties such as intelligence and beauty and the "idealization" of wealth or sexual virtuosity? We consider the former as virtues, as innate or acquired marks of character, while the latter are adventitious, but there is overlap, and idealization occurs for both sets of features. A person might desire wealth solely for philanthropy, while beauty may lead to vanity and intelligence is often nefarious. We know there is an important distinction in loving someone for their qualities and loving or desiring them for their money, but the distinction in properties is less important than the process through which these attributes are valued.

To love someone for goods is not to truly love the person, though true love may wither if material needs are not satisfied. Moreover, to love a person for goods is no less a sign of need than to love for the attributes of character. In one case the desire is for what the individual *has*, in the other, for what the individual *is*. An individual who is desired for goods or as a bearer of those goods is a means for others to acquire them. In this, such people become goods themselves. In this respect, the desire for goods as a justification for loving a person reduces the person from *someone* to *something*. In contrast, attributes of character are enjoyed and admired but are not transferable, like goods, to the lover. The love of non-material qualities elevates the person from a something to a *someone*.

For things, the desire is to possess or accumulate. The desire for animate objects is for shared feeling, not ownership.[1] Unlike a child or a beloved, things—jewelry, a home—are fungible or replaceable, though certain things, such as artworks, can be sole exemplars and take on unique value. Some people are attached to cars or other such items, but if lost, the item can usually be replaced without an emotional reaction. There is an obvious difference in how fungible a thing is compared to a loved object (person, pet). Art occupies a middle ground, and shows greater subjectivity than ordinary objects. One can love a piece of music but not a performance. One can love a novel in spite of a ragged copy. There is, of course, immense value in an oil painting by a master, or an original literary or musical composition by a great artist. They arouse the desire to own or experience the works, which are much prized by art lovers and collectors. There is estimable value in the work, and reciprocity in pleasure and instruction, but we would not say they are objects of love. For the artist or the connoisseur, a sculpture, a fine book, a particular song, can be an obsessive preoccupation similar to loving, where the value of the thing or activity is personal, even idiosyncratic, and perhaps far greater than the worth of the thing to others. It is not uncommon for a pursuit of the inanimate to replace the love for family. The boundary of love and art is nicely captured in the myth of *Galatea*, where the unreciprocated feeling for a sculpture leads to the wish to animate the object so as to receive the love one gives to it. This story illustrates a central difference in the desire for the inanimate and the incapacity to achieve true love in oneness when the loved object has no self to be assimilated with that of the lover.

The worth of things, except things of sentimental value, is often closer to economic worth and consensual value, while the value of the beloved is not market-based, and is generally independent of opinion and advice. The economic approach to object worth rests in supply and demand. When things are purchased with money or goods, the worth of the thing roughly corresponds to its price. This is clear when things alone are desired, less so when a person is desired for having things. One could say, cynically, yet with a grain of truth, that there is a cost to everything in life, even in true love, which, if it is not freely given, is exchanged. The kernel of truth in the remark concerns the reciprocity and need-satisfaction from which love arises and on which it depends. The more a person's goods are the target, the less likelihood of oneness, partly due to the concentration on goods and the disparity between lovers that motivates desire in one person and enticement in the other, partly because just having goods does not imply sharing them, so that some features of character, for example, generosity, inevitably come into play, and finally, because the core attributes of the love-object will be secondary to the possessions, the reverse of true love in which goods are ancillary.

We speak of things as having worth to justify our desire for them, and we speak of others as being worthy of our desire. The distinction hinges on value as external and impersonal or value as personal and subjective. People can be perceived as things and their inner life ignored, that is, not revived in the imagination of the observer. Generally, the distinction of animate and inanimate or living and non-living objects holds, but it is not just the animate or inanimate nature of an object that defines the quality of feeling. The subjectivity of the animate transforms it into an object with feeling, but an extreme objectivity can shift an animate object to the status of an inanimate thing. In the depersonalization of schizophrenia, people are robots, zombies, or automata. The ready transformation of feeling from the intensity of love and passion to disinterest or cruelty reflects the dominant locus in the transition from mind to world, core to surface or need to impersonality.

Conversely, an inanimate thing can occasion desire, even love. For someone who believes that nature is infused with mind or spirit, things are animated with feeling. This is essential to totemic and animistic belief. An inanimate object such as a painting can be loved in a way that is not dissimilar from the love for a person. Indeed, the inanimate or impersonal can mark a path to genuine love. After all, falling in love must begin somewhere, with a smile, a gesture or with golden hair. A person desired for sex, or one who traffics in sexual favors, may be discarded after the service is rendered and replaced by an approximate other. Without love, functional value supplants romantic interest, but love is most often preceded by sexual desire.

There is a fluid shift from objects suffused with value and signification to those devoid of worth, and either state can begin or eventuate in the other. When love is gone—dead, one can say—the loved object dies in the imagination. Value is extracted from the object as it externalizes, voiding any shred of subjective idealization. Put differently, in the generation of perceptual objects, a phase of inner valuation is traversed with little residue in the final perception. Feeling dissipates in detachment, with indifference to a thing-like person or, at best, desire for a person-like thing. Like a material entity in the world, the other has a purely utilitarian function. Feeling can be so reduced that there is no sign of feeling at all. In a violent sociopath or in soldiers during combat, dehumanized others may lose all rudiments of humanity, becoming thing-like creatures that can be exploited or killed without remorse and disposed like useless commodities.

In spite of many differences in the desire for things and others, deeper similarities reveal a continuum of feeling. In both, the value that goes out with the object in its formation reflects need and/or wish. Desire (hate) for things is selfish, in that giving and sacrifice are not required. In love, these attitudes are essential. For inanimate objects, the extreme of desire is selfish or *ego*centric need, as in self-indulgence, ambition, and greed. Acquisitiveness is self-assertion, aggression, while acquisition in love is in the service of dependency. Receiving and possessing are primary in the desire for things; giving and acquiescing are primary in the love of others.

The pursuit of things

Every religion teaches that the things we seek to possess eventually possess us and must be relinquished for the sake of happiness and the love of god. The Buddhists hold that the first third of life is for growth and education, the middle third for ambition and family, the final third for renunciation and meditation. This recognizes the near-universality of striving, acquisition of worldly goods, the dissatisfaction with what one has and the pressure for more. Were this not so, denial would not be a central tenet of the teachings. While Buddhism is a life-path and a metaphysic, not a religion, the relinquishment of goods and a detachment from material pursuits is, in all religions, a preliminary to god-experience.

The hedonic urge for non-libidinal objects of pleasure or the money and position to acquire them, the greed and self-interest, the envy of those with more, are so much a part of the human condition that love, compassion, and religious values are often trampled by the unreflective striving for personal advantage. The complimentary state in the desire for animate objects is the other-centered or *exo*centric feeling of love and compassion. In everyday life these are not exclusive tendencies. One can desire goods to attract a lover and the love can mature to be independent of its lures, and one can desire goods to reinforce genuine feeling.

As to means-end relations, the beloved is an end, not a means, while goods are conceived, overtly or implicitly, as means to power or self-enrichment. Goods account for little in genuine love, and a thirst for them can replace a desire for the beloved. However, the distinction is tricky. A genuine love may be so dependent on the beloved that its reciprocation is a means to one's very existence, while a quest for the material can grow to a genuine love. One can reduce love to a constellation of needs and desires and argue that the other is a means to their fulfillment.

For those in grinding poverty with few acquisitions or cravings beyond those of survival, there is little or nothing to surrender. In such instances, renunciation comes at too small a cost. The self-justification in disavowal and the satisfaction of petty sacrifice are achieved when the burdens of life, not a chosen path, are the basis for the lack of material desire. The acceptance of the teachings may be heartfelt, which is what matters most, but should the goal of salvation or redemption be an escape or an advance, a way out or a way in? To give little when there is little to give has greater merit than to give much when one's coffers are overflowing, but what of those with much to give who give all they have? Does merit accrue in relation to the portion of the whole that is sacrificed? Buddhism accepts that acquisition should precede abnegation. Like the princely Siddhartha, the greater the wealth, the greater the merit of renunciation.

What forces are at play that lead one to acquire objects or states of power, authority, and position that go beyond ordinary need and comfort—food, shelter, and the like—and how do these forces relate to feeling and the structure of emotion, specifically the desire for a beloved, and the complex affective states in love and loss? We know that greed and ambition can reach the point where they replace or undermine other spheres of feeling, the love of friends, partners, and family. To the businessman, the pious individual may look weak and sanctimonious, while to piety, acquisition of wealth is sinful or distasteful. At the opposite pole, the ascetic is a *rara avis* in western society, not so much scorned as dismissed as an eccentric or crackpot. Nothing exceeds like excess, the pun goes, but even those who seek more will admit, and all evidence supports it, that material goods do not bring happiness (though their lack is one source of unhappiness), but only reinforce the desire for further acquisition, leaving a kind of emptiness or loneliness that can only be filled with love. Surely, a strong love that pays no heed to commerce will, when the flame burns less brightly, often turn to surrogate objects. If the materialism of wealth is found wanting in emotion, the totality of true love, when endangered, may find renewal in acquisition.

The self of loving is biased to process; the self of acquisition is biased to substance. Yet it is often said that the desire for material wealth conceals a deeply rooted sense of inadequacy, compensation for childhood deprivation, a reaction to an "inferiority complex," insecurity, and so on, as if love, or all striving, could be "explained" in the same way. The temptation to explain adult behavior in terms of childhood experience should be treated with caution, since a similar juvenile profile can lead to markedly discrepant outcomes, and events not consciously recollected may figure in determining the adult pattern. The major problem with such accounts, apart from their vacuity, is that they can be applied to all behaviors, and the same behavior can be attributed to opposing attitudes, even to those who relinquish all possessions to join a cult or religious community. For example, in a cult, the desire for love or things is replaced by the need for belonging, for approval and deference to authority and/or a sense of moral superiority.

However, the substitution of intangible for tangible goods is merely a shift in need-satisfaction. The most compassionate voices in public are often scoundrels in private life. For the self, others and material objects are modes of self-completion: in love, it is the beloved; in avarice, it is money and things. The major difference is that love is satisfied in *giving* while greed is satisfied in *taking*. Is the need to take others into one's heart, for self and other, just an emollient for solitude? The cynic would say there is an overt or tacit negotiation over price in both; in love, the resolution of competing needs and favors even when the match is most harmonious.

The self is the "pump" of all acts and objects. The value of an object is indebted to the self as the source of its valuation. The self distributes into objects that mirror or supplement its needs. Why does one person seek love at all costs and another seeks goods or profit? Why for one person is feeling primary, and for another the satisfaction of mercenary pursuits? One person achieves wholeness in sharing; another attempts to replicate this state with goods (Figure 5.1). Yet the oneness of love has a completeness that material acquisition can only simulate; wholeness entails giving while acquisition is only a strategy for more grasping, since there is no end of things to acquire. We see this contrast in the "social butterfly" or philanthropist at one extreme and the misanthrope or miser at the other. For one, there is satisfaction in participation and aiding others, even as a substitute for loving and giving, while in the other, the self is reinforced when others are treated with indifference or contempt. The extremes of self-realization reflect need and incompleteness, one inclined to lifeless objects, the other to feeling and vitality.

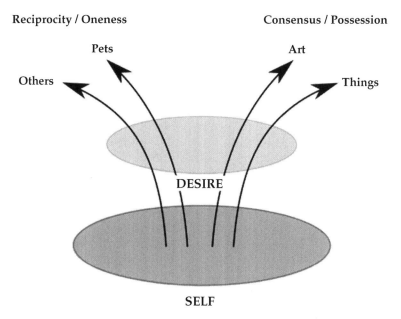

Figure 5.1. Generally, love needs love in return. Material things offer comfort, pride and pleasure but do not return affection. Pets occupy an intermediate role in relation to loved ones, while art-works occupy an intermediate role in relation to things.

This introduces the observation that even the strongest love may not last, and even ideals depreciate over time, while treasure often appreciates in value. There may be compensations to a lover for a beloved who is aging, but the worth of a valuable object tends to increase over time. This presumes that objects of desire are quantities, and that there is a quality/quantity distinction in the love of others and the desire for things, or a distinction of process (feeling) for its own sake and acquisition for the sake of possession.

How does one compare the qualitative value in the intoxication of a brief but unforgettable love with the quantitative worth over years of a prized object? The mystic or ascetic who sacrifices all for the possibility of transient oneness with god or nature is like the storybook lover who gives a kingdom for a beloved, which can only occur with profound and genuine love or faith. Love that depends on judgment, or faith that depends on a calculation of probabilities, would not take the risk. Indeed, the way once-loving couples fight in a divorce over the scraps of a marriage implies that love was inauthentic when it was in full bloom. The attitude is that if love is lost, at least some profit should be extracted to compensate for the years that were "wasted." A love that once was shared is perceived as an investment, and motivates a shift from giving to taking in which the material trumps the spiritual, and transforms love to commerce. This is a common turn of events, and makes some wonder if most love affairs do not have their covert beginning in mercenary strategies with a veneer of illusory passion.

The egocentric tends to over-ride the other-centered, as the moral high ground eventually collapses through failure, ineffectiveness or disillusionment. The maxim, "love thy neighbor," being anti-Darwinian, must be inscribed early, and instilled and executed as a faith. Societal values spread outward from familial and tribal loyalties and a nucleus of dependency, the benefits of which are evident when survival requires cooperation. In developed societies, social cohesion is herd mentality, as in religious and political movements, when the self is immersed in an impersonal collective. Such occasions do not usually require personal sacrifice, for the mindset is centered on shared goals.

Love, sacrifice, and charitable feeling must overcome the conflict of ego and other, autonomy and dependency, and the biological imperative of drive to self-advancement at any cost, an attitude for which love is a weakness that saps a healthy egoism. The outcome is the relegation of love to contractual benefits for the co-signatories. The differences in character that underlie self- and other-centered acts reflect the degree to which the humane and the selfless are instilled to offset the ruthlessness of Darwinian norms, which pose a danger to all, especially the weak and vulnerable. An excess of other-directed values may provide a short-term profit but a long-term risk. Unless love and charity are decisive, the natural tendencies to covetousness and acquisition will prevail.

Drive and egocentricity

The hunger-drive replicates the self; the sex-drive replicates the species. Self-replication is causal persistence in that the self is re-instated each moment in a slightly novel recurrence. To an egocentric attitude, successive reinstatements augment self-valuation. In avarice, every acquisition reinforces a wealthier or more powerful self. In love, self-renewal has less freedom, decisiveness, and autonomy. The accrual of things enhances self-esteem by virtue of possessions; the beloved enhances the self by assimilation. Greed reinforces the egocentricity that love dissolves.

Take the saying, "you are what you eat." This does not mean the body turns into alfalfa or a pork chop, but that food morphs into tissue that enables the organism to survive and reproduce. Ingestion in hunger goes to penetration in sex. In hunger, food is assimilated, in sex, there is merger. One can say that assimilation is prior to contact or that wholeness is prior to splitting, in the sense that unity is prior to autonomy and/or multiplicity. The body assimilates food in hunger but assimilates the self of one lover to the other in genuine love. The assimilation of psyche in love may endure for a season or a lifetime, but the bodily fusion with food is irreversible, while the penetration of sex is temporary.

As a general rule, the more food an animal obtains, the more fit and capable it becomes. Food is the underpinning of sex, enhancing the strength and agility needed for successful mating. Language employs similar terms for feeding and sexual activity. The sharing of a meal with others is a sign of caring. Over a meal, acquaintances can become friends, and friendships are reinforced. We speak of sexual appetite as hunger, alluding to the importation of the drive of hunger into that of sexuality. Hunger and sexual drive are elaborated to desires, as the animal *need* for sex and food develops to the human *desire* for love-objects and things. We say that the *hunger for a lover* is comparable to the *appetite for things*. One drive develops into and with the other. The term "hunger" is also applied to ambition and other forceful strivings. Predation refers to sex and hunger. The word *taste* applies to eating and the selection of foods, wines, mates, etc., as well as to things acquired with discernment.

Unlike hunger, the sexual drive in animals is not a daily occurrence. What becomes of animal libido when females are not receptive? In humans, psychoanalysis presumes libido is displaced or diverted to other goals. Variations in the expression of sexual drive are held to explain behaviors that are not obviously sexual, for example, ambition, envy, etc. For psa, the architecture of the mind is a product of the vicissitudes of libidinal drive. Even when hunger is ceded as primary it is sexualized. For microgenetic theory, infantile nursing is a pattern of instinctual nourishment carried into sexuality and not, as in psa, a sexual behavior grafted to feeding. In a word, the capture and ingestion of prey, which are the non-sexual implementations of hunger, transform to the acquisition and hording of material goods. Put otherwise, as desire and romantic love develop out of sexual-drive, the "love" for things develops out of the hunger-drive, though the transition from one drive to the other, and the regression of the later (sexual) drive to the earlier drive of hunger accounts for the overlap or mixing in a given behavior and the confusion in interpretation (Figure 5.2).

Appetite applies to nourishment, but also to ambition, power, and greed. The self-assertion that arises from the combination of hunger-drive and aggression appears in confidence, vanity, pride, and arrogance, personality traits that are implemented in the acquisition of power and wealth. To a variable extent, these traits can be offset by unselfish values, such as philanthropy, *pro bono* work, service to others, tithing, charitable donations, and so on, but a genuine act of charity or kindness (see: Ch. 8) is uncommon. Many non-profits are fraudulent, with the greater share of income going to salaries, conferences, and furtherance of the group. For the donors, the moral value of contributions is undercut by their status as tax write-offs. Self-interest extends to arenas that mask self-aggrandizement in the guise of munificence, such as social networking and political patronage. We also think of donations as compensations that balance competing values and assuage guilt. While the discharge of other-centered values placates and restrains the natural impulse to self-advantage, this does not go to the root forces of

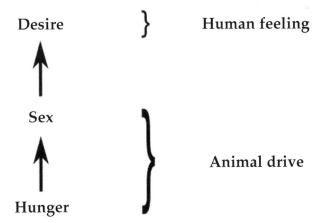

Figure 5.2. The relation of the hunger to the sex drive, and of both to desire.

giving and confuses charity with therapy. Happily, now and then an enlightened philanthropist, disinterested in self-promotion, preferably anonymous with no strings attached will genuinely use largess to help the unfortunate.

Hunger in relation to acquisition

The relation of hunger to sexual drive and the account of this relation in psa (Ch. 6) are helpful to understanding the microgenetic approach to the roots of acquisition, that is, the desire for things in hunger as opposed to the desire for the other in sex. We are so accustomed to thinking of love in relation to sex, an observation that recurs so often in everyday life, that we readily accept the bromide that ambition, greed, and materialism generally are adjuncts to sexual desire or surrogates for suppressed or sublimated sexuality. We speak of ambition as a "lust" for power or money or a displacement of sexual drive, rather than appetitive hunger. In so doing, we miss the origins of acquisition in non-sexual hunger and satiation.

According to Jung (1961), the break with Freud was largely over the exaggerated role in psa of sexual drive. Freud's emphasis on libidinal drive as the foundation of the theory owed, in part, to the expectation that prurient interest would lead to greater publicity. In spite of the current disregard into which Freud's theory has fallen, one legacy of the theory remains almost a cliché: namely, that many forms of striving and acquiring are viewed as signs of repressed sexuality, not specifications of hunger into non-edible objects. Hunger and its derivatives constitute the primary force in human (and animal) mentality. Hunger is derived into sexual drive and much of what is routinely explained in terms of sexual drive can be better understood if the derivatives of hunger and its vectors of aggression and defense are conceived as *fundamental* to the everyday manifestations of sexual drive.

As reviewed in Chapter Six, the major fault-line in psychoanalytical theory is that libido was interpreted in the *Metapsychology* and elsewhere on the model of the synapse (Brown, 1998), as energy that activates otherwise static perceptual and memory traces. With libido as fundamental, it became necessary to expand its scope to very early (infantile) cognition in spite of the absence in young children of sexual drive, actual knowledge of sex, or even fantasy. In childhood, hunger is primary, along with the organs of ingestion and evacuation. There is a preoccupation with feeding (or refusal to eat), elimination, the psychic correlates of digestive organs and their functions. This is not to deny curiosity and pleasure in bodily exploration in pre-latency children, but to maintain that it is secondary to the claims of hunger and its derivations, of which the sex drive is one. Specifically, instead of speculating that infantile sexuality is imposed on hunger, it is more reasonable to assume that the drive to predation in animal hunger develops to predation in animal sexuality, and that the evolutionary pattern in animals is exported to human drive-maturation. The complex of exploration, consummation, and satiation is common to both hunger and sex, with a shift from internal to external organs, and a shift from devouring for pleasure in animal satisfaction to retaining the pleasure-giving object for another occasion in sexual satisfaction.

The primacy of hunger is consistent with its frequency and universality compared to the periodicity, relative intermittency, and variability of the sex drive. Hunger sustains life, while in humans sex is chiefly for pleasure, not reproduction, and many seek the intimacy and contact that sex affords, not the sex act alone. Sexual drive wanes in aging, while hunger remains and eating continues to be a main source of enjoyment. Dinner and candies are often preliminaries to sex and seduction. For most, gastronomic pleasure may not compare with orgasm, but hunger in those who are starving is stronger than the sex drive in those who are abstinent. Such observations are consistent with the foundational nature of the hunger drive and a transition from hunger to sexual drive.

The ethological features of animal sexuality—appetitive behavior, the gestalt of the "releaser," discharge, consummation, and the refractory period that follows—are all comparable to, and preceded by, the same patterns in hunger. Sexual display in mating has its correlates in the diverse strategies of predation and evasion. Sexual adventure has a correspondence, if at times remote, with that in hunting and prey-capture, and the avoidance of predators. Variations in taste for food or drink are analogous to those in sex and perversions.

We may not see a connection between the "love" of a rare wine or cheese and the desire to be trampled by high heels, but they both reflect the ramification of a sphere of desire that is generated out of each class of instinctual drive. The popularity of "health" foods, natural produce, minerals and vitamins, indicates how a basic drive leads to a multiplicity of aims and desires that, like fetishes, appear remote from the source drive as they compound in the imagination. Conceivably, bulimia and anorexia correspond in the sphere of hunger to sexual addiction (nymphomania, satyriasis) and abstinence in the sphere of sex.

The parallel of anorexia to abstinence is imperfect, as anorectics do not feel hunger; the idea of eating often nauseates them. In abstinence there can be strong desire. As a spiritual discipline, abstinence has no value if there is no desire to be denied. One does encounter people with no apparent capacity for sexual pleasure who frequently, like anorectics, feel distaste in the presence of sexual behavior. It is fashionable to speak of such people as "asexual." Unlike the anorectic, such a person is not endangering his life by abstinence.

The role of hunger, its derivatives, and implementations in the psychic life, constitutes a new avenue in analytic psychology, one that goes beyond the voyeurism of sexuality to its origins in primitive hunger and its mutations to surrogate fulfillments, much as the vicissitudes of sexual drive implement a diversity of satisfactions. Hunger is critical in self-preservation and the struggle for survival. A theory grounded in evolution and biology should not begin with sex and mating strategies, but rather should trace sexual drive to its roots in the hunger that insures individual survival. Obviously, one needs both drives to perpetuate the organism and the species, one for self-replication, the other for progeny that are adaptations to changing environments.

A note on libido

In psa, libido is the primary force in mental life. The supposed primacy of sexuality and the need for theoretical consistency led to the argument that libido is exerted not only in adult behavior but "all the way down" to infancy. The strength of the theory was that its diachronic or developmental aspects became more important than the synchronic ones, since adult behavior was explained by sexualized events in childhood. The chief problem with childhood sexuality is its lack of evidence, though the central role of sex in psa required the sexualizing of infantile behavior. These behaviors, inferred by observation, were then forgotten in latency to re-emerge later on and play a pivotal role in adult behavior.

The forgetting of early childhood sexuality was explained by repression. This presumed a withdrawal from memory traces of the libidinal energy that was responsible for their activation. The postulation of an on-off switch or innervation and denervation of cathectic energy is tantamount to claiming that X is not activated because its mechanism of activation is canceled. The argument further entails that a *neural* mechanism (cathexis) is reversed (decathexis) by a *psychological* reaction (shame). This is inconsistent with Freud's anti-dualism, in supposing that a psychic reaction can induce a change in a brain process, and not just any process but one claimed to be the most powerful force in mental life.

Gradually, repression became the linchpin of the theory. The amnesia for sexuality in early childhood was attributed to repression in latency even if forgetting is for all events, not just those construed as sexual, and regardless of whether the child's upbringing was loving or traumatic. The possibility that childhood amnesia is due to normal cognitive maturation, with a lack of adult access to state-dependent learning, received scant attention. Yet state-specificity is quite plausible given findings in many areas of cognitive study on altered states, immature or primitive cognition, rapid exposure or masked stimuli that show the effects of unconscious learning on conscious behavior. The lack of access occurs because antecedent cognition is not conveyed *in statu quo* to rational thought but undergoes a qualitative shift in the transition to consciousness.

From drive to desire: hunger and sex

We tend to focus on the sexual because most of us are well-fed and do not feel intense hunger, nor do we hunt or scavenge for food. In humans, when sexual gratification is direct and immediate, the activity is closer to drive and aggression. When sexual activity is more refined or individuated, it is closer to play (when creative) or perversion (when stereotypical). Both play and perversion allow a surfacing of submerged phases or transient regression of the personality without disintegration. Sexual conquest can be postponed for the pleasures of teasing and courtship. Hunger as a drive can, like sex, be expressed with aggression, even brutality, but hunger as desire refines its objects, including the rituals (manners, ceremonies, etc.) that accompany eating, preparing, and serving meals. The profit in the delay of feeding lies in the anticipation of a meal and the enjoyment of subtle taste. A breath or few sips of fine wine may precede a night of wild inebriation, a tender kiss or gentle foreplay may end in sexual abandon. The part is a window to the whole that is ever lurking below.

Sexual relations heighten and reinforce valuation with feelings of love, hate, jealousy, esteem, or rejection. These also occur with the objects of hunger. The shared pleasure of dinner with friends is a remnant of the cohesion of a pack that hunts and devours a prey. It can also be a prelude to romance. Drive is ordinarily cultivated as it partitions to desire. The frenzy of drive-based hunger is parsed to the enjoyment of wish-fulfillment. We see this in the derivation of hunger to its refinements or to a desire for non-edible objects, as well as the transition to sexual drive and desire. For example, the precursors of sexual desire appear in the priorities of eating, hierarchic order, food selection, competition, submission, and deference. The variety of emotions associated with the desire for things appears in non-sexual envy, pride, greed, competitiveness, etc. Generally, sexual drive is for animate objects, though inanimate ones—a shoe, a stocking, perfume—can serve as aides or surrogates. Hunger as a desire that is not for feeding is usually for inanimate objects, that is, things one wants.

The "pangs" of hunger are referred to the stomach and sated by an acceptable object in an edible class, while the "throes" of sexual desire are referred to the groin or genitals and are sated by an object in a class of appropriate members. Sex in the male is assuaged by discharge; hunger, by ingestion. A person who is famished will eat almost anything as the category of the edible expands. This is true to a lesser extent for sexual gratification, though it can be achieved in solitary by masturbation, postponed indefinitely until a suitable partner comes along, or denied in celibacy. The seizure of prey and the avoidance of predators in the context of drive-based hunger are polar reactions that generally do not admit of intermediate stages. This is also likely for sexual drive in animals. Humans have options in feeding when hunger is not pronounced. In sexual choice, implicit or explicit options give rise to ambivalence and uncertainty as drive mitigates to desire and its vectors. Aggression and defense in sex, for example, in control and submission, are parallel to attack and evasion in feeding.

The shift from polarities to intermediaries, from the pronounced to the subtle, from extremes to gradations, from diffuse to focal in the urge, or to greater specificity in the aim, is expected if hunger is the ground out of which sexual drive develops. Aggression in hunting, fighting over food or territory, tracking a prey, aggressive postures and displays, for example, baring the teeth, are derived to mating behaviors. The male biting the nape of the female in sex is reminiscent of one animal crushing the neck of another. The reflex sucking of nursing is derived in adult sex to voluntary pleasure. We see a transition from behaviors relating to hunger to those relating to sexual drive and desire. Much that is attributed to sexual drive or desire develops out of a mixture of hunger and sex (drive and desire) or from hunger alone. This chapter attempts to right the imbalance in the interpretation of behavior that, since Freud, has tended to over-include the sexual to a neglect of the primacy of hunger. The observations described to this point support the hypotheses that:

1. Hunger-drive precedes and is derived to sexual-drive.
2. The objects of hunger-as-desire are things to enjoy and possess.
3. The objects of sex-as-desire are others to love and possess.

The constellation of the hunger-drive and aggressive/defensive vectors is carried into the sexual-drive with the same vectors of implementation (Figure 5.3), conforming to the evolutionary principle that functions do

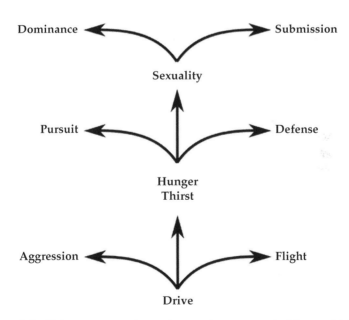

Figure 5.3. Drive energy gives rise to hunger and thirst, which are transitional to sexual drive. The polarities of approach and avoidance, in relation to drive, discharge into aggressive and defensive behaviors. In hunger, this translates to pursuit and defense; in sexual drive, to seizure and dominance, or submission and acquiescence.

not appear *de novo* but exploit, that is, are derived from, more archaic systems.

Hunger, sex, and their objects

Hunger and its derivatives are directed to inanimate objects or animate objects treated as things (to eat), while sexuality is directed to animate objects or individuals with a certain value. An animate object can be the target of either drive or desire. A dog can be an object of affection or a thing one eats. In Korea, where I lived some years ago, people kept cows in the house and ate the dogs! A thing is also a possession or property, an object of desire or one of passing interest. A starry night can deeply stir the emotions, or as Hegel remarked, is a "rash on the sky." In one instance, feeling is felt to go out to the object, or the object is incorporated in the affective life of the observer. In the other, the observer is indifferent to the object or has disdain for the emotions of others. We speak of having a connection with nature and its objects, an attitude that ranges from mild interest, to a hobby as in gardening, to reverence or, in Wordsworth, to the most sublime poetry. An object (thing) may have value only in its utility. A thing evokes impersonality or self-interest. An affectively charged object evokes personal feeling. The former is closer to hunger and the desires to which it gives rise, the latter to sexual drive and its desires.

The progression from hunger to sex is from aggression to pursuit or from flight to submission. In hunger, flight is escape from death; in sex, flight can be rejection, defense or a lure to pursuit. There is a transition from the digestion of things to fusion with others. Hunger devours and assimilates. Sex penetrates and detaches. For hunger, the object has no importance other than as food. Once ingested, the object no longer exists. In sex, objects have greater autonomy and are distinct from subjects, though in the intricacies of sexual relations, one individual can be subsumed in the other.

The shift from hunger to sexual drive goes from objects as things without value apart from nourishment or drive-satisfaction, to objects with value other than the consummation of drive. This direction is natural if hunger is antecedent to sexuality. We say we are nourished by love. A person in the throes of love may not feel like eating; gain or loss of weight is often a sequel to parting. A girl is a dish. Hunger and sex are combined in daily life, in myth and religion. Gods devour their children. There are offerings of human sacrifice, especially virgins. Vampirism merges sexual longing with thirst for blood to achieve a state of immortality. Even the last supper is a feast where the love of supplicants is tested.

In hunger, the object is always a thing. One has no pity for what one eats, though in tribal communities, blessings and respect are often bestowed on living things to be eaten, a practice that carries over to grace at table before a meal. The acknowledgement of spirit in things to be eaten includes grains, fruits and vegetables, as well as animals with inferred mental states. The animistic mentality of the native, which extends into religious practice, invokes the spirit that inhabits the once-living organism. In a prayer or blessing before a meal, mind or spirit moves from nature and sequesters in deity. When we give thanks to god for the bread and the wine, there is a shift from the concrete to the abstract, from mind (spirit) in a particular object to mind-universal in which all objects have a share.

The desire for things has more to do with hunger than sex though, as noted above, in a kind of inverse confirmation of the thesis, ambition, greed, and covetousness are often interpreted as compensations for a lack of sexual fulfillment. There is displacement from one drive to another. It is important that desires not exploit others as means, but approach them as ends. In the desire for things, this is a response to the charm or beauty of the thing. In sexual desire, love is an end in itself. Hunger is naturally oblivious to the other, whether alive, dead or in the course of being killed. Ambition and greed are like this. Sexual desire is often for the other as a means to self-indulgence. For sexual desire and hunger, and their ramifications, the challenge is for love and beauty to be constantly before one's eyes, not provocations to egocentric pleasure.

As a desire, hunger is for thing-like objects rather than persons. One exception is cannibalism, but the object of cannibalism is less a person than an enemy, a rival, a religious or ceremonial figure, or just a meal. In some tribes, eating the organs of the dead is thought to convey the qualities associated with that person. Unusual cases of psychopathology (e.g., Jeffrey Dahmer, or the fictional Hannibal Lecter) remind us that cannibalism and sexuality are intertwined.[2] Religious and cultural beliefs extend spirit or sacredness to all living things, even to microbes in ascetic Jainism. For some vegetarians, it is shameful to eat fish or snails. Some individuals infer feelings in plants, but the Rubicon is vague at the lower levels of life forms. This illustrates the affective sharing or incorporation of the other in the self irrespective of the lack of reciprocity. The vegetarian scale depends on the presence of psyche in living things—animals more than fish, fish more than plants. This establishes a link with love and sexuality, however tenuous, since the assumption of psyche in others is the basis for compassion.

In the development of hunger from drive to desire, the ingestion of a thing evolves to its possession. The desire for jewelry, clothes, art, develops from hunger, where having or owning the thing makes it part of the self, rather like eating it. The pleasures that develop out of hunger-as-desire take the object far from the drive in which it arises. As with love, objects of hunger can be idealized, for example, in art. The love of art is the desire to possess, as well as the will to create, which owe as much to hunger as to sexual desire. This was nicely put by Mark Strand:

> *Ink runs from the corners of my mouth.*
> *There is no happiness like mine.*
> *I have been eating poetry.*

In psa, possessiveness is referred to the influence of oral and/or anal stages and their relation to digestion, retention, and evacuation. Possessiveness in love is closer to hunger than sexuality, even with a sexual character, since the signature of true love is surrender, not ownership. A desperate need for a beloved or a pathological jealousy may appear as great passion, but it derives from the transition of predation to sexual capture. In animal hunger there is aggression with rivals over a scarce supply of food. In jealousy, there is aggression with rivals to the beloved as a unique repository of feeling. In animals, the competition in mating arises in the same way, though aggression is targeted and ritualized by the sexual complement.

In human love, there is devastation if the beloved leaves or is lost, but even in the despair of a parting that is a misfortune for the self there is, ideally, a wish for the happiness of the beloved. However, a lost love may evoke an aggression that turns inward in suicide or self-abasement, especially when there is dependency and/or betrayal, or when the beloved dies and there is no person or circumstance to serve as a focus of anger or grief. To paraphrase Goethe on love, "a confusion of the real with the ideal never goes unpunished." In sexual drive and desire, the other can be treated as an object that is loved or a thing that gives pleasure. The objects of hunger that seem valueless except as food can prevail over the objects of unselfish desire. The valuation that is no longer for a person but a thing displays the roots of sexual drive in hunger.

The desire for a partner, as in the desire for food, is satisfied by other things of the same class. A fetish as an aide to sexual gratification is such a thing in which hunger conflicts with or supplements sexual desire. In perversion, the fetish as a thing and the other as an object are essential to drive-satisfaction. The interpretation of perversion and fetishism in psa takes the sexual act in the adult and relates it to sexual conflict in childhood, whereas the tension between the *need for a thing* and the *desire for the other,* which is a mix of hunger and sexual desire, occurs when one desire facilitates or blocks another. This is especially so when neither desire alone—hunger, sex—is sufficient for consummation; the inanimate things of hunger and ownership are aides to the unloved objects of sexual desire.

The use of things as aides or substitutes in sexual behavior, where the needs of one person trump those of the other, is an egocentric bias in object-relations; the object—the other—is insufficient to bring the act to completion. Masturbation eliminates the other with images or fetishes (things) as surrogates. The fetish arises in the need for a hunger-based object in a sexual context. The fetish is usually inanimate, such as shoes or clothing, things that are allied to hunger as inanimate possessions. Scent is clearly related to hunger and may also aid arousal. The importance of odor in animal hunger is transmitted to human sexuality in the erotic appeal of bodily odor, exploited in the use of perfume to enhance sexual attraction. Similarly, an "accessory" for a woman, for example, high heel shoes, may be given a sexual interpretation, but buying a pair of shoes or a bottle of perfume is, for a woman, the satisfaction of hunger as desire, while for a man, the use of a shoe as a fetish takes the object into a more explicit sexual setting. As with perfume, the knowledge that objects of hunger can provoke sexual feeling just as sexual desire exploits hunger, for example, giving presents to a lover, shows how the refinements of one drive or desire infiltrate the other.

The sex-drive lapses into the equivalents of hunger, as hunger advances to modes of sexuality. A person used as a means of sexual relief brings the aggressive underpinnings of hunger to the fore. We speak of sexual hunger, of thirst and of cravings, as if the sexual urge is comparable to hunger. The song, "drink to me only with thine eyes," combines love and thirst. One says to a lover, "I could eat you up." Sexual drive can combine the origin of sexual desire in hunger, or permit intentional feelings derived to desire to undergo play in the imagination. In this case, the other is invested (re-created) with feeling tones that supplement rather than discharge the self.

One could say that when the other is a means of satisfaction rather than an object of affection, sexual need, especially in perversion, is more truly an expression of hunger than sex, for the sexual drive is incompletely differentiated. We see the mix of hunger and sexuality normally when the latter is incompletely resolved. This is expected if the approach and avoidance of sexual drive, which are shifting and reversing in the attraction to others, evolve from hunger and the polarities of fight and flight. The forward direction of drive-resolution into a complex of desires, some closer to hunger, others to sex, imports the mental state into contents that narrow down to the tributaries of conceptual feeling. Drive passes to desire, desire unfolds to a multiplicity of imaginative contents, and the bridge from the primitive to the refined is obscured.

Transition to sexual drive

The principle that incomplete resolution of stages in the maturation of young children creates a nidus for later deviance is generally true, but speculation on the stages in resolution, and the phenomena that occur in the process, give a complexity to psa that is so divorced from psychological reality as to be almost cartoonish in the way conflicts are postulated irrespective of neurological or cognitive theory. Yet we see conditions in the psa account that point to the hunger-sex relation. Take castration anxiety, which is central to the theory of sexual function and perversion. The fear of castration is claimed to have its roots in the ambivalence of the oedipal wish to love and be loved by the father and at the same time to murder him. However, some theorists have argued that fear of castration is not for the punitive father but the devouring vagina. Kaplan (1991, p. 58) described this as "the unconscious fear of being swallowed up into the womb." She also discusses the "anal birth" theory of small children, that is, that babies emerge like excrement, or that the mother eats something that develops like a seed inside her. Spanking children who do not eat, the punishment of naughtiness or disobedience is carried over into adult sexual activity. These observations support the account, in that the digestive functions of hunger are the origins of libidinal drive energy and the basis of the child's imagination of sexual and other mysteries. In this category is the fascination of small children with fairy tales of giants that eat children or dragons that devour brave young men who try to win the heart of a princess.

The development of desire out of drive, the priority of hunger over sex in development, even if overshadowed by the sexual adventures and fantasies of adult cognition, the interplay in the derivations of both drives, their elaborations in conceptual feeling and imaginative growth—are problems for a theory of mind grounded in evolutionary thought. The time is ripe for a re-interpretation of the emotions from the standpoint of the development and the specification of drive into desire, the predominant phase at which feelings and behaviors arise, and how early events are carried into maturity.

Implications of the theory

As noted, an object does not have to be inanimate to be a thing; it requires the observer to not share in the affective life of what is perceived. Any object can be a thing, but only living things share feeling with a subject. The degree to which feelings are inferred, felt or reciprocated depends on individual attitude. Ordinarily, we do not ask if a rock or spoon has feelings—though in some sense they do. Some vegetarians have compassion for plants; perhaps they imagine that carrots feel pain when cooked. They may feel compassion for a fish on a hook or in the frying pan, and empathize with higher animal forms. However, they do not participate in the "affective experience" of lower life forms and rarely expect reciprocity from the advanced ones, save for pets and humans. In humans and other organisms, a lack of shared feeling, or a failure to assimilate the feelings of the object or other in the self turns it into a thing.

In sum: The hunger drive has its own line of development, but also extends into sexuality. The hunger for food develops to the desire for things. In sexuality, it colors desire with acquisition, and shifts sexual desire to thing-like objects, or treats objects as things, in which the value of the object is secondary to the needs of the self. When the sexual drive is relatively independent of this influence, it is free to develop to objects of value.

Animate and inanimate objects have value but only the animate can reciprocate feeling. Any object can be treated indifferently, like an inanimate thing, but inanimate things, though objects of desire, do not become objects of affection. There is no clear demarcation between loved objects and desired things, or the value of animate and inanimate objects, but as a general rule, loved objects reinforce value by reciprocity, while the value of inanimate but desired things is influenced by consensus.

The beloved becomes part of the self, so that self-realization is the realization of a self fused with the other. The self can assimilate occasions as well as others. Some individuals can become so entangled with things they become the things they desire. This is the case, for example, of a person so bound up with work or money there is little left of the self if these are lost. In this sense, there can be despair, even suicide, as when a loved one is lost.

The value in a thing is its value for the self. One can speak of the intrinsic value of a home or diamond, but this economic value differs from that of a beloved, where the worth of the person is only to the lover and is not the result of a comparison. The love of things is a desire to possess the thing, while the love for a beloved is a love of the ideal. Ordinarily, things are not idealized to the same extent as loved others, nor is the value of a thing comparable to the value of the beloved.

These differences between the desire for things, the love of things, and the love for another person, fall on a continuum from drive-like objects to objects-of-desire, and within desire, for those objects that one desires and those objects that one loves. Indeed, in a certain sense, the aggressive or acquisitive vector of self-satisfaction that develops out of hunger gives way to acquiescence, that is, a vector of submission or self-denial, as represented in the medieval concept of *Frauendienst*, the abject service of a man to his beloved (see Lewis, 1936), that for some is the very essence of true love. The self gives its self to the beloved in a way it cannot give to other things. In submission to the beloved, romantic love approximates religious devotion.

Notes

1. There is some evidence from pathological dissociations that different regions in the brain mediate animate and inanimate objects (Nielsen, 1936).
2. The anthropology of eating (Lévi-Strauss, 1964) offers insights to the diverse manifestations of hunger in everyday life; for example, the origin of table manners in the deterrence or taboo of cannibalism. Even cannibals are not immune to the delicacy of cuisine. Professor Anton Leischner of Bonn related to me a visit to the Brazilian Amazon, where he was taken by a guide to a tribe of cannibals, who told him that above all they prefer the soft, tasty flesh of Jesuits!

CHAPTER SIX

Love and pathology: a note on psychoanalytic theory

No one who disdains the key will ever be able to unlock the door.

—Sigmund Freud (1905)

Introduction

The different modes and objects of loving are a challenge to the uniformity of feeling, as well as to the simplicity of any theory that might be applied to explain the diversity of human experience in the sphere of emotion. The difficulty is compounded by the rarity of a true and lasting love, and the obvious question, apart from literary flights of fancy, whether such love is mere fantasy or a real possibility. The prevalence of selfish need over unselfish giving, the uncertainty of love or its pretense, the diversity of unions between and among the sexes, and the natural evolution of love over time, and at different points in the life cycle, are all responsible for the cynicism that attends to discussions of true love. There are also the covert motives, the self-interest, the counterfeit, the delusion, and the covetousness that drive most human behaviors. How is love to flourish in the modern era when people are treated as commodities that have a certain economic worth, values are

127

expendable, and attributes are less marks of character than skills to be marketed?

To the extent love is a conscious decision, the feeling is diminished, while to the extent it is a passion, it is mocked for lack of discernment. Love as rational appraisal cannot be resolved with the union of genuine loving, though the natural relaxation of passionate beginnings allows reason to creep into feeling as desire wanes and is refined to subtler affect-ideas. We do not all find love, or if we find it, keep it, and we may have to choose between a rapture that passes and an affection that is less passionate but enduring. There is also the opposition of desire with a calculus of utility and the consumerism and corruption of the deeper sensitivities, which make us believe that love is for the young, the innocent, or the guileless. There is the fact that unfulfilled desire may persist, but once satisfied may not recur, so that the sought-after fusion of lovers is the death of longing. If autonomy and self-sufficiency are the goal, love can be seen as pathology. If it is interpreted as a need, it is a weakness to be compensated. If a distraction, it is not worth the bother; if an obsession, it needs a cure. The analytic mind asks if love is an illusory surrogate for an uncompromising objectivity in which a life without illusion is a life without meaning. Yet even as a topic of ridicule, the ideal of a true love is deeply rooted in the heart of even the most hardened cynic. One has to ask, then:

1. Why people seek love even as they deride it, or why they long for love after many disappointments.
2. What are the main reasons that people cannot find or cultivate genuine loving?

As to the former, there is, as we observe in animal nature, a foundational drive to coupling on which all dyads or ensembles are based. Mating and the sexual urge continue to exert their effects long after the reproductive capability and the sexual urge are exhausted. The impulse that is founded on instinctual drive undergoes many adaptations as it adjusts to experience and circumstance, but the basic parameters are biological and driven by the animal inheritance.

Beyond this, and at least before advanced age sets in, we are usually searching for someone or something we value, a lover, a new job, health, fitness, wealth, acquisition, or merely a vague happiness in which love in one form or another, as passion or enthusiasm, is no small part. Common to all these objects of striving is that the mind/brain is an engine of meaning and value-creation. To love someone or something deeply is to experience, in the extension of desire into objects, the uttermost point in human valuation. Similarly, being loved by another satisfies the same need, for it affirms the uniqueness of the self. To be loved is to be reassured one is exceptional, that is, is a self distinct from other selves, and at the same time it justifies the value given to those who are loved.

Some hold the "pleasure principle" as the motivating force, and it is true that we seek and derive pleasure, *inter alia*, in giving and receiving love. But valuation is prior to the urge for pleasure, in that it determines those objects and activities that are sought after and from which pleasure is derived. Pleasure may trump love, but love is still the ultimate value. Thus the process of value-creation and the implicit beliefs it entails, which begins in drive, then passes to desire in the object-concept, and accompanies the forming object outward as value or worth, the process through which value (and meaning) is "assigned" to objects, the Will directed to what it wants, is the fundamental force that accounts for the need to love another as the goal of personal valuation, as it accounts for the need to be loved, in which the self is, itself, affirmed as an object of ultimate valuation.

The latter question concerns the capacity or incapacity to give and receive love and is more intricate if not more complex than the first. In Anna Karenina, Tolstoy wrote, famously, that "happy families are all alike; that every unhappy family is unhappy in its own way." The incapacity to love, or the habit of loving badly or incompletely, has its sources in the vagaries and misfortunes of life, some brief though traumatic, others trivial but cumulative, with the result an unwillingness or inability to fully surrender the self to another person. The impulse to self-protection leaves no room for the vulnerabilities on which love depends. Selfishness, isolation, lack of generosity, and the displacement of feeling to surrogate pursuits are some of its manifestations. The misanthrope and sociopath are the extremes. The fundamental defect of character is a resistance to the assimilation of the other that is essential to the attainment of oneness. This corresponds to a lack of openness that could allow the values and beliefs of the other to infiltrate the self-concept. The assimilation of the other requires a suspension of egocentric feeling. To accept the other in one's heart is to relinquish the self and disavow its completeness.

The variations on this theme also involve a disparity between expectations and needs, or one could say, between rational judgments and emotional dependencies. For example, what are we to think of people who describe the man or woman of their dreams in terms of an inventory of traits, and to appraise others according to the degree to which the inventory is approximated? Once in a while, a person comes along who may actually fit the description, which is more like a shopping or wish list than a coming-together of souls, but what of those occasions, probably frequent, when there is a disconnect in the list of hoped-for attributes and the beloved who is actually chosen? Naturally, there are cultural similarities in such inventories in spite of the paucity of partners who could satisfy them. Most people would say they are seeking a beloved who is intelligent, generous, caring, or has a good sense of humor, but how often, for the lover, and from an impersonal standpoint, are these expectations satisfied?

Into the mix of need, choice and despair comes psychoanalysis (psa) to the rescue, in which, so it is argued, the manifestations of love, its distortions and pathologies can be explained by oedipal conflicts and the traumas of life experience. It is the richness of these individual histories, the actual histories and the dreams and parapraxes that further enrich them, which opens the door to clever reconstructions based on memories, symbols, what is acted out and what is withheld, that makes the psychoanalytic interpretation so compelling. The "conjuring trick" is to begin with the content of thought or behavior and trace it, by dream images, free-association, hypnosis, and other devices, to psychic trauma in childhood. Diverse behaviors are explained in a formulaic way depending on which events are conceived as decisive. In this way, the same event can have a variety of outcomes according to the conditions that need to be explained. A child reared by an unaffectionate mother can develop a personality similar to the parent or it can go in the opposite direction and become an individual who needs and gives affection. In one case, the path is direct, in the other, compensatory. The theory does not predict the adult pattern from the source event—one cannot predict, from the mother-child relation, the pattern of adult behavior. Instead, one seeks the source events to account for outcomes in maturity.

It is also the case that psychoanalytic theory has taken different positions on mental processes that are critical to the interpretation of a behavior. For example, in early theory, a memory trace underwent transformation in the passage from unconscious (Ucs) to conscious (Cs) thought, while in later theory the trace remained static, becoming Cs as a target of libidinal drive (cathexis). On the first theory, diverse behaviors could be explained by vicissitudes in the micro-development of thought, while in the latter account, memories are selectively illuminated and assembled *post hoc* to explain behavior. If one accepts the foundational principles, the explanatory power of the later theory is greater even if it lacks an evidentiary basis, while the early theory, which was linked to evolutionary concepts that were subsequently abandoned, is more accurate but less powerful in the account of variation. The basic shift in psa from early to late theory, say from the work on symptom formation, the metapsychology and topographic theory to ego psychology and structural theory, was from a formulation based in mind/brain process to one based on psychic content. A theory based on content always has the advantage that it can re-assemble the elements of Ucs life to a narrative of the etiology of Cs behavior, while process theory, like evolution, gives the main lines of psychic process, not the specific contents it delivers. The one (substance) theory goes from content to content with the mediating process concealed or collapsed to symbols and mechanisms, while for the other (process) theory, behaviors are markers of the process that deposits them, not inherent elements.

Microgenetic theory is more cautious than psa, preferring a sketch or framework to a finished composition. The main themes of development conform to laws or regularities in mind/brain process that are common to all individuals. Events in life impact this development by restricting, suppressing or eliminating an adaptive line of growth. The events do not fill an otherwise empty shell with content, but shape instinctual patterns to unfold in different ways. Specifically, the effect of experience is to delimit an act of cognition to an habitual line of expression, which may be more or less healthy. Ordinarily, the healthy is what is adaptive, but an adaptation can also be what is essential for survival. This interpretation differs from psa in that it begins with a general theory in which experience constrains recurrent acts of thought rather than with a nucleus of infantile experiences as the building blocks of mature behavior. Evolution postulates phyletic universals or principles that guide the interpretation of unique outcomes. Microgenetic theory postulates that the diversity of behavior reflects a sculpting by sensory experience of unconscious need, which constrains its derivation to conscious desire and enforces the adaptation of both to the exigencies of the immediate occasion.

Psychoanalytic theory of love

The principle goal of this work on love and its perturbations is not a theory of pathology, but rather an attempt to develop an account of love as a sublime emotional experience, along with its manifestations and object-relations, in a way that is consistent with microgenetic concepts. This account may not provide sufficient detail to satisfy those seeking explanations for every variety of love, or hate, or other emotions and sexual experiences, but what is described, however restricted in scope, can serve as a starting point for an understanding that maps to process theory. A direction pointing at truth is preferable to one that attempts to explain a great deal but has no relation to psychological theory or research. Psychoanalysis is a theory of behavioral and emotional states with a wide explanatory reach, but with little relation to psychology or a theory of the mind/brain state. This applies to the account of love. In a letter to Jung (Bergmann, 1987, p. 157), Freud wrote, "I do not think that our psychoanalytic flag ought to be raised over the territory of normal love." The psychic conflict on which psa is built is inconsistent with the wholeness of true love. Since psa does not explain "normal" behavior, only pathology, it must turn normalcy into a form of pathology and deal with it as a variant.

Conflict is pervasive in all psa interpretations but consider the entities in conflict. Every object is a contrast. A table and chair are perceived as outcomes of a process of successive contrasts in which a multitude of other possibilities are eliminated as the final ones individuate. Contrast is essential to theory of mind, but contrast only becomes conflict when the contrasts through which objects (ideas, acts, feelings) develop, especially at early phases, are postulated to persist as parallel forces, latent or overt. Like psa, microgenesis has its roots in (organic) pathology, but unlike psa the disorders are ante-cedent phases that are revived; they do not persist as combatants in perpetual conflict.

In spite of these and many other reservations, however, the psycho-analytic model does offer some insights that can be translated to the vocabulary of process thinking:

1. In psa, the drive-representation is the result of a cathexis by libido of a memory trace. In process theory, the drive-representation is a combination of drive as a foundational emotion, and category as a foundational concept, not a trace that is activated by sexual energy. The relation of drive or feeling to concept or object is one of inherence, not attachment. The concept of a durable trace that is targeted and cathected by libido is replaced by a succession of phases in which the memory trace is a developing configuration—from image or concept to act or object—each having an intrinsic, affective tone. The "trace" is the entire sequence from unconscious core to world surface.

2. In psa, there is a shift of energy from self to object or an attachment of libidinal drive from one trace or object to another. The circulation and redistribution of libido is an essential component of the theory. For example, loving and separation entail the attachment and detachment of sexual drive energy, with objects remaining more or less unchanged. However, attachment and detachment are just terms for the observable; they are not models or interpretations of mind/brain process that underlie what is observed. Indeed, the transfer of common sense descriptions to explanatory constructs is the bugbear of modern psychology.

3. A similar problem bedevils the theory of a conscious idea as an illuminated copy of the unconscious trace. Sensory constraints on the object-development insure that the beloved will be perceived more or less the same before and after s/he is loved even though the perception of the object is primarily an internal process. When love is gone, the individual may say, what did I ever see in him or her? The attributes of the other are no longer idealized. This inner life of the object, its experiential and conceptual meaning and affective history, are radically altered even when "physical" appearance is little changed.

4. In process theory, libidinal drive individuates categories and concepts to intentional feelings in a graduated series with intermediate phases. The object does not remain unaltered with only its affective charge modified. This includes all objects. The shift from one valued object or idea to another entails conceptual growth or branching, or an exchange of one affectively charged category for another, not a transfer of energy. The energy-transfer theory requires that energy (drive, libido) is the sole source of the dynamic in change, while

traces, ideas, and objects remain solid or static entities. This is the fundamental defect in psa.

5. To take a personal example, my interest (value) in neuropsychology as a young man shifted to philosophy in later years, but this was not a result of energy transfer, rather a slow maturation in which one field expanded to another by overlapping concepts. The shift is more like an over-inclusion of a semantic category or a bridge from one concept to another by way of shared attributes than a release of energy from one field of interest and the attachment of that energy to another. In internalizing attention as libido, or externalizing libido as attention, a shift in one becomes a shift in the other regardless of the idea or object to which it is applied.

6. The shift from one loved object to another is similar to the growth of ideas. Suppose I fall in love with someone and then my interest shifts to another person. This may seem a simple transfer of attention or drive energy, but the situation is more complex. Perhaps the newly beloved fulfills an ideal that before was only partly satisfied, or incompletely idealized. Both love-objects may overlap in many ways. I may be seeking the passion that naturally fades in a transition to friendship. A slight, a feeling of rejection or incomplete acceptance, the feeling that love has become conditional, selfish, exploitative can lead a person to seek a substitute or supplement. Is libido transferred, divided or shared? There may be ambivalence or uncertainty; perhaps both objects are loved. The point is that each concept or object has an affective tonality, as do the intervening ideas or states across them. It is not a question of attachment, release, and re-attachment, as if feeling is the beam of a flashlight that is allocated, first here, then there.

7. In the microgenetic account, when an object or person is no longer loved, the "physical" appearance may not change, since the sensory sculpting of the perception goes on as before, but this is not the case for the attributes that distinguish that person as someone who is loved. The ideal of the beloved erodes as qualities objectify to give a more realistic appraisal. This can result in friendship or enmity, but in any case it clears the path for another love-object. With objectification, the beloved leaves the imagination of the lover and enters the object world where, like any other object, it is not so beautiful or caring. This may continue to separation or divorce, or to a loveless companionship or a dispassionate accord. Perhaps, love persists as a new love is taken to resolve sexual or other needs.

8. While it may be unobjectionable to say love seeks the union of infancy, this need not be framed in terms of revisiting or resisting incestuous wishes. Life begins in a series of partitions; first, the intrinsic splitting, individuation and expansion "inside-out" of the fetus within a membrane. Great complexity is achieved in a continuous fractionation of successive wholes. This trend eventuates at birth in the anatomic splitting of mother and child, a separation replaced by a psychic unity in which the nurturing adult is essentially an extension of the child's mind. The cellular mitosis that leads to parturition (partition) of infant and mother recurs, from the infant's perspective, in the psychological whole of mother and child, a wholeness that once more leads to gradual separation as the child detaches from its caretaker. This separation establishes the seeds for further individuation and the autonomy of later life.

9. I have written of the "force lines" of embryogenesis (Brown, 2011), in which the elimination of redundancy in cells and connections in fetal and post-partum brain growth leads to functional specificity. This trend continues in specification by the inhibition of an established connectivity. The same pattern recurs in the actualization of the mind/brain state as a whole-part transition from unconscious core to world surface. The appearance of this basic pattern in fetal growth and psychological maturation, and its relation to whole-part shifts in the phase-transitions of the mind/brain state, make one wonder if patterns that guide the growth of individuality are manifestations of foundational laws that trace to the germinal phases of life.

10. Along these lines, I have also speculated on similar patterns in brain and skin, both derived from primitive ectoderm. There are analogous patterns of arising and perishing, in skin the shedding of cells at the surface of the body and their replacement from below, in brain the development of objects from core to surface, their perishing and replacement from deeper phases. Perhaps this is merely an analogy, but it may point to differing manifestations of fundamental regularities in the process of mind and nature.

11. In psa, love is explained largely as a residual of the mother-child relation, in the transfer of libido from incestuous to non-incestuous objects. The parent-child relation is taken to explain nearly all behavior. Sexual love, its varieties and perversions, trace to an incestuous wish, in which the oedipal complex is one component. Although we are admonished by advocates of psa not to interpret such relations in overly simplistic terms, sex, love, and related states,

indeed all behaviors, depend on varying degrees of irresolution in the struggle among competing claims on the infantile memory of the adult brain, as revealed in dream report, observation, and analysis. Certainly, patterns of early cognition laid down in the core of the mind/brain state configure consequent phases. However, the mother-child relation and the experience of childhood can also be interpreted in terms of an infantile cognition that differs from that of the adult. We should avoid a vocabulary of conflict among hypothetical entities that are little more than internalized homunculi, but rather uncover the archaic configurations that implement unconscious needs in a transition to conscious and intentional wants by a series of adaptive contrasts. In this regard, the search for Jungian archetypes in myth and legend is, I believe, a step closer than psa to a theory of the mind rooted in nature, brain, and psyche.

12. Attachment theory is a variant of psa ostensibly grounded in biology and experiment. Though it espouses a representation of the other in the self, the approach is largely interactive, contrasting with Freud's (and my own) intrapsychic model. No doubt some interesting studies on mother-baby interaction have been done, for example that of Jaffe, Beebe, Feldstein, Crown, and Jasnow (2001) on rhythms of dialogue, but the field seems largely a platitude in search of an argument. We know well that parenting is important in other creatures. I have written on the isolation cry of the infant macaque separated from its mother (Brown, 1986), and affection, or its similitude, among the higher mammals. This is familiar to all who watch nature programs on television. So what is new about attachment theory that expands our knowledge of the psyche? Not much. The theory is so impoverished it is difficult to understand why it created such a stir in the first place. At least Freud's story has psychic complexity and arguments as to outcomes. If it is true, as Steele (2003) writes, that "arguably attachment experiences in early childhood never lead directly to the attachment emotions, beliefs and behaviors in adult," what is the import of the theory? With regard to the effort to map psa, and especially attachment models, to brain or chemistry, this in my view is hopeless. Before we even attempt such an enterprise, we need to replace the unconscious apparatus of psa with a description that is coherent with findings in related disciplines.

13. The fundamental strategy of psa is to install in the unconscious the conscious objects that result from the interpretation of behavior, including dreams, and postulate a conflict between opposing beliefs, when the true conflict, if that is the correct term, is in the failure of the precursors of those objects to fully actualize in consciousness. The sub-surface conflict is inferred from its symbolic representations, mis-directions or derailments in everyday experience. Conflict, tension, cognitive dissonance, refer to the anxiety that occurs when we do not have a clear picture of alternatives, usually because the option-to-be has not yet fully resolved. Conflict is presumed to result from the mismatch of two irreconcilable ideas, desires or conditions that, like opposing factions, compete for control.

14. There is another way to interpret the conflict that is central to psa. Every phase in the mental state involves a specification of ground to figure, with each figural content (virtual unless it actualizes) serving as ground for an ensuing specification. The development from ground to figure, from whole to part or from context to item, that is, the process of specification, differentiation or individuation, is the basic process of microgenesis. This can be thought of as a struggle among hypothetical entities, but there are no actual entities, only biases in the direction of the entity that actualizes. For example, when we search for a word or name we do not ordinarily select among two or three choices. If we do, we are selecting or deciding, not searching. In word search, there is often a sense of the length, syllabic content, and initial sound as a background for other possibilities. Unconscious conflict is the tension that occurs in unresolved situations like that studied by Zeigarnik and Lewin in problem-solving. This is not a struggle between opposing objects or choices, but the tension that occurs in evoking a solution or choice when it is not yet known. Tension occurs when we are not conscious of the alternatives or the sources of decisions. Tension and anxiety refer to the incomplete resolution of one object with clarity. Once the options are clear, the struggle is almost over. We see this, for example, when a person passes through an agitated depression on the way into or out of a morbid depression where there is loss of objects but without anxiety. The agitation accompanies the losing or gaining of objects, in deterioration or in recovery. Once the object is clear, or fully lost, the anxiety changes to an emotion like fear or it disperses in object loss.

15. This tensional state was studied long ago by Sander (1928) in percept-genetic research. The methods that were used involved brief visual exposures too rapid for eye movement or object identification. With a gradual increase in exposure time, the subject goes through various stages on the way to full identification. Increasing anxiety gives way to relief when identification occurs. If we are choosing among conscious objects, say whether to take one job or another, one partner or another, one vacation or another, the "choices" have objectified and the conflict is less intense than when they were unconscious possibilities. The anxiety that accompanies the desire for love without an object, or the uncertainty over a new love or the loss of a current one, illustrates this phenomenon. Objects not available in a state of anxiety are imported in psa to the mind as hypothetic entities in the expectation that the state of tension (conflict) can be resolved when the object is provided or suggested, or is seized upon by insight. If this were true, insight would lead to cure, that is, resolution of conflict, but most analysts would admit that any benefit of psa is largely due to suggestion, impressionability, or gullibility, which in turn has consequences for a theory of love (see below).

16. An act of cognition leads to objects, acts, thoughts, and images, as habit and bias adapt to the sensory surround. An unconscious bias reflects the adequacy of neural configurations to specify out of preceding phases. The problem with conflict-theory is that the specification from whole to part is not a domination of one path over its competitors, at least not in the unconscious where the drama is assumed to occur, but is a partition of the potential for multiple routes of development that are instigated by need and guided by necessity. The affective weakness or strength of an object is a function of its clarity or obscurity, its psychic depth or objectivity. The object-formation is adaptive when internal pressures are resolved with external demands. It is maladaptive when the internal bias is inappropriate to need, or there is a relative equivalence of possibilities and tension cannot be resolved, or the demands on the individual are unrealistic given the character or personality.

17. The literary and romantic imagination postulates shadowy, nefarious entities that are then installed in the creative recesses of unconscious mind. The more pressing need is to better understand the structural relations of the infantile core, its gradual development and transformation, and how these early constructs are realized

in adult discourse and behavior. Like the linguistic universals of topic and action that, arguably, are the kernel of an utterance, core vectors such as dependence and individuation (wholeness and apartness), like the demands of social engagement on self-pleasure and egocentricity, provide a valence for the instigative phases of acts of cognition. A good place to begin is with the intersection of the animal inheritance with the affect-laden, early-experienced, largely unconscious patterns of childhood behavior and memory. The implicit beliefs, values and orientations of the core provide a context for the originating drives and their derivation to the concepts and desires of later mentation. The centrality of the child-parent relation in early experience, as well as the formation of character, disposition and moral feeling, reflect the solidification of trends in object-development, as an archaic cognition prepares the way for the ideas and objects of conscious experience.

18. From this standpoint, the bond or oneness with the mother (caretaker) can be strong or weak, healthy or unhealthy as to outcome, but there is no reason to term it incestuous, or to speak of love as a shift to non-incestuous objects, which implies a taint of sexual perversity in the separation of child and parent or the search for a loving other, or the relation of the individual to the wider social environment. A neutral approach merely holds the mother-infant bond as an early phase in object-formation (Mahler, Pine, & Bergmann, 2002). The breast, bottle, and warmth of the caretaker shape early phases in the passage from core to rim in the subjective space of the infant mind. These phases forecast the particulars of the inner field, and the objects, properties, and valuations of the outer one. Objective space evolves from the subjectivity of the observer along with the feelings and values that accompany its objectification. In this iterated process, the proximal segment stays behind as the subjectivity of the observer while the distal segment externalizes as the observer's world. The objectification of the outer segment of subjective space is not only for objects but for the affective tonality that accompanies them in their outward migration.

19. The return of the repressed, as in the regaining of mother-child union, figures in areas other than love and sexuality, for example, in mystical descent to loving oneness with god, or unity with nature (Brown, 2008). We can think of religious feeling as sublimated sexuality, but then we get the whole briccolage of elements that go with it. Love of god is an idealization of the beloved (thus, the

similarity of descriptions to human love) that goes beyond the individual when the category of the other expands to the perfection of deity. To claim that love of god is sublimated sexuality is really to say that the love for another person and for god share certain qualities such as idealization, the assimilation of the values of the other, devotion, and sacrifice. It is not necessary to relinquish or sublimate sexuality in order to love god. They can readily co-exist, though devout love, whether for a person or for god, can exclude all others from the sphere of interest, well put by Augustine when he exclaimed, "make me pure, Oh Lord, but not yet."

20. Modern formulations (e.g., Kohut, 1971) argue that love strengthens the self. This agrees with the microgenetic idea that installing the values of the beloved in the self augments its own valuation. But is this a strengthening? The dependency and dissolution of autonomy in true love increase vulnerability. If self-love or confidence is necessary for true love, how does love add to that strength? If we take wholeness seriously and the beloved contributes a major portion to the lover's self, how strong was the self prior to falling in love? Once in love, what are the limits of self-reliance?

21. The narrative of psa depends on an appeal to the analysand or reader just as its interpretations depend on the experience, temperament, and needs of the analyst. In this respect, psa is removed to an extent from other fields of psychology and science. Apart from the detail of the approach, its foundational principles are open to question. The role of suggestion and transference in the analytic setting provides a model for a path to loving. In transference, the individual absorbs the values and beliefs of the analyst, which are installed overtly or insidiously in the therapy session and gain traction in the aftermath of the imagination. Listening and implicit caring are taken as signs of reciprocity. Autonomy and control are relinquished in the loosened defenses, the relaxation and the openness. These changes, along with the dependency and vulnerability are predispositions, if not essentials, to the devotion of unselfish love.

22. For Freud, the current of sexual drive, or libido, explains overt or sublimated sexuality, which in turn explains everything else, even the motives of its critics. Regarding libido, the mantra is that quantities of libido are attached to incestuous love objects. Since the self is also a libidinal target, the transfer of libido to objects depletes narcissism. This is a needlessly complex way of saying that interest shifts from self to other. Moreover, the view that libido flows from

self to object like an electric current mechanizes the trajectory of the object-development. Efforts to identify intermediate phases in this transition, such as those by Paul Schilder or David Rapaport (in Rapaport, 1951), went largely unnoticed by the orthodoxy. My view is that the passage from drive-categories to conceptual-feelings is one of increasing specificity, not transfer, not that self-love underlies object-love but that objects develop from the self and that the narcissism of self-love is the autonomy that true love breaks down.

23. As mentioned, Freud's theory of love and sexuality involves shifts of libido from one object or content to another. If libido theory is wrong, the entire edifice collapses. The problem is that the shifting, subduing, activating, displacing, implementing, or transmuting of libidinal drive energy from one locus to another can explain almost any constellation of behaviors. These on/off, push/pull, plus/minus, excitation/inhibition concepts of energy can be applied to any assortment of entities to activate or suppress a specific behavior or mental event. What is also problematic is the treatment of the content the libido is presumed to effect. For example, what passes as a psychic element or symbol, for example, phallic fear or envy, can as well be interpreted in relation to metaphoric extension or paralogical thinking at intermediate phases in thought- and object-development. Von Domarus (1944) explained dream symbol or substitution in terms of primitive logic. For example, a knife "stands for" a penis by way of shared attributes (shape, penetration). The resemblance of some attributes leads to an identification based on the overlap. Put differently, the actual object (a knife or penis) is now an adjunct to its properties, which have become object-like. This occurs in the non-sexual thinking of primitives (Lévy-Brühl, 1935/1983; Brown, 2000), for example, in the identification of a man and animal based on shared properties such as swiftness, strength, etc. The priority of predication over topic or object is consistent with the description of inner speech as largely predicative, since the topic is already known to the speaker (Vygotsky, 1962).

24. The more general critique of psa concerns the process-substance debate. In the project and papers on metapsychology, Freud postulated libido in an attempt to achieve a dynamic psychology that could provide an alternative to the association thinking of his day, but all the process in the system went into sexual drive energy,

while the trace or idea remained static; the energy is fluid but the objects of attachment (cathexis) are unchanging (Brown, 1998, 2000). A fully dynamic theory has feeling and idea undergoing change as a unit. A related issue is the problem of interpreting the content, say of an analytic session, in terms of the process that explains it. Content has infinite variety, process is uniform. Process theory can account for the main lines of thought-, act- or object-development, not the specific events that occur. For this, one would need a different theory for every mental event.

25. In contrast to psa, there is much evidence in neuropsychology that hallucination and dream arise from the same core and travel the same path as perception, except that dream, lacking the adaptive effects of sensation, does not complete the journey. Dream is a form of mental imagery that differs from other forms in meaning and narrative. The other forms include hallucination, illusion, eidetic memory, thought and imagination images, autosymbolic images and afterimages, not to mention the imagery of reverie and transitional states. For theory of mind, it is important to relate the dream to these other forms. Terms such as repression, oedipal conflict, super-ego, cathexis, and especially the significance of dreams, can all be interpreted in relation to the recurrence, deviation or accentuation of phases in a common process of momentary actualization. We should also keep in mind that the dream can be interpreted like a myth or a work of visual or literary art, but it is the substrates of dream, not its interpretation, that mediate the preliminary phases in an act of cognition.

In sum, while certain themes have greater or lesser resonance, such as the conflict between narcissism and object love, or the relation of homo-erotic to heterosexual impulses, much of psa is a re-statement of what is or, over the years has become, self-evident, but presented in a specialized vocabulary. The shift of egocentric feeling to an other-centered locus follows the phase-transition of microgenesis. The ingress of the other to a subjective locus and the assimilation of the other to the self of the lover allow the affect in the love-object to dominate and help to explain why the love for the other prevails over self-love.[1] The relation of self-centered to other-centered feeling is the relation of autonomy to fusion when the other becomes part of the self's own valuations. A common thread underlies those states in which egocentric feeling in one person is mitigated or subdued by the incorporation of the other, so that lover and beloved actualize out of a single mind/brain in the passage from core to surface.

Psa tends to appeal to the infantile in every explanation. To say character formed early in life determines or influences feeling, thought, object choice, moral action, etc., is one thing, but it is quite another to regard sexuality in relation to the parent-child relation as decisive, even taking other contexts or traumas into consideration. Even if true, this merely substitutes adult prototypes for archaic patterns in the child's mind, and nothing is learned of the psychic structure of character development and how it transitions to thought and action. The forgetting of the infantile is postulated as a sign of its force. Patterns of experience in early life are forgotten precisely because they build up the personality. The self cannot recall early experience because the self is constituted of that experience. An important question is what Ucs configurations of neural activity constitute good and bad mothering or its outcomes, and how psa advances the understanding of psycho-neural activity. Psa is a story of inner events told from a perspective outside mind, that is, the interpretation of final content or behavior by subjective experience, but what are the actual configurations that carry the cognitive process from Ucs to Cs realization?

The agility of Freud's theory enables one to interpret a variety of outcomes with almost any childhood experience. Does a man who had a loving mother and happy childhood search for the maternal type, does he need more love than he gives, does he long for the maturity of an adult, or does he attempt to re-create the infantile? Does he search for a model of the loved parent, or seek the opposite to avoid the incestuous? Does he shun women to retain fidelity to an idealized mother, or renounce them and become homosexual by identification with them? Does he become bi-sexual from the retention or lack of individuation of infantile mentality? While it is more likely that an individual who is raised in a pathological environment will not have a healthy outcome, psa does not predict the outcome and there are enough exceptions to question any given interpretation. In any event, the analyst appeals to context and to other occurrences in life to disambiguate a multiplicity of possible outcomes from a few source constructs. The theory is retrodictive, not predictive, often reducing adult stereotypes to the mother-child relation, with other life experiences inserted *ad hoc* to reinforce and justify their interpretation.

Except for a few memories, the first five years of life are largely forgotten. This is not, as Freud thought, due to the repression attached to early sexuality. The cognition of the child is transformed to a mode that is inaccessible to a mature consciousness, that is, it is state-dependent. This was discussed in an important paper by Schachtel (1947). Early forgetting is not specific to trauma, but involves all experience. Events are not selectively repressed; they are normally forgotten as a novel mode of cognition appears. What is recalled of childhood in dream or analysis is transmuted to adult cognition, either directly or by the analyst in symbol-translation. Each person feels unique and desires a unique interpretation that relates to the personal life story. The interpretations must adapt to the demands of the individual, if not to general theory. A central problem with such conformance is that psa does not overlap with other concepts in psychology of memory, forgetting, conceptual growth, etc. The unique narratives required to explain individual thought and behavior are difficult to reconcile with a general theory to which all narratives must conform.

For this reason, it is preferable to under-specify the psa components of sexuality rather than systematizing them in a theory uncoupled from other psychological concepts. Mayhem in the basement does not explain clutter in the attic. Instead of the complex forms, outcomes, interpretations, and pathologies of narcissism, we need clarity on the nature of the self, the self-object relation and object-valuations in terms of mind/brain process. In psa, we have inherited a rich, multi-faceted theory, much like cognitive psychology in this respect, in that the wealth of data and observation and the propagation of detail can afford to sacrifice elements in the model for the preservation of the whole. The narrative of psa is rooted in the literary imagination, while that of cognitive psychology is based on neuroscientific concepts and philosophical materialism, but each in its way impedes rather than furthers efforts to understand mind in its complexity. Better a skiff that rides true on the waves than a tanker spilling oil at the seams.

Note

1. We speak of internalization of the love-object, but the object is not actually internalized. The dominant focus in the mental state is antecedent in the object-development. The object can develop fully, but internal phases, being accentuated, tend to replace those that objectify.

CHAPTER SEVEN

Pornography and perversion

The tragedy of sexual intercourse is the perpetual virginity of the soul.

—William B. Yeats

It is an everyday truth that a healthy individual has a richness of mind, internal and external, with a fluid motion to the depths and an active engagement at the surface, a capacity to revive earlier phases of novelty and renewal to conscious thought, and an impulse to purpose in the world that carries the self into action. Some are fully engaged in activity and social interaction, while others believe that inner mind and detached repose are the path to true reality. A person busy with objects will have occasion to consider their worth or meaning, while those fixed on inwardness must still adapt to circumstances in the outer life.

So it is with love, which begins with an object, withdraws to an ideal and then more often than not travels outward again as the ideal objectifies in judgment. Those for whom the other is not idealized as a unique exemplar fall back on an eroticized category of replaceable members. In some, the ideal can be an unusual bodily feature, obesity, emaciation, scars, even a shriveled or a missing limb. The same person (or object)

145

transforms in relation to value, and similar objects can have differing concurrent valuations. We describe the dominant behavior in individuals as a kind of personality type, which is the average of all behaviors, when what matters is the form of a *momentary* object according to the phase that is privileged and the valuation accorded to it.

Consider an individual who genuinely loves someone but enjoys pornography or uses it to enhance private or consensual pleasure. Would we say that the use of pornography, or even infidelity, raise questions as to the validity of feeling for a beloved? Can one have genuine love for a partner yet engage in clandestine sexual acts with others, or sexual fantasies about others, that may be insignificant for the person, yet would be damaging were they to become known to the beloved? The *filial* or companionable sort of love may co-exist with sexual fantasies of others, as well as affairs, but is this so for true love? Is pornography a form of infidelity in the absence of temptation? With infidelity, the presence of an actual other is an attack on the sanctity of a loving union. Is pornography an adultery in the imagination in which the ideal of the beloved, or sexual fantasy that could be devoted to the beloved, is replaced by the image of another person? For the subjectivist, an adulterous thought is the near-equivalent of an adulterous act, especially if the distinction rests on a lack of opportunity. Conversely, if the prurient arouses the same drives and desires on which authentic love is grounded, can pornography reinforce fidelity by providing an outlet for sexual drive or serve as an aid to erotic enjoyment with the beloved, that is, can it be excused in that it is independent of loving?

Without love or affection a coupling based on sexual desire that arises unfettered from drive has little to do with true love and loving sexuality, except for the common foundation in drive. There is a range of behaviors from the use of objects or images in pornography as aids or substitutes in fantasy and/or masturbation, to the pleasure of triads, prostitutes, or loveless affairs. Can activities in which the other is an instrument of a self-pleasure that does not involve reciprocity or mutuality of feeling co-exist with genuine love? Or do they betray cracks in the authenticity of feeling for the beloved as signs the ideal has objectified? Pornography is a form of impersonal sexuality. In the absence of an actual other, the fantasy or idealization of the sexual object can remain fully sexual. When the other is a prostitute or casual partner, there is no love-object. Desire is egocentric; the imagination is realizing drive-based needs. In this respect, it is the opposite of self-giving for a beloved. In the former, the aggressive trends of taking and satisfaction dominate the passive or receptive tendencies that lead to shared experience. One could say that the pleasure of taking replaces the pleasure of giving. The assimilation of the beloved to the self gives pleasure when the beloved is pleased. In loving sexuality, the needs of the beloved are paramount. For the carnal impulse, the other is an object for personal use (Figure 7.1).

An image is active at a phase of desire or fantasy in the pleasure-seeking of sexual need or the idealization of love. The pornographic object (picture, text, etc.) engages the aggressive (acquisitive) trends. The love object engages the receptive (submissive) trends. The instinctual vectors that specify the passage of drive to desire can be ego- or exo-centric, the former with an absence of love, the latter in submission or dependence on the beloved.

With the pornographic object or a purely sexual partner, in fantasy or actuality, feeling is egocentric in the lack of reciprocity. The object recedes to fantasy but does not punctuate autonomy. With the beloved, receptive tendencies predominate and solitary enjoyment is subordinate to

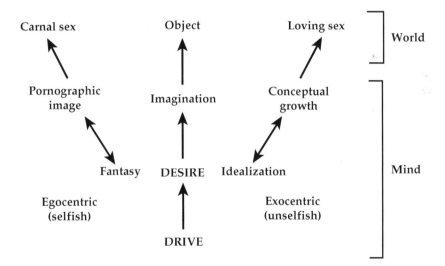

Figure 7.1. The bifurcation of sexual drive into pornographic and loving sexuality. In one, ego-centric desire leads to fantasy; in the other, exo-centric desire leads to idealization. In both, the transition from mind to world is continuous.

shared pleasure. Infidelity is closer to love or pornography depending on the quality of feeling for the lover and the beloved. In a triangle, a lover can be a sexual aid or replace a love that has grown stale.

Perversions

In the mental life, an aberration is often more illustrative of a principle than the commonplace, in that it draws out to the extreme some aspect of theory that is obscured in the narrower range of ordinary behavior. For this reason, it is useful to discuss the psychoanalytic account of perversion in relation to process thinking, to see if there could be an alternative approach to these behaviors which, in many ways, are the foundations of classical theory. Every perversion points to an admixture of the drives, the desires, and the process that delivers objects. In this light, the perversions, and psychopathology in general, serve as a test of a theory of cognition rather than an exception or supplement to a standard repertoire. Heretofore, the account of deviance has focused on some pattern in development, such as isolation, parenting or abuse, on which the special history of the individual turns. The history can assume greater or lesser importance depending on the gravity of the pattern. For example, severe abuse in childhood can explain a host of adult behaviors that are conceived as relatively independent of the transition to maturity.

In this respect, that is, in the attribution of an adult behavior to a nucleus of infantile experience, the theory is comparable to attempts at the correlation of mature cognition or language with genome or brain area, in which a complex adult pattern is collapsed to an earlier or lower-level system with little or no attention to the laws, events, or algorithms that translate one level to another that is qualitatively unique and no less complex. When no single trauma or pattern of trauma can be discerned, subtleties of the life story are invoked as explanatory, such as the mother-child relation, castration anxiety, sibling rivalry, and so on.

No doubt these interpretations have their place, and in some instances, as in psychoanalysis, they can make for fascinating stories that seem to lead inevitably to the ordained outcome, when it is the outcome that invokes the childhood experience as the causal factor. The various elements that are postulated as the reasons for deviance are not well-integrated in a theory of emotion. Psychoanalysis does not offer an explanation of the structures and mechanisms of perversion, how it develops and why one outcome is selected rather than another. This was a challenge that eluded even Freud. Does an absence of perversion follow from a lack of castration anxiety? Do all men have such anxiety and, if so, why do all men not share perversions? Does the degree of anxiety determine the presence and nature of perversion? What would such anxiety have to do with a general theory within which the pathological has a place? An additional problem is the dual role of the father as protector of the child and family (the origin for Freud of the concept of god), and his role as the one who destroys the child's narcissistic wish by forcing adaptation to reality (see Leowald, 2000). Whether the protective or destructive function is emphasized is dictated by interpretive need. Indeed, Karen Horney wrote that vulval fear is more elemental than fear of castration, that is, the fear of being cut off is not as primal as the fear of falling in.

The childhood event or pattern is a kind of object in direct causal relation or association with the adult behavior, independent of the process of drive expression and object formation out of which the childhood and adult patterns develop. The "normal" is the absence of occasions from which deviance results. In contrast, microgenetic theory gives a general account of brain and emotion, taking some forms of deviance as evidence of its validity; that is, the theory precedes the pathology, which is an accentuation or de-emphasis of certain lines of normal development.

Historically, the description of perversions owes much to psychoanalytic theory with homosexual behavior playing a central role.[1] The usual definition is of a pattern of sexual behavior that differs from the conventional, in which genital union is avoided or is secondary, and fetishes or ancillary erogenous zones serve as the primary sources of gratification. Castration anxiety and oedipal conflicts are invoked as causal factors. The perversion is derived from infantile sexuality, with a regression to pre-genital levels of sexual excitement, that is, the pre-genital zones are sexualized. There appear to be no significant differences in the occurrence of perversion in primitive and advanced societies. In some cultures, from the ancient Greeks to modern societies and primitive tribes, the submission of boys to anal intercourse is considered a rite of passage to adulthood.

For Freud, the sexual organs achieve primacy in maturity out of a background of erogenous zones—initially auto-erotic—in which oral, anal, and other bodily regions—skin, eyes—recede to a secondary importance, mainly in foreplay. Perversion occurs when secondary zones, or fetishes, take precedence. It can occur with regression to, or arrest at, a pre-genital phase. Freud wrote that neurosis is the negative of perversion, and inferred that it can also protect against psychosis. This implies that perversions isolate or sequester the anxiety that would otherwise lead to neurosis, and that they neutralize or contain a thought disorder that could lead to psychosis, that is, perversion is a safety valve against other psychopathologies.

A working definition of perversion is a pre-occupation with some facet of behavior that is out of the ordinary, that is, abnormal in most definitions, recurrent, encapsulated or circumscribed, and with sexual intent. For Kaplan (1991), at least one of the following must occur: the use of a non-human object for arousal; real or simulated suffering or humiliation; and sexual activity with non-consenting partners. A perversion is not necessarily part of a general psychopathology, nor does psychopathology entail perversion, though perversions are pathological symptoms. The perversity usually lies in the bizarre and/or distasteful quality, though the degree of acceptance in a culture can determine whether the behavior is labeled as perverse. Homosexuality is typical in this respect, accepted in some cultures, not in others, though it exhibits many of the classical features of perversion.

Some perversions are obvious, especially when pronounced, such as self-mutilation, lust murder, necrophilia, bestiality, cross-dressing, exhibitionism, voyeurism, and sado-masochism, but there is often no clear boundary with normal behavior. Self-mutilation is common in tattooing or piercing, but to cut one's own or other's sexual organs crosses the line. Sadism contrasts with the aggression, domination, and control that occur in normal sexuality, even the pleasure derived from inflicting some pain. The line between the collector and the fetishist, or the distinction of a benign fetish, such as savoring a woman's shoes, or with religious and other rituals, totems, and charms, is when the fetish has primacy over attachment and becomes indispensable to orgasm. The fetish will arouse sexual excitement and stimulate erection, but the curve of the breast or buttock can have the same effect. Perhaps even an obligatory image or thought can be equivalent to a fetish. That one is clothing, another is a part of the woman's body, and yet another is a surrogate or symbolic replacement—may be trivial distinctions. For some analysts (Alexander, 1965), the perversion is an end in itself, while the fragment of interest in normal behavior is a means to an end. Thus, pain in sadism is an end while in criminal activity it is a means. However, the distinction fails if inflicting pain is perceived as a means to erection or orgasm. The difficulty in distinguishing perversion as pathology from behavior that, though eccentric or unusual, is still acceptable, supports the thesis that perversion and psychopathology realize some facet of the ordinary, or that aspects of the ordinary are dis-inhibited. On this view, the perverse is a nucleus of cognition that is submerged or concealed within "normal" sexuality.

Aggression in perversion

Sexuality can be driven by varying intensities of aggression or defense. Aggression can, of course, be non-sexual, but in violence that is unusual or outside the norm there is often a sexual element. Freud wrote, "there is an intimate connection between cruelty and the sexual instinct." He considered sadomasochism the most significant of the perversions, with masochism a form of sadism directed to the self. These tendencies are subdued, perhaps inherent in ordinary sexual behavior. In this, my approach follows Schilder (1942), who believed that sadomasochism represented an accentuation of normal tendencies of activity and passivity, aggression and defense.

Control and domination, submission and acquiescence, are in delicate, often shifting, balance, with one partner assuming control in all matters or one sphere of activity, or the other assuming intermittent control. The step from role-playing to instances in which domination leads to aggression, with verbal and physical abuse, to a deliberate hurt and, finally, to pleasure that is achieved, not by genital union, but by inflicting pain on others, is a gradual accentuation of normal trends. Similarly, submission can give pleasure, but it can also become a need that changes to masochism and self-punishment. We see comparable behavior when the mortifications of a spiritual quest are sexualized as signs of worthiness for a love-union with god. In masochism, there is direct pleasure in submission, and indirect pleasure in self-denial and pleasing the other. The vectors of aggression and defense that invade the sexual drive alter behavior in one direction or the other to the point where pleasure and satisfaction depend on the prominence of one tendency over another or their admixture.

Pars pro toto

The relation of whole to part in the phase transition of the mental state appears as well in the relation of part to whole. Synecdoche is a term that characterizes this relation in a literary context, when the part stands for the whole. This relation can be innocuous, as in the Eucharist sacrament or circumcision, and in magical thinking, such as voodoo, totemism, and primitive logic. The emphasis on the part occurs in fetish when, say, a shoe, a stocking, or lock of hair stands for the person who is an object of intentional feeling (love, hate, etc.).[2] Many fetishes develop like totems, in that they appear in conjunction with observing the genitals, say a woman's shoe or stocking when a boy peers up her dress. This implies that the mechanism is not primarily sexual, but that a general process dedicated to sexual drive is given a sexual interpretation. The part/whole relation occurs when a sadist selects one feature in a sexual occasion for particular brutality, say cutting or causing extreme pain in the breasts. The fetish can be said to concentrate on detail to avoid exposing the whole of the situation or the pathology (Kaplan, 1991).

Is it possible to find a common thread in perversions that would account for the deviance from conventional sexual behavior, for example, one that could explain the extremes of sadism and the curiosities of voyeurism and fetish? For Freud, the unifying principle was castration anxiety, leading to reluctance to insert the penis into a devouring vagina and avoidance of genital union. There is also the question of whether a male perversion masks a shameful feminine wish. Disgust at the female organ or the failure of the vagina to stimulate erection, indeed, to suppress it, may encourage a fetish as substitute. The fear of genital contact could explain the diversion to other routes of satisfaction, exhibitionism, the use of aides, devices or fetishes as substitutes or adjuncts of pleasure and/or to facilitate coitus. However, the phallic emphasis on loss, lack or mutilation, might well serve as a symbol of differing masculine and feminine social roles, the individual's desire to achieve or avoid them and the anxiety induced by the disparity.

A derailment in the derivation to desire of the sexual or hunger drive gives deviations in the instinctual goal. The deviation can affect the object of desire or the resolution of the object out of the series of whole/part transitions. The prominence of antecedent drive—sexual, hunger—and the vectors—aggression, defense—along with the individual experience, determine the form of the perversion and whether it is implemented in an active or passive manner. The derailments that eventuate in surrogate or ancillary objects or behaviors serve to displace or dilute the fear of coitus and mitigate anxiety.

Is there a basis for the fear of natural coitus other than castration? Anxiety is a sign of the irresolution of an object or path without clarity. In this there is the tension of ambiguity, where contrasting possibilities have not yet materialized. Indecision or ambivalence among conscious well-defined choices is less likely to generate anxiety than a state in which choice has not yet actualized. Ambiguity is essential to anxiety, but the tension cannot persist indefinitely, and the ambiguity must consolidate to one outcome or line of perversity. Where does the anxiety come from? For Freud, it was the fear of castration, but why not a tension between the aggressive and defensive attitudes? An excess of aggression characterizes sadism, an excess of the defensive attitude gives masochism, but there is more to aggression than aggressiveness. There is the active, outgoing and energetic attitude, and with defense there is fear, flight, or passivity. The degree to which sexuality is not an adaptation of one extreme to another or the toleration by one partner of the other's peculiarities but a shared or mutual pleasure depends on a reasonable balance and conformance of attitudes as a full expression of unconscious hunger and sexual drive.

Freud postulated the penis as a focal point and source of anxiety, but fear of genital union could arise from various sources, including the fear of impregnation, revulsion for the female organ or impotence. The central point is that anxiety does not yet have an object. It results when an object has not resolved. The concept is in line with the theory that anxiety is eliminated by understanding or resolving its cause, as in the talking cure, but the friction in pre-object resolution involves constituents that have not yet objectified.

Relation of perversion to general theory

My aim in this section is merely to uncover, by way of the perversions, the main outlines of a psychological account of emotion consistent with a process theory of the brain state, not to provide the details of a personal history that may explain why one mode of perversion—sadism, fetish—is chosen over another. The literature on perversions is rich and complex and permeated with Freudian concepts, even if they do not explain a specific perversion or fetish, or why one sadist induces physical pain, another psychological pain, while others prefer to observe pain, or to maim or kill.

In the figure below (see Figure 7.2), the basic drive of hunger leads to aggressive and defensive outcomes. This drive develops to further layers of refinement. Examples of the drive expression on the aggressive branch are greed or ambition; on the defensive branch, passivity, or asceticism. The derivation to the sexual drive also has aggressive and defensive orientations. The aggressive branch leads, for example, to varieties of sadism and, when de-sexualized, to other forms of criminal activity and/or violence. The defensive branch leads to masochism, with pleasure in pain, and to de-sexualized manifestations in religious suffering (stigmata) and penitence for salvation. The process leading to the aggressive or defensive outcomes is, as mentioned, a sequence of whole/part transitions. The relation of part to whole can be sexualized in fetish or de-sexualized in totemic, religious, and magical thinking.

The transition from hunger and sexual drives to desire gives increasing refinement and specificity to the vectors of expression, to the objects selected and the process through which the selection occurs. Even with greater specificity and deliberation, the whole/part relation is primary. What appears as displacement of interest, substitution, or derailment can be explained on the basis of whole/part relations, such as synecdoche, metonymy, and metaphor. The relation of hunger to sexuality in perversion is clear. We see this naturally in the convention of dinner before sexual relations, or candy as a means of seduction, and in the "fluid exchange" of genital sex with oral and anal sexuality. In the perversions,

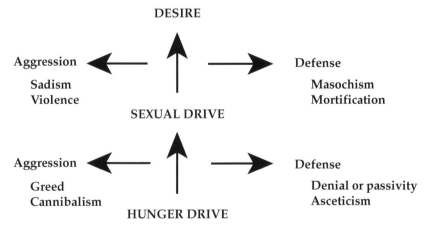

DESIRE

Aggression ← ↑ → Defense

Sadism   Masochism
Violence   Mortification

SEXUAL DRIVE

Aggression ← ↑ → Defense

Greed   Denial or passivity
Cannibalism   Asceticism

HUNGER DRIVE

Figure 7.2. A sketch of perversions as diversions in the microgenesis of desire out of hunger and sexual drive.

the relations are stronger. Sade wrote, "There is no passion more closely involved with lechery than drunkenness and gluttony."

Toward a theory of perversions

The masochistic turn in religious activity, detaching sexual pleasure for love union with god, takes voluntary suffering out of sexuality and allows us to think of it as basic process, de-sexualized and linked to separation and fusion or autonomy and oneness. If mortifications are submissions to an all-powerful but not sadistic god, or if dependency and surrender lure god to fusion, what of nature mystics whose mortifications are at least as severe, yet union with the Absolute, Nature or Emptiness are the justifications? If masochism has no sadistic response, it must be closely tied to relinquishment, an indifference to distraction and proof of worthiness, not an invitation to a sadistic urge.

The central process in growth entails fusion and individuation. The fractionation of parts within an envelope or whole is the fundamental manifestation. This process is carried out through successive stages in maturation, and takes on differing colorations according to stage, gender, personal experience, and the directives of the underlying drives. The vagaries of fusion and individuation give a variety of paths in development and the expression of individual trends that appear to have little in common. The perversions are an example of how explanation depends on the representation in metaphor of more basic tendencies that distribute into behaviors that implement drive-expression. The fractionation of wholes does not just occur and move on, but recurs. The whole is revived as each partition is renewed. The revival of the whole and the recurrence of partitions allow a certain balance to be established in the process of specification.

In everyday life, we speak of togetherness and apartness, isolation and longing, separation and oneness, abandonment and reunion. The natural tension of autonomy and individuation with merging and union opens the door to a different way of thinking about perversions, indeed, all of psychology and psychoanalysis. For example, the castration anxiety—and its correlate in penis envy—that are so important in psychoanalytic interpretations are sexual caricatures, or an objectification in sexual parts, of the underlying tension of wholeness and loss, independence and engagement, personal autonomy and sexual union. The underlying division of wholes into parts, along with the recurrence of the whole-part transition, takes on a different guise as it objectifies in the sex organs in relation to the personal life story.

In perversion, there is avoidance of the natural genital fusion that is entailed by the biology of procreation. The sadist is not motivated by a need to love or belong to the other that would involve surrender, but by impersonal desires and egocentric feeling. The masochist not only endures but needs (or exploits) humiliation and rejection, fearful of loneliness and loss, tolerating abject submission, often relinquishment of self, to be one with the other, a need manipulated by the sadist to maintain control and insularity. Psychoanalytic interpretations literally explode this core process to novel realms of fantasy in the individual and in the analyst.

Relations to art and science

Pornography has interest in its relation to science, with which it shares a radical objectivity, and with art, where theme, use and intent are the primary distinctions. We are familiar with the debates over pornography and art, but the relation to scientific objects is more surprising. It is not without reason that a preoccupation with the external in science corresponds with a similar attitude in the personal life, for example, when feeling in the object is excluded or when pleasure is aroused by objects detached from human affection. The transition from thought to fact that is fundamental to science and in the correspondence of true propositions with the facts of nature, which is the trumpeted aim of philosophical logic, replaces the transition in love from fact to thought. One might say the pursuit of the objectively real in science differs from the pursuit of the subjectively real in love, or that the idealization of truth threatens the idealization of the beloved. Science in some respects is the equivalent of pornography in that the sexualized images of pornography externalize to the de-sexualized objects of science, or that an immediacy of solitary pleasure in pornography objectifies to the expectation of worldly success in science and philosophy.

Science is said to be a disinterested search for truth, not just any truth but one that is impersonal and can be confirmed by observation or experiment. This boils down to a consensual validation of fact. The extrinsic verification that is essential to science is also important to art and pornography. The judgment of an artwork, indeed, what counts as art, is no longer decided by individuals but is left to connoisseurs. This is also the case with the scientific study of sexual behavior or the study of the human body as a collective enterprise. If people agree that an object is not primarily erotic or that it has redeeming artistic or scientific qualities, it will not be judged as pornographic. A consensus is required to label an object as pornographic. If one in ten think it pornographic and nine in ten think it art, it will be art (or science), and the reverse. This differs from external judgment in love, where personal value trumps fact and commitment is reinforced by reciprocity.

Science presumes an absence of emotion to an extreme of objectivity so that its topics are putatively mind-independent. Feelings and motives uncontaminated by personal belief or value are essential to scientific work, though the belief that fact is not colored by emotion or that interpretation is independent of value is more hope than reality. The submissiveness of true love corresponds, in science, to the assimilation of belief and the acquiescence to like-minded colleagues. The worship of an idea, a movement, a leader, has similar roots to that for a beloved. In both, assumptions of dubious validity are rarely questioned, especially when promoted by a strong personality or a beloved. How many scientists or philosophers examine a topic outside the leading paradigm? The objects of pornography, of fetish or prostitution, if animate, are not actual others, but things of utilitarian value, while those of science are always things, that is, quanta of the real. In science, objects stimulate thought, in pornography they stimulate desire, in art they stimulate the creative imagination.

There is a difference in the proximity to sexual drive and the degree of self- or object-centeredness, but in all instances emotion in the object, if any, is subordinate to that in the observer. In art, what is vital is the transmission of feeling, in love, absorption of the other, in pornography, discharge of feeling, in science and philosophy, the relation of thought to object and the absence of feeling or its mutation to interest, competition, and ambition. These activities, which appear so disparate, differ in relation to the explicitness of sexual interest, the quality and intensity of feeling in the object and the degree of objectification, that is, closer to thought or nature. The differences point to continua, supporting the contentions of psa and common sense that phenomena common to one mind, or all minds, replace or dominate one another. Extremes make the case, but transitions reveal the process.

The data of science do not exclude sexual objects. Pornography and sexual behavior can be studied and classified. A creative psychoanalyst might compare nuclear fusion and energy release with copulation and orgasm, but the salient points of overlap are that scientific, artistic, and pornographic objects elicit subjective reactions to "mind-independent" objects. Science stays in the material world, art wavers between the inner and outer, pornography incorporates the outer in the inner, and love remains internal. A turn to the subjective elicits the sensual as erotic or esthetic. The esthetic has beauty as an ideal, while the erotic ideal is the one who is loved or desired.

For the skeptic, the final truth of sex is conformance to evolutionary pressures, with love the bait to bonds of family that endure, all else being an overlay of denial, escape or fantasy, a point of view in which all thought and feeling not grounded in survival is illusory or fictitious. The tributaries of sexual fantasy have a complexity that grows ever more distant from the simplicity of true love. It is likely that what holds for sex without affection applies to artifice, devices, triads, orgies, exchanges, bondage, and other practices. When a disunity of partners leads to unusual practices or accessories, private need prevails over spiritual union and the door opens to deviance. Once down that path, redemption is near impossible. It is a short step from self-pleasure and egocentric sex to manipulation, control, rape, and exploitation. When the unselfish tendencies are lacking or in abeyance, the other is an instrumentality that can be used and discarded. The only limits on carnality are law, punishment, lack of imagination, and self-restraint. The end of sadism for the Marquis de Sade was to kill and devour the sexual object. The other has no humanity, becoming an "it" rather than a person, serving exclusively as an instrument of drive-satisfaction.

The objectification of sex has subtler consequences. Baudrillard (1979) wrote that it reinforces the distinction between the female and the feminine. Accordingly, the female is phallic-centered and sexual, organized around male sexuality or phallocracy. Libido is masculine; interest wanes with orgasm. The emphasis on equal rights and equal pleasure mirrors phallic power and destroys or trivializes the feminine. In contrast, the feminine is diffusely sensuous, continuous, and sexually indeterminate, outside the world of sex and power, its strength that of seduction. Here, we have the aggressive (masculine) tendencies of acquisition and the defensive (feminine) ones of acquiescence, the balance of conquest and submission or demand and enticement. The aggressive is tied to action, the passive to perception, but either trend or mix of trends can prevail.

Thought is no guarantee of thoughtfulness. What ensues on a retreat to beliefs and values does not depend on psychic proximity but on their role in character. Healthy or unhealthy values, or beliefs that incline to good or wicked acts, are implemented when the inner life takes an egocentric (selfish) or exocentric (unselfish) path. Yet the egocentric is not necessarily selfish, for example, in self-denial, while the exocentric is not necessarily passive or giving, in that objects can be despised or persecuted. What matters is object value, not inwardness or extroversion. With solitary obsession or a deluge of the impersonal, thought provides deliberate villainies or strategies for empathic service. Antecedents need not objectify to be finalities.

Some prefer wish to actuality, or to revel in the lure of the possible. In matters of love they are indecisive, perhaps fearing that the loved object will be lost or that unknown others will be missed. Some prefer desire to acquisition, longing to having, or the reverse, immediacy to want. Some do not idealize in mind but categorize in the world, others target concrete particulars. Desire is framed by the objects it pursues. Becoming does not take on shape until it becomes what it is. The variety of desires results from the infinite number of satisfactions. Once feeling becomes an object or an idea, once desire fills its object, wanting is subdued and the object, not the feeling inside it, takes precedence. When a "container" of feeling—the being that the process of becoming deposits—shifts from idea to object, from inner to outer, feeling withers and desire passes to judgment, as in a love that is lost or one that never ripened. Without an object, the potential in feeling can increase; one imagines what might have been without the judgment of what was.

The subjective in love and art

Love is a gift of a shared vulnerability that mitigates loneliness and eases the confrontation with grim fate in a hostile, indifferent world. True love is like a work of art, with the lover an artist who creates an ideal of the beloved as a personal masterpiece. In turn, the object of that love bestows on the lover the love the artist deserves, much as if a painting, a musical or literary work should reciprocate the devotion given to composition. Anyone who works as an artist, Freud wrote, feels a father to his works, like a parent who loves a child without reciprocation. To create love in others that outlives one's life is like creating an artwork that survives its creator. To instill or draw out affection is akin to an esthetic act. Love, however, is more than a cure for solitude or a bridge to otherness; it is a work of beauty that lives on as an ideal.

As the artist aspires to leave a work as a token of immortality, the lover inspires others to reminisce if only for a moment and in this small way lovers and their love live again in the minds of others.

The comparison will seem less far-fetched if one considers the passion, sacrifice, dedication, selflessness and receptivity that go into the conception and composition of the work of art and how the devotion continues even without reciprocity. Whether loved by few or many, the art is pursued in a state of wonderment and with an awareness of the fragility of the gift. The transience of admiration and unworthiness of most opinions at least constitute a consensus of quality that is a substitute for the feelings of a beloved. A love that lasts for a lifetime outlasts most works of art. A great artwork is an expression of the deepest emotions, with art and artist—creator and creation—one. As with the end of a love, the artist despairs, or begins again, once more to fall in love with a new work. In the same way, the lover possesses and is possessed by the beloved in a love that is an artistic unity without an actual object.

Hofstadter (1996) wrote of the love affair as a work of art, using love letters as a concrete expression. But what of the feeling, unrecorded and intangible, conveyed between lovers? In art, the paper, tones, or paint provide visible or audible proof of the creative impulse. Is the feeling that is channeled into the beloved similar to that in music, literature, or film? Is the work of art a gift to the artist's muse? Love and art are created in the imagination in mystical trance (Brown, 2008/2010). The spell cast by love envelops the lover in a dream where all objects, save the beloved, disappear.

The creative person seeks and rejoices on occasions when, lost in thought, the pen is passively guided by ideas unforeseen to surface organically into composition. Hölderlin wrote of the dangers of contemplative poetry, the risk of falling into a chasm from which one might not return. Such risks are real to those with depth of insight. A strong love has features of creative descent. As with creativity, love is intermittently intense. There are moments, as in creative trance, when objects dissolve and lover and beloved are all that remain.

Notes

1. What follows comes largely from Friedman (1959).
2. The classic reference is Krafft-Ebing (1965).

CHAPTER EIGHT

Kindness and compassion

A pity beyond all telling is hid in the heart of love.

—Yeats, *The Pity of Love*

Introduction

Having discussed the character, the intensity and the fragility of love, and its relation to other emotions, as well as an excursion into psycho-analytic and microgenetic theory, I will now explore some modes of selfless or charitable giving in order to see what light they can throw on feelings related to love, such as kindness, sincerity, empathy, compassion, mercy, or forgiveness. Take kindness as a feeling common to many of these states. We can think of kindness as a sense of caring or generosity toward others, in which the selfish tendencies are suppressed in favor of other-centered interests. Kindness is an attitude with conceptual underpinnings, say, the belief that other people have value apart from, or at the expense of, self-interest or the belief that whenever possible we should help the less fortunate, that is, that we are truly our "brother's keepers," or that we should attempt to alleviate suffering and facilitate the betterment of others, at least when we have the power to do so and intervention can make a difference.

161

Kindness develops out of conceptual-feeling. At one moment, affect prevails, at another, the concept. The concept of kindness, the belief in charity or compassion, enfolds the feeling but a person can believe in kindness as an obligation or value without a desire to be kind. A person can profess a belief in many things, good and bad, without ever acting on them, and can assert many feelings that do not find their way into action. For this reason, action is the primary warrant of feeling. Action that appears as generosity can be implemented by selfish ends, for example, feigning munificence as in giving people the "opportunity" to work harder for a relatively small increase in wages when the person's goal is disproportionate profit. We see this pattern in charitable giving, for example, in the support of elite, self-beneficial, and tax-deductible organizations such as the opera, rather than people in distress, or when the desire to help others is satisfied by a negligible donation to a beggar with no relation to the donor's means. This *token* kindness merely serves to assuage guilt, avoid confrontation, and substitute for participatory engagement.

In common with other feelings of the same type, kindness entails selflessness or other-centered values. Other-centered feeling that leads to kindness, irrespective of a lack of self-interest, determines its *moral* value. What counts for moral value is the priority of the other over the self, or the abeyance of self-interest. Goodness is not the child of innocence. The claim that the goodness that overcomes temptation has greater moral value is countered by Aristotle, who states that the truly good are not tempted. This goes to the nature of core or individual character. The concern for others has greater moral value according to the degree of self-denial, but one could argue that kindness should be measured against apathy or disinterest not self-denial since ordinary acts of kindness involve politeness, respect for others, even manners, without compromising the self. Shaw said, the greatest sin is indifference.

It might further be claimed that any act of kindness rebounds on the self, mitigating guilt, enhancing self-esteem, earning respect or admiration. Even the saint believes good acts do not go unnoticed by an all-seeing god. A cynic reflecting on these observations might say that self-interest is the covert motive in all such acts save those that exact a severe price on the giver. But one should be cautious about inferring or conflating sub-surface motives. For example, a business owner can turn a healthy profit and still be kind, generous, and gracious to employees. A balance of self and other is preferable to an excess in one direction. Too great a deference to the needs of others can encourage exploitation by those who are not so unselfish. Excessive generosity can lead to bankruptcy. There are hurtful if unintended consequences of an unselfish act, and the reverse, as when an action that appears selfish has beneficial consequences that stem from unselfish sources. In love, a different argument ensues if jealousy or possessiveness is construed not as selfishness but as insecurity, a fear of being unworthy, or of losing the beloved. Even the opposite of love and kindness, murder, can be viewed in a compassionate light when it is a "crime of passion" rather than the worst of crimes, "cold-blooded murder."

A quality of feeling that is intrinsic to love, namely, concern for the welfare of the other, is the basis for viewing kindness as a form of loving. However, a focus on the other can be malicious, deceitful, or exploitative as readily as caring and merciful. A person can be the object of love, but also of hate, contempt, pleasure or disinterest, and a goodly number of other emotions. What counts is not the other-centeredness but the feeling that accompanies the other in object-formation. Since the self gives rise to all objects, the perception of others is constrained by character, which exerts an influence of approval or disapproval, direct or indirect, on every act and object. This effect determines the balance between advantage to the self and to the other.

A similar argument for love is that it is a mode of self-interest or personal gain. The brevity, intermittency, and fluctuation of actual feeling and the permutations of love-relations encourage competing interpretations, but genuine loving is genuine giving and by definition unselfish. True and passionate love evokes a joy that lovers seek to renew in giving and pleasing the beloved. Ideally, there is no means-end relation in which self-interest is primary. The pursuit of the beloved and the insistence on sexual, even social, exclusivity can be construed as selfish and deliberate but, from the lover's perspective, this behavior forestalls the devastation that would follow on loss of the beloved. Unlike true love, kindness does not pursue its object and has no fear of loss. The giver has a choice; there is appraisal and decision, and the principle conflict is with self-interest.

Kindness and love share a concern for the well-being of the other, but an overlap in one attribute is a contact only with respect to that attribute, not a *family* resemblance. An identity of objects on the basis of a shared attribute is fundamental in primitive logic and metaphorical thinking, but in rational thought it need not point to a deeper commonalty. Nor is the difference a matter of degree, that is, the "amount," persistence and scope or delimitation of kindness, even though increased intensity of kindness to one person can internalize the qualities and accentuate the value of that person and lead to idealization and greater subjectivity. When this occurs, an intensification of kindness can lead, with reciprocity, to a mode of loving. Kindness can generalize from individuals to communities and depending on the objects and quality of feeling we speak of devotion, compassion, even saintliness. The paradox is that the giver must feel something, and that feeling should be the pleasure in giving, but if self-pleasure is the reward of giving, it is not then entirely without self-interest.

Quantitative changes have qualitative consequences. In an act of kindness, an individual or group is selected out of other potential beneficiaries. The isolation of the recipient, along with the enhancement of giving (feelings, goods, etc.) can idealize the other(s) in relation to competitors. The person is seen as more responsible or deserving, or shows more gratitude. For reasons other than kindness, for example, attractiveness, loneliness, the other can become an object of affection. The transition from kindness to fondness to love, and the fact that kindness is ingredient in love, obscure the fact that modes of giving differ from true loving in other and more fundamental ways. Generally, when self-interest is not the guiding motive, all other-centered feelings share the quality of kindness, or at least are so felt by the recipient.

In some respects, the luxury of romantic love in a life in the subjective and in deference to the beloved contravenes the self-interest necessary to survival. In purely evolutionary terms, it seems an open question if restricting the male's access to females offsets the advantage of sustained coupling that a lasting love provides. Traditionally, this tension has been resolved by marriage. Surely, there is a tendency to associate falling in love with marriage, and to associate love and marriage with the young. Love seals the fate of men and guarantees parentage, but the linkage of true love with youth is explained, partly, by the fertility of young women, and partly by the lack of insularity, or a failure of the self to reach the autonomy of a later maturity. Love requires a self that is porous, and this is prevented by full individuation. Put differently, incomplete specification of the self facilitates the infusion of the beloved so that two selves can become one.

Thus, if parenting is associated with relative youth for biological reasons, so is true love similarly associated because of the greater openness, innocence, and plasticity and the lack of habitual reactions. The coincidence of passion and mating in the young is encouraged by naïve attitudes toward love and marriage. Young women who think passion is a prelude to procreation want a child by the man they love. The other is less a partner than a soulmate. Yet the worldly woman and the circumspect man realize that love is not a bond to get through anything, but an antidote to the inevitable strains of family life. Only in the last century has love been seen as important to mating, coupling, and child-rearing; historically, love and passion were perceived as a threat to the requisite docility and stability of marriage. Indeed, the majority of the world's population has marriages made by families.

The ideal is marriage and children, not love and romance, though such fantasies are still rife in those who, in spite of experience, still harbor a Cinderella dream. In the fuss over marriage, in the pomp and ceremony, the bride has the thrill of being a queen for a day, gathering and savoring the memory of a love in full bloom as compensation for the troubles that lay ahead. It is always a little sad when we hear a woman or man say in reference to their wedding, "it was the happiest day of my life." The worst thing is that it might be true. With these observations we turn to some other similarities and differences between love and kindness to better comprehend the nature of these various feelings, and the significance of love as an acme of valuation.

Disjunctions and commonalties

> The quality of mercy is not strain'd,
> It droppeth as the gentle rain from heaven
> Upon the place beneath. It is twice blest:
> It blesseth him that gives and him that takes.

Shakespeare wrote in the *Merchant of Venice* that in mercy (kindness) there is or, one might think, ought to be a mutuality of feeling. Yet, kindness is most often asymmetric, the one who bestows, the one who receives. The one who benefits from an act of kindness has nothing to offer but gratitude, and even gratitude should remain unexpressed. In some countries such as India, a beggar does not give thanks for charity since generosity alone is a blessing. Love can also be like this, though the lover hopes to be loved in return. Love and kindness share the quality of giving which, in some individuals, encourages a reciprocity that accrues to the selfless giver. But in love, other-centered feelings are more intense and mutuality is the rule; indeed, being loved often heightens loving, as gratitude complements giving.

Love differs from ordinary kindness in the emphasis on inwardness and subjectivity. Kindness inclines to objectivity—a focus on the outer situation and action to ameliorate it. Kindness is a response to a set of external conditions, love is imaginative absorption. The lover does not merely respond to the attributes of the beloved but invents and idealizes them as an internal image. Kindness depends on an unadorned realism that demands action and relief. Love is an illusion of the other that arouses desire. In kindness and in love, the other often accentuates certain attributes to incite feeling. The beggar may act in an obsequious manner, exaggerate needs or feign disability, just as a beloved will employ strategies to attract the lover, such as gifts, love letters, cosmetics, or clothing.

The distinction of love and kindness is a mark of the degree of objectification. The object of kindness is usually someone whose life-situation evokes concern, pity, or compassion. The person is fully objectified and there is evidence of need. This is not the case with the beloved, whose needs, other than to be loved, are largely unconscious and unknown to the lover, and whose attributes are not perceived with the realism of other objects. The objectivity of a future or former beloved, that is, before love sets in or after it is exhausted, is unexceptional, but objectivity in a state of love is poisonous. The ideal is unrealized or shattered in a beloved who fails to internalize and inhabit the lover's imagination, or one who objectifies among innumerable others. Love devolves to friendship or caring when the other moves from the subjective to a locus in the world. When this happens, love passes to a feeling similar to kindness except as nuanced by the history of the lovers. The flux from subjective ideal to objective appraisal determines if love becomes kindness, or if kindness grows to love. Kindness to one person that recurs with intimacy can assume the quality of love. The giver and the recipient grow closer, the giver transforms to the lover, the recipient to the beloved. There is, in fact, no longer giver and recipient, only giver. What begins in kindness as asymmetric feeling passes to mutuality in friendship or love.

When there is no mutuality, when love goes on in spite of loss or rejection, we suspect a psychological disorder. This is captured in the refrain of an old French song that contrasts the fleeting pleasures of (erotic) love with the lasting sorrow of loss: *"chagrin d'amour dure toute la vie"* (the pain of love lasts a lifetime). Love hopes for but does not require reciprocation. Love unconsummated is a common theme in artistic inspiration. Beethoven's "immortal beloved," Dante's Beatrice, Yeats' Maud Gonne, are some of many examples. This is parodied in Don Quixote's love for Dulcinea. The beloved remains ideal when spared the impurity of sex and the dulling routine of daily contact.

A person who, in the broad sense, is charitable or empathic should exhibit such qualities on a sufficient range and number of occasions and not exhibit the opposing tendencies. When kindness is habitual, or at least is typical of the individual, it is considered a mark of character. When we say a person is kind we refer to character; recurrent acts of kindness express a kindly character. When we say a person is in love we refer to a specific person and/or occasion that may or may not endure. Love is unexpected, episodic. We do not attribute a state of love, or even the capacity to love, to a person's character. We might say a person has a loving character, but this implies kindness or caring, not romantic love. A loving person might not fall in love; a person who falls in love might not have a loving character. Indeed, having a disposition to love forfeits love's immediacy and the felt uniqueness of the beloved.

One could add that a person disposed to fall in love or someone who readily falls in love, is mistaken in belief, unselective in choice and/or superficial in feeling. It is true that timing and openness are important. Many would say a person who is aggressively and sincerely pursued is likely to fall in love just from the aphrodisiac of being loved by someone so enamored. Proust put it this way: *"in his younger days a man dreams of possessing the heart of the woman whom he loves; later, the feeling that he possesses the heart of a woman may be enough to make him fall in love with her."* People who are selfish and unkind to others may, to the astonishment of onlookers, fall deeply in love with one person. Kindness and love dissociate. One can be kind to a stranger and cruel to one's partner or family, and the reverse. One has to look no farther than the relation of Hitler to Eva Braun. The misanthrope of Moliere's play, *Alceste*, is quick to criticize everyone, including himself, and *Celimene*, whom he loves. The disdain for others does not offset the need to love and be loved. One can detest humanity, as a category of beings more or less alike, and still have genuine love for one person. Kindness that is local, episodic and uncoupled from love, or co-exists with meanness, is unlikely to be genuine. Acts of kindness in such individuals have a secondary gain or advantage, for example, ingratiation, deceit, or are compensatory gestures so the person does not feel irredeemably hollow.

Suffering is often thought to be part of loving, but one does not suffer from ingratitude. Kindness to someone who is ungrateful leads to disappointment, but a passionate love that is rejected leads to sorrow. Kindness does not have the intensity of love, nor does it undergo growth and decay, as is so common in love, when excitement fades, expectations are unfulfilled and individuals seek novelty. Since kindness is an attribute of character, and does not idealize its objects, it does not show a descent from initial passion to the humdrum of domestic routine that, in love, is a common seed of discontent.

In love, the individual trumps the community. Kindness should not be limited to a specific type or person, especially a friend or relation but to anyone in need. However irrational, the attributes of the beloved are believed to be unique, possessed only by that person, while the attributes of an object of kindness are shared by others with similar needs. Such attributes in the beloved as beauty, charm or intelligence are shared by many others, as is the case with the attributes of the needy, such as infirmity, poverty, or a reversal of fortune, but the former are idealized and perceived as specific to the beloved, while the latter are illustrative of a group. Love concentrates on the beloved; kindness for someone who is poor is felt as kindness to the poor. Unlike love, the attributes of an object of kindness can be recognized and satisfied by others without jealousy. Put differently, others can be kind or generous to the same person without jealousy among them.

All that love has to give is love. True love has no need of proofs or tokens. These are the artifice of seduction, the gratitude of a lover or compensations for disinterest once passions have subsided. All the beloved wants is for the lover to accept and give love freely. In contrast, kindness requires an act of kindness in which something apart from feeling is given that signifies the act as kind. One can love secretly or without acting on the feeling, and we would still say the person is in love, but what is kindness apart from kind acts? William James wrote of the ladies with a foolish and misplaced compassion for singers in an opera while their coachmen were freezing outside. To feel kindness, compassion or generosity but not act on it is hypocritical; to feel love and not act is a sign of timidity or shyness.

In kindness, the object of giving is not usually idealized except as a particular example of a type in which the objectivity of the person's condition is so pronounced as to evoke a subjective ideal in the giver. While the object of kindness is a member of a category, for example, the poor, the suffering, the ill, the handicapped, we often feel greater tenderness for one person than another not necessarily based on the person's need. Gender, age, loyalties, and cultural variables influence the strength of kindness. The object of kindness is perceived in a realistic, even hyper-realistic mode and is not usually internalized as a subjective image or ideal, though an individual who shows extreme kindness or compassion may be idealized, even beatified. The need of the person may be exaggerated or the person may be selected for reasons, for example, obsequiousness, that tap into emotions in the giver unrelated to the category of need. The individual represents the category. Needs, defects or deficiencies replace the individual so that the property, for example, a deformity, an illness, is the basis for the kindness rather than the person who exhibits the property, unlike the beloved who exists, or whose attributes exist, as objects of love in the imagination.

A major difference between kindness or empathy and love is that kindness is generic, while love is for the individual. Kindness or mercy may be bestowed on one person, but individual qualities are less important. Indeed, forgiveness or compassion may have greater moral value when bestowed on the undeserving, for example, kindness to someone who is cruel. In any event, it is the generosity of the donor that matters, not the attributes of the recipient, save that he or she falls within the appropriate category. We say that someone is kind or merciful more readily than we say a person is loving or has a loving nature, for love is exclusive to the beloved who is irreplaceable, and whose qualities are beyond compare The beneficiary of an act of kindness is not unique in attributes of personality but circumstance, for example, poverty, or in exemplifying a condition or category, for example, suffering. The beneficiary represents a class, say of the disempowered. The interaction is one-way, from the unselfish to the needy, unlike love which feeds on mutuality.

In romantic love, sexuality ordinarily accompanies and enhances the feeling of love, and strengthens the bond between lovers. In love, kindness is a given; it is part of the overall state of loving. When kindness is distinct from love, sexuality conflicts with unselfishness and threatens to convert an act of kindness into one of exploitation. Unselfish kindness does not have an overt sexual element but it can mutate to sado-masochism. The self can perceive advantage in the needs of the other, induce obligation and abuse the trust of the recipient. What begins with kindness can end in dependency or enslavement, as the needs of the recipient enable donors to enrich their advantage. Similarly, the recipient, from a different perspective, can interpret unselfishness as weakness and exploit, sexually or otherwise, the generosity of the giver. The need can be constant and increasing, and motivate an abject submission, or it can become monstrous and devour the one who feeds it. Needless to say, love too can degenerate to pathology.

Idealization occurs in relation to objects of feeling, such as a parent, a friend, or in admiration for an artist or politician, where feeling is primary and accompanied by caring and self-sacrifice. Objects of kindness, if idealized, are in some sense negative ideals, like the beauty of deformity in a Goya painting or the horror of war in the *Guernica*, exemplifications of suffering and the human condition. In love, occasionally in compassion or altruism, the idealization of feeling creates occasions of giving in which the other becomes more important than the self. Compassion can lead one to risk one's life, as in a suicidal act of altruism. In conceptual idealization, such as the idealization of truth or beauty, there is no impulse to give, though there may be an impulse to love, a love that like philosophy, the love of wisdom, is abstract and conceptual, far from actual feeling.[1]

Love is allied with compassion in that the drive to individuation is opposed to that for community, which is manifest in the reciprocity and security that family afford, not only for children but in the shared labor and mutual aid essential to family life. Community reaches its limit in abdication; individuation reaches its limit in alienation. We see these competing pressures at work at many social levels; autonomy of self and oneness with the other, individuality and dependency, solitude and companionship, and the claims of the individual versus those of the community that are central to so many legal and moral issues. We can also examine anger, jealousy, and rejection in this light, that is, in the tension of self-giving and self-protection. But then one asks, what is the self that gives and what is there to protect? When a couple sees itself as the sum of two distinct individuals, assimilation is incomplete. If to be complete is to incorporate the other, what can the self point to as its own? The self is an outcome of an individual and social history, an amalgam of inherited traits, parents, friends, teachers, a stew of acquired beliefs and values that achieve a relative coherence or constant identity. Each of us, as the descendent of others, as of our own former selves, is already a community of more or less harmonious attributes.

In sum, we often speak of compassion or love for humanity as forms of loving and, certainly, the commitment to others and passionate caring do resemble love in their sincerity and devotion. Further, this point of contact can enlarge to become love or friendship. The continuity of kindness with love is important to a theory of emotion, but human objects of kindness differ in important ways from the beloved, including reciprocity of feeling, uniqueness, idealization, passion, elation, and sorrow. The beloved is a singularity with attributes as paradigms within a class, while objects of kindness are arbitrary members of general categories. An object of kindness, say a person who is sick, is the category member to the nurse. With love, the beloved alone is the category, the members of which are his or her attributes that attract the lover. Kindness to a stranger may evolve to love, for example, when a nurse falls in love with a patient, but the illness is not the attribute that is idealized; rather, other features such as attractiveness, gentleness, or intelligence form the basis for the love. The illness brings the couple together, the care involves some degree of intimacy, the intimacy allows the qualities of the couple to transcend their roles, that is, patient/nurse, and gradually the devotion of the caretaker and the needs of the patient evolve to a love in which the illness or disability is now a secondary feature of the bond between the lovers. We have all seen such occasions, some of which are loving, some opportunistic, but more often love devolves to kindness as the beloved objectifies and de-idealizes to become an object of friendship, pity, sympathy, or compassion.

Ordinary kindness and the uniqueness of love

It is essential to understand the nature of love if one is to consider the diverse modes of kindness as forms of loving. To review, we speak of those who show compassion as loving, and of compassion as a type of love that is felt and given to those who are in need, yet there are as many points of contact with romantic love as there are differences. For example, lovers are aware of desire but their needs are unconscious, inferred from the strength of their love and the excursions into sexual and other behaviors. For the most part, need in lovers is tied to prior experience, personality, and subjective value. In compassion, the needs of others are clear and perceptible, and they are addressed directly in relation to the life situation. The objects of compassion are generic, those of love are individuals. One can say the objects of compassion have objectified, as well as the feeling. The saying *"he wears his heart on his sleeve,"* describes a person who is (too) caring. The suggestion that differences of kind are differences of degree is moot when the latter form a qualitative series of states. In this section, the central features of romantic love are reviewed with the goal of further elucidating and hopefully bridging the divide that separates genuine love from kindness and its manifestations.

Love is only one example of an illusion that replaces a direct gaze on the objective—the objective as an external or impersonal perspective—not the objectively real, which is inaccessible. We all have illusions, some of which we might concede, such as the illusion that our lives (work, play, sport, family) matter when all comes to dust and the earth itself is dust in one of many galaxies or universes. Some illusions are stronger than others, such as the belief in free will or a physical world outside of its mental replica. Some illusions we perceive, such as a rainbow or duck/rabbit figure, others occur without awareness, such as perceptual constancies, and still others, such as dreams, are a natural part of the mental life. But of all the illusions, and all that is illusory, that of love and the feelings allied to love are the most essential to human nature and the desire to go on in life, whether love for a beloved, a friend, a family, a pet, a book, an idea, or a sunset. Love may be an illusion, but it is the engine of life, of hope, of longing, of joy, fulfillment, and renewal. One cannot say this of kindness or compassion. Nor would we claim that needs satisfied in love, which are inferred rather than known, are comparable to the needs satisfied in kindness, which are evident to the observer.

Animals are guided by drives that aid in survival; some show affection and social bonding, some appear to show grief, but in humans a life is lived, enjoyed, suffered, for goals other than the immediacy of drive. The capacity to transcend the drives, that is, to live for the desires, for concepts and the derived affects, consists in the ability of the drives to remain in the shadows even as they individuate to partial feelings. This entails the partition of categorical primitives or imperatives of drive to concepts, and the specification of drive-discharge to the postponed satisfaction of desire.

Feeling takes on direction to future or absent objects. Anticipation, expectation, choice, and decision come into play. The drive-representation individuates to conceptual-feeling, the affect giving the desire, the concept furnishing the goal. From this standpoint, in contrast to the evolved feeling of genuine love, kindness may have developed out of an instinctual group mentality; communities of Bonobo, tribal loyalties, the cohesion required for survival in hunter-gatherers, perhaps as some version of the animal faith of Santayana. The mentality of animals and their tight fit with the environment are buried in the human psyche, left behind in the growth to autonomy and yet revived each moment as the state recurs.

Love is the ultimate valuation of a thing, to which all desires are subordinate. There is nothing more important than what is loved, which is to say that love, regardless of whether or not it is implemented, realizes a value of immense signification. Apart from the self-preservative drives, a genuine love for a person, for a thing or an occasion, from the perspective of the individual, announces an object of the greatest possible value. Kindness differs from love in that it is realized for members of a category in need, while love concentrates on a category-member of surpassing value. The feeling in compassion is distributed over objects that are inter-changeable. Some claim that the beloved is also fungible, but how often in a lifetime is one truly in love? Some argue that kindness is a higher unselfish emotion in that the individual has nothing to gain. But the humanity of kindness is closer to an idea than a feeling. There is no specific object to which it is "attached" except when it is implemented. Compassion is closer to an ideal in the abstract, unlike the idealization of a lover. In this, as an idea at which the intentional is aimed, it resembles the ideal lover one dreams about. Perhaps the compassion for others is like an expansion of non-sexual love, or the affection for family members, that is, the "family of man," a vastly extended family with some needier than others, for whom an individual feels a responsibility to care, with the relation of caretaker to those in need being asymmetric. After all, most families serve as the stage on which the drama of life plays out.

Desire for an object is generally in relation to its value. The more we desire an object, the greater to us its worth or value. However, intense desire is not a mark of love. Ambition can supersede or exploit most feelings, even those of intense value to the individual, but we would not say that their value is love or its equivalent. Love is accompanied by intense desire in longing for the beloved. A love that begins with attraction, like an intoxicating perfume, lingers when the beloved is gone. The idea of the beloved evokes feelings of love. In kindness, the desire to help is usually weaker in the absence of those in need, and even when they are present. More generally, desire occurs for diverse objects and is often transient, and like drive, may focus on objects of immediate satisfaction.

The objects of desire are exchangeable like those of kindness, while those of love are exemplary. The former come and go, the latter persist (recur). The desire to possess an ordinary object or a sexual target tends to be transient and depleted for that object when it is possessed, while the desire to have and keep the beloved endures. The transition from need to desire elaborates a private space of imagination, where the wish for an absent object forms an image of what is wished-for, and what is wished-for becomes an ideal of the beloved. Kindness does not occur in the absence of an act or object. The desire to help may be present in solitude, but except in the throes of a personal or religious calling, it does not compare with the desire for the beloved.

Love is intense, often over a long time, while an act of kindness is episodic, but duration, intensity, and quantity do not capture the conceptual growth and imaginative play that love demands. Kindness does not engage in the vivid fantasy of love. Intense love approximates drive, but a strong desire in love, when it is sexual, is paradoxical in that it entails a prominence of self—the "I want"—antithetical to self-offering and sacrifice. The effectuation of desire independent of love is self-realization, not surrender. Desire may precede or anticipate a beloved, or concur with sexual need, but in genuine loving the self dissolves in the other. The self-other relation, the "I love him or her," is buried in the all-or-nothing. The self is infiltrated by the other, loving and being loved, giving not taking, wanting the other, and relinquishing the self.

The intentional self of desire is the self of choice and judgment, which is why genuine union is not a fusion with the other but an awakening of a deeper unity out of which, like Siamese twins, conjoined lovers arise. The beloved individuates an archetypal oneness beneath conscious mind. There is no reason to think the archetype is dyadic, though coupling in animals may evolve to that in humans. The deeper unity could as well be the humanity that is the "sympathetic identification" and underpinning of compassion. Archetypal oneness is revived in love as a fusion (incomplete separation) of lover and beloved. Prior to individuality, the subject is one in a ground of community. If the identification with the other in compassion taps the depth of psyche when autonomy is suspended or when love has not partitioned and sequestered in one individual, sympathetic identification may arise from the ancient sea out of which humankind emerged. Romantic love plays out this participation as a pathway to compassion when love ceases to concentrate on the other but infuses the All out of which the One, as shared individuality, arises.

The self-realization to which individuation leads conflicts in some respects with love, for it entails an individuality that resists incorporation of the beloved as part of the lover's self. Being one's self and belonging to the other may be irreconcilable. The realization of a desire other than the desire to be in love, or to be with the beloved, involves a relation of the self to what is desired, not a collapse of self into the other in a moment of intense loving. Once a desire is satisfied, judgment resumes and other desires press to satisfaction. The sympathetic identification of kindness puts one's self in the place of the other; it does not assimilate the other to the self.

Oneness: love and compassion

Desire achieves its goal by displacing love from mind to world, or shifting the object from the imaginary to the objective. We may think of desire as equivalent to love, or as the agency through which love is manifest, but the principle desire in love is to remain in love, or to be with the beloved, so desire is submerged in the actual or pending joy of union.

The *lass mich ziehn* of Tannhauser in the grotto of Venus makes sense as an appeal from erotic bondage or sexual exhaustion, but it is not typically the lover's lament. Since the desire for the beloved is confounded by sexual appetite, the stronger the sexual desire, the greater the proximity to drive. A love that depends too heavily on sexual attraction is in danger of reverting to drive-satisfaction, and having the uniqueness of the beloved sacrificed to undisciplined appetite, with the beloved replaceable by others who fill the same sexual role. Conversely, we question the authenticity of a love that dissipates as the sexual passion wanes, that is, does not transition from *eros* to *philia*. Diminished sexual appetite may signal a change in feeling, but reduced libido can occur with aging, medications, illness, yet love can be unaffected if intimacy remains.

Sexual union achieves a transient physical bonding that can facilitate or substitute for psychic oneness. Lovers will hold each other tightly and sleep with their bodies in contact to replicate, somatically, what exists or is hoped for in spirit. The ease and frequency of sexual union, the melting of boundaries in the flesh of the other, is the unity of core drive that we hope to achieve at the phase of self and desire. The rarity of true love and the fragility of oneness in relation to the egocentric forces of drive-satisfaction give hasty couplings in the hope of enduring unions. For the cynic, the sexual is the actual and real, and love achieves reality only by remaining a fantasy. For the young, the confusion of love and sex exchanges one for the other, usually sexual coupling for loving oneness rather than the reverse. The "sacred and the profane" do not, for them, have clear demarcations. Gradually, one comes to see that love is not fundamentally sexual even if, as desire, it develops out of sexual drive, just as the latter can be—most often is—independent of loving.

Many would say the greatest, least selfish, sacrificial and non-sexual love, and one free of desire, is not for a beloved but for one's children. There is no wanting other than to be with them, their success and happiness. We simply feel love when we gaze at them. With a beloved, desire arises as feeling goes in the direction of action, in a courtship that leans to the future, or companionship or marriage, or in an absence that accentuates the desire for the ideal over the actual and, true to the platitude, makes the heart grow fonder. Desire is fundamental in love but in desire, as noted, a self-other relation obtains that, in unity, love seeks to dispel. Love's formula, $1 + 1 = 1$, requires lovers to return from the external relatedness of appearances to the deeper well of indivisibility.

Except for those in a morbid depression, acedia or the summit of (Buddhist) enlightenment, desire is fundamental to human thought and feeling. A desire is closer to the world than a wish, which can be for the improbable or unattainable. We make a wish on a birthday cake, less hopeful it will come to pass than we would be if it were a desire. One can wish for a desire, such as a wish to fall in love with someone who is desirable. Many search for a beloved, or to be in a state of loving. They seem to be in love with love. There is a distinction between being in love with love, or wanting to be in a state of loving and loving for the sake of love, as the Mahler song goes, *"love not for youth, or beauty or treasure, but love for love and be loved forever."* The other-worldly or wish-like quality of this state is reminiscent of the Rodgers and Hart song, *"falling in love with love is falling for make-believe."* Falling in love with anyone is make-believe. But to be in love with love is to want the exhilaration of love or the devotion to non-self without an object. It is also submitting and accommodating the ideal to the qualities and limitations of a beloved without an actual other.

In many if not most people, there is an idea, often unconscious, of the lover they are seeking, or the qualities they want in a lover. For some, the need for love is constantly seething, now and then erupting, and the feeling of love or wanting to be in love is so powerful that almost any person will do as an object. If love is subjective idealization, it is an image of the beloved, not the actual person that is its object. One can love a person or celebrity one has never met as in *erotomania*. Love goes on after the beloved dies. How important is the actual beloved to the lover's feeling? Put differently, is love truly dependent on the beloved, or does the lover come upon someone who fulfills an ideal that is waiting to be satisfied? Is the man or woman of one's dreams a veritable dream image that is implanted on an actual being, a person who possesses one or more of the several attributes that have been idealized in the imagination?

This implies that one can meet a potential beloved, apprehend qualities that are appealing, internalize those qualities and fall in love with the ideal version of the person, or one can have a subjective ideal beforehand, meet someone who shares some of the internalized qualities, and fall in love more or less immediately. Perhaps this is the basis of love at first sight. The lover retains, probably in the unconscious, an idealized image of a future beloved, and on perceiving some or most of the already subjective qualities, promptly falls in love. That is, the beloved arises as a creation of the ideal, or the ideal creates the beloved. In either case, it is not the actual person that is loved but an internal replica that satisfies a preconceived image.

Desire liberates an individual from the tyranny of the drives as it distances the self from objects of immediate gratification. The landscape of desire is populated by options, which can lead to indecision as readily as to choice. Freedom and torment are the extremes of the many phenomena that attend to desire. The will to meet and love a person who corresponds to the image of a wish transcends the biological imperatives of immediate action. There is possibility, there is the choice of acting or not acting, there is the wish of reverie and daydream, the surrogates and distortions of dream that guide the person to a manifold of incipient or effective acts. These phenomena add to the agent's sense of a self uncoupled from causal necessity, one that hovers over a body (brain) that implements final thought and feeling. In this escape from chance on the one hand, and predictability on the other, the self is free to desire all things possible in this life or the next. Into this psychic arena comes love as a bridge from desire to necessity; the desire to have and the need to submit, to possess and to relinquish. The feeling of complete volition with an inability to resist is a kind of voluntary compulsion that touches the spirit-life above and animal-hunger below. Love is a sacrifice of autonomy in merger but in mutual dissolution it rescues the self from isolation and despair.

Love and the human condition

> *Past touch and sight and sound, Not further to be found, How hopeless under ground Falls the remorseful day.*

A. E. Housman, "Easter Hymn" XVI

Unlike our animal predecessors, we know that one day the passage of life will cease and, as in Housman's poem, the sun will set on our dying day. Love is inevitably a response to annihilation, nothingness, and the consciousness of mortality. To live fully is to know death in selflessness and overcome death in transcendence. To "love unto death" is to stave off death by loving. To "die of a broken heart" when the beloved is lost implies the self cannot be reconciled to separation. The escape in love from ever-present death is immortalized in the *Liebestod*, the love-death, the arising of love from a perishing into death. Love and death, arising and perishing, creation and destruction, are thematic in life and literature. A metaphoric death at a moment of great passion is a feeling not unknown to most people. As pleasure is the antidote to pain, love is the cure for emptiness; the eternity in a moment that removes lovers from the incessant drumbeat of time and aging. We all need a reason to live. For most of us it is to find something or someone worth loving, which is to escape death, in love, and find value in a world where all paths lead to final passage. Love is the flight from decay and putrefaction to the arms of illusion, an ideal of perfection, timeless, deathless, and everlasting.

To feel love is to be fully in the present, even—especially—when thinking of an absent lover. To be in the present is to feel acutely the loss of the moment and the effort to hold on to it, prolong its sweetness or feel the moment as eternal. We take snapshots at times of pleasure to save the object and original feeling. We want to safeguard the experience from decay and transition, demarcate the object from the self to preserve one as the other ages and dies. The snapshot validates the experience and gives permanence to reminiscence, trusting the imagination to provide context and meaning to a dismembered slice. Yet with all this, even in the perishing of immediacy, we are reminded of the gift of presence in the loss of all that matters including our own lives.

Love is the quintessential value, but whatever is valued has a share in the process of loving. No doubt the ubiquity of love and the facile extension of the term dilute its meaning when applied to a beloved, but the scope of usage reveals a common undercurrent of valuation regardless of the object, and regardless of the positive or negative attitude the valuation assumes. The pervasiveness of valuation, the ease of loving, and the common use of the term, for a book, a movie, a vacation or a job, allow a more equitable distribution of feeling or, put differently, entail an over-inclusion of objects and a flattening of the peaks (depths) of true love. This makes romantic love all the more precious when we find it. A lover will hesitate to say, *I love my garden*, in the same breath as, *I love my sweetheart*. The easy application of the term for non-equivalent objects saps it of meaning, except as an affirmation of value. The more pernicious effect is an uncoupling of love from its expression in ordinary language, with the consequence that to say, *I love you*, is without meaning and is taken with skepticism if not truly felt by the speaker and truly believed by the beloved.

When the ideal of love is forced to confront an objectionable reality, especially if it comes as a surprise, say, when a person discovers that a lover of some duration is married, or discovers some unsavory facts about the beloved, what becomes of the love, and what does the response say about genuine feeling? Naturally, situations differ and a distinction could be made as to the quality of the beloved's marriage, the tolerance of the lover and the shock of the betrayal. Still, a sudden rupture implies the love was inauthentic, that is, conditional, in that the love aimed beyond loving with a purpose or motivation. If more was expected, love was not enough. There was more hope than acquiescence and the love was not genuine. If there is no change in the lover's feeling save for the assimilation of this knowledge, and if the fault was not one of deception, there seems little justification for a breakup.

The lovers remain as before, except that they understand the situation and do not judge the beloved by the past. When the knowledge is such as to threaten the ideal, the love may weaken and pass to distrust; judgment replaces intuition. An abuse of trust makes lovers uncertain that love is justified or if there is reciprocity, that is, that protestations of love are just so much talk. Whatever undermines trust will infect the belief that one is truly loved. The upheaval in trust and the ambivalence of feeling allow judgment to enter where faith ruled before.

Take the story about the young woman from Galicia—whose inhabitants do not have saintly reputations—who confessed to her rabbi that she had not told her fiancée that she had formerly been a prostitute, and what was she to do? Tell him, said the rabbi, he will understand, but don't say you're from Galicia. Some bits of knowledge are more destructive than others, but love is guided by intuition, not by knowledge which plays a role in appraisal, not immediate feeling. Lovers are notoriously resistant to the admonitions of others, but when such warnings are heeded, love becomes "reasonable," judgment prevails and the insularity of the self has precedence over the needs of the beloved. The influence of advice is also a test of the extent to which love arises spontaneously from need, or is dependent on qualities in the other to which those needs are matched.

Hunger and sexual drive, the life-affirmative values, rise out of the absence, emptiness, or physical relationality that is the death of organism. The proximity of love and death, as of the incompatibility of the valuations of self and world with *acedia,* apathy or disinterest, owes to death's nullification of the reproductive drive, as well as the opposing vectors of privation and acquisition. The arc from birth to death is iterated each moment in the arising and perishing of the mental state. Love is defiance. Sex, love, and value struggle against ever-present decay and the inevitable triumph of death when the core fails to revive. Every act of love or sex, every moment of value, is an affront to non-existence.

There are many ways of dying in love: sexual death and rebirth in orgasm; the passage of all feeling; hopelessness and suicide; the becoming that erases prior being in novel form; the loss of self in other; grief and mourning; the succession of states of loving and of the beloved kept alive in the imagination; the perishing in actuality. There are also ways of not dying for the sake of loving; the clinging to life when all is lost, the excitement of another round of creation, the futurity of desire that fills emptiness with longing, and the ineffable sweetness of reunion.

The morality of love: passion and compassion

Love can be moral or immoral depending on its objects, moral in the goodness of unselfish giving, immoral or amoral in deception and sexual exploitation. For some, the carnal impulse is a stage in the evolution of moral feeling to unselfish caring. Yet, it is not primarily the sexuality, possessiveness, perversions or abuses of desire that question the moral dimension of love but the sacrifice of lovers and the continuum with compassion that reinforce it. Love of the good is love for an ideal, like love for the idealized attributes of a beloved, but in compassion, the ideal is severed from the sexual and generalizes beyond the individual. This involves a shift from a particular to an idea. Love proceeds from the particular to the general, from individual traits to a category of such traits and from there to ideal categories that subsume but are distinct from the individual. Compassion goes in the other direction from the general to the particular. It begins with an idea or concept and individuates to the particular. Put otherwise, the endpoint in the expansion of a romantic ideal is the starting point of compassion.

Why is love not at the heart of our humanity? The moral basis of compassion is its direction from the ideal to the particular, from what is good for the many to what applies to the few. Kant's maxim, which is similar to the *Golden Rule* or the biblical "love thy neighbor.," is not a command to love others, but to treat them as you want to be treated. In compassion, the other can be an empathic focus but the love for humanity is not love for an individual. Individual love creates loyalties and biases that go against the love for humanity. The beloved is reified to an ideal category. For romantic love as for parental and other forms of individual love, the value for the one comes at the expense of the many. The beloved—a parent, child, even a pet—is loved to the exclusion of others.

What does it mean to love humanity? In what way is the passion to help others similar to that for a beloved? Is love related to compassion? We may profess a love for all people and declare that, similarly, god loves his children equally, but love distributed over humanity dilutes the intensity and alters the quality of individual love. Perhaps the ideal of the beloved as a human being or living thing independent of attributes, or the idealization of attributes that all humans share, is the basis of compassion, which ignores individual traits for generic categories. It is possible to show continuity but at some point romantic love is so transformed it is unrecognizable. Hegel wrote, "the heart which seeks to embrace the whole of humanity within itself indulges in a vain attempt to spread out its love till it becomes a mere idea, *the opposite of love* (and that man) ... can only love a few particular individuals" (McTaggart, 1901, p. 211).

C. P. Snow once said something to the effect that one could say the life of a genius is worth the same as an ordinary man, that is, that all people have the same value, but not that two ordinary men are worth twice as much as a genius. One can't make a quantity of a quality. A qualitative significance is given to the individual but the quantity of significance does not trump individual value. People may empathize with the plight of a single person in a catastrophic situation and shrug at the deaths of thousands in a disaster. Stalin is quoted as saying that the death of one man is a tragedy, the death of millions is a statistic. Feeling intensifies when it sequesters in a single individual and dissipates in a category. Politicians well understand this device and use it to advantage in rhetoric. Love is for the particular, and even compassion is most powerful when it seeks to alleviate the suffering of a single person or animal.

As discussed above, the love of humanity is often conceived as a nobler vision of romantic love. It might be, however, that compassion arises in the privation of feeling for the one. The great soul who inspires millions is often accused of mistreatment or neglect by his family. Promises to the many are withheld from the few. Perhaps the absence of individual love and/or the presence of overweening ambition is the foundation on which concern for the masses rests. The vow of celibacy in the church is an example of the conflict between love for the individual and love for the universal (god, humanity). Compassion is no less immune to cynicism than romantic love. The great saints and mystics are often described as selfish, their devotion and sacrifice conditioned on a conscious pretense to more of god's love than is freely given to others (Leuba, 1925). A person genuinely in love also forgets the needs of others, but at least there is no hypocrisy.

Passion can arise for a categorical ideal that does not extend to the valuations of its members. Many Continental and European intellectuals were passionate about communism, but rationalized or were indifferent to the fate of millions in Stalinist camps. A passion for ideas requires that particulars dissolve in generalities, so that ideas can gather force in the imagination. Once liberated from the particulars, they carry the full weight of passionate feeling. Both passion and compassion occur for individuals but only compassion is for populations. Compassion for individual suffering loses force when widely distributed or when it goes outward to the many yet finds a home in the few. The nobility of such feeling is that it gives love but does not seek it; it does not assimilate others to the self but identifies the self with others, perceiving them as instances to be loved and cared for.

Some argue that a love-union creates a new entity, a "we," composed of self and other, lover and beloved. Is the formation of a "we" a nucleus of co-dependency that nurtures multiple others? Does the "we" form the basis of the inter-dependence of compassion? I believe the "we" is not a transpersonal entity but a revised self that assimilates the valuations of the other, though it still could be the seed of communal feeling.

The self is now constituted of values native to the lover, along with values magnified by the ingress of the beloved. The "we" is an "I" in which the other is assimilated to the self, or usurps a portion of the self-concept. Compassion may occur when this assimilation creates values of selfless giving that extend beyond an individual, or replace the love for an individual with asymmetric caring.

The formation of a "we" has implications for other interpretations. Alberoni (1981/1983) argued for an expansion of the monogamy of true love to the formation of triads, say a man with two lovers, and that the "communism" of nascent love—the giving, sharing, equity, communal property—extends to society. The argument is similar to that for compassion. There are differences, such as the uniqueness of the beloved—who is unique to the lover, but who also requires to be loved uniquely—in comparison with the interchangeability of individuals in the mass, but the process of falling in love is similar, entailing the sharing of values and a self subordinate to the other. However, the comparison is of little interest without a psychology of how feeling ramifies from the love of an individual to compassion for multitudes.

How does falling in love relate to falling out of love, to mourning, loss, grief, jealousy, anger, to parental and other forms of love or affection, to focal attention or interest, indeed, to almost any show of feeling? Love and its perturbations are central to all activities. It is the "spiritual" correlate of the sexuality that Freud related to a wide array of behaviors. Alberoni (1981/1983, p. 43) touches on an aspect of love that helps to explain such connections when he writes, with some intuition, that "*the happiness savored in the nascent state of falling in love is always there in us as nostalgia."* Love is restrained by reason, but grows stronger in reflection. A love that evolves to everyday caring and affection persists in nostalgia as the memory of, or longing for, an earlier passion. The impulse for a surrogate mode of togetherness is the spark in the imagination that, like the perfume that lingers in the poem of Aragon, is a reminder of the intensity of past love or separation.

Staying in love

We all know couples who have been in love for life. Perhaps such couples are the true models of love, while the rest of us settle for some imitation. We tend to think that the one you fall in love with at twenty is not the one you will love at thirty or fifty. It is not so much that the self is changing, though it does, or that the beloved changes, though that occurs, but that different stages in life experience bring other needs to bear on old or new loves.

Bradford (2011) has written that getting out from under trivia can, in composite, be worse than isolated tragedies. Though often fatal to passion, the routine of constant togetherness is not necessarily destructive to love. The trivia of daily life and marriage can sustain feeling even if original passion cannot be revived. A famous composer, when bluntly asked why most of his music was worthless, replied that it was necessary to write trash in order for a few good pieces to be composed. I doubt that real genius rests on a foundation of mediocrity, but does love require a tacit bond of compatibility, reliability, trust, in a complicity that endures even if it is not conducive to passion?

I have known loving couples where the vitality and creativity of one partner is in stark contrast to the dullness of the other—a virtuoso cadenza against a soft orchestral murmur—yet somehow the marriage works. An eventless duration of trivia, routine, and quotidian responsibility replaces momentary bliss as an anchor without which the ship of love is adrift.[2] The erotics of early infatuation are replaced by shared goals, security, and amity even if the bonds are closer to the *philia* of friendship than the *eros* of romance. Inevitably, passion fades but an exploration of the beloved may uncover qualities that support the continuance of loving feeling. This mode of enduring love should not suffer by comparison with the fabled ascent to a brief erotic paradise.

If unconscious needs are satisfied there is hope the union will continue, though the desires of the conscious or empirical self, the self of the moment, may divert attention to the qualities of others. This marks the dominance of the intentional over the involuntary or the triumph of volition over necessity. What do we make of the person who rejects the stability of union with one lover and goes from one conquest to another?

It is possible that the pleasure in desire is commensurable with the satisfaction of need, that drive and desire are concordant in seeking novelty over stability. There might be an unusual degree of wholeness or insularity to which the transience of the other is superfluous, or an exceptional degree of shallowness to which the other cannot descend. The object of momentary desire actualizes at a superficial plane in the lover's imagination where physical attributes, egoism, availability—for excitement, risk or predation—and volitional desire prevails. Lovers who cannot stay in love may find the other unable to fulfill their needs, or they may be attracted to attributes that do not satisfy the core. In a word, the union is imperfect or of insufficient depth.

Santayana (1923) wrote, "all beauties attract by suggesting the ideal and then fail to satisfy it." Put differently, the lover idealizes one or several attributes of the beloved but is unable to sustain the idealization. Perhaps the ideal is eroded by contradictory attitudes, or, for lack of imagination or commitment, the lover is unable to maintain the ideal or live with it, or the attributes of the other do not fulfill core needs. The idealizations of the lover may not mitigate unappealing characteristics. Or, the value of the other is for the idealized attributes—physical, psychic—while the person as a whole is ignored. A relationship is superficial when a desire does not become a need. An individual can adore the body or intellect of the other, but even if such qualities are idealized, the limited scope (depth) will focus on particular functions or features. In true love, the particular is an attribute of a category that actualizes the core, where it grows in the unconscious at a depth that is blind to other characteristics. The growth augments a conscious desire with the intensity of unconscious drive. The attributes of the beloved are part of the core self. The ideal is not a mere abstraction. It is no less vital than the lover's own life. The intensity and duration of grief over loss reveal the extent to which the beloved inhabits the core.

On a practical level, staying in love implies sensitivity to the history of the couple in shared experience, encouraging the best in the other as in the self, increasing the feeling of worth (value) in the other and building-up trust. For love to last, similarities not shared in the beginning must be recovered. Aristotle thought the mirroring of the self in the other increased self-knowledge. However, the admirable qualities of the other can also betray insufficiency and incite a striving for wholeness that does not rely on dependency. The opposite can fill what is lacking in the self for a more perfect union or provide a false therapy for one's shortcomings. Completing the self by incorporating the beloved can have the unintended effect of leaving a residue of felt inadequacy in which assimilation provokes an awareness of disparities that are a source of conflict.

Notes

1. However, "Platonic" love consists in channeling erotic passion toward Beauty itself, rather than a beautiful person (who is never completely beautiful and never remains beautiful), but this does not entail stifling the passion, just channeling it "upward." Socrates is very passionate, a seducer of sorts, truly guilty of "corrupting the young" as he is charged. For Nietzsche, philosophy deprived of passion is a game of no real importance.
2. Perhaps this relates to Nietzsche's horror of grey monotony. The idea of Apollonian and Dionysian culture is built on the idea that the "beautiful dream" and "intoxication" are the only means of escape from the deadening weight of the routine of ordinary life.

CHAPTER NINE

Belief and value

Love looks not with the eyes but with the mind and therefore is wing'd Cupid painted blind.

—William Shakespeare, Midsummer Night's Dream, 1.1

Preliminary remarks on belief and value

A belief is an attitude *about* or *toward* a thing or the concept of the thing, whereas a value is the feeling invested in a thing or aroused by it. The attitude in belief can be implicit and unconscious, or it can be conscious and explicit. Belief is a psychological process taking place in the brain, but the belief that is the outcome of this process is lifted from the psyche and subjected to a personal or impersonal judgment, an acceptance or rejection, or affirmation or denial of the truth, goodness or utility of the belief. This ordinarily requires the belief to be framed in a proposition, but most beliefs are dispositional and implicit. An *explicit* belief limited to the truth value of a certain statement is not the conscious equivalent of the unconscious belief from which it develops, but is rather a mark of the dispositional nature of the implicit belief that eventuates in the conscious fragment. A statement of the form *I believe that x is true* is closer to an expression of some item of knowledge than that of a belief. What we know can be put in the form of a statement for purposes of making a truth-judgment, but that is not necessarily what we believe, while what we believe is not necessarily something that we know. One can believe in an afterlife without knowing anything about it or whether or not there is any such thing, and one can know how to speak or write, which do not involve belief, except in the most particulate manner. A belief without evidence is opinion or faith; a belief supported by fact is knowledge.

Belief that takes the form of a propositional attitude or a statement submitted to a determination of truth is a limited account of belief without psychological import. The truth of a conscious belief is tied to logic or evidence; the "truth" of an unconscious belief is tied to meaning, survival, and signification. A conscious belief in the form of a statement realizes only a portion, and not an exact one at that, of the unconscious context that initiates and guides the behavior. An implicit belief that is conveyed into a statement for purposes of a truth-judgment is an extreme of conceptual realization; the statement is drained of the implicit valuations, feelings, and experience that characterize the unconscious context in which the potential for the belief, in the form of a statement, is embedded.

A conscious belief that is judged to be true is close to the extra-personal limit of mind in the need for objective data and consensus, which are extrinsic events that are brought to bear on what is otherwise an inclination or bias. The prime example of this implicit bias is common sense, which is the set of core assumptions that are inherited or acquired in the evolutionary history of animal and human thought. These assumptions are adaptive tools for survival. A single fact that reinforces a common sense belief is accepted without question, while those that challenge it must be multiple or profound. Contrary facts that cannot be reconciled with common sense or folk theory are initially dismissed or, when persuasive, are treated as an alternate perspective, not a refutation. The older set of beliefs is set aside, perhaps replaced, as Kuhn argued, but if they are in conformance to common sense they are not usually rejected. To paraphrase Niels Bohr, the opposite of a falsehood is a truth, but the opposite of a great truth may well be another great truth. Yet great truths aside, the implicit biases that issue from common sense beliefs are the everyday assumptions that guide behavior, for example, that a person is identical across periods of sleep, that the self is slow to change in spite of a changing world, that time "flows," that free will is real, that some things matter more than others, and so on.

For a belief to be true it must confirm to common sense, or to iron logic or fact. Facts are the evidence for true beliefs, but if, as Dewey argued, facts are irreducible values, belief is bound up with valuation. Facts are not impersonal data; they are settled and consensual values, states of affairs from which originating values have largely been extracted. The residual value in a fact is what makes us believe it is true, and so too for the belief the fact supports. But to say a belief is true requires more than naked fact; it requires the dynamic or direction in the fact that prompts a judgment as to its truth and the relevance of the fact to the belief. This dynamic is the value that guides the belief to the fact, or the dispositional feeling of the implicit belief that underlies the attitude. The propositional account of belief ignores the unconscious dispositions that frame our conscious beliefs, and the presuppositions that reflect the belief-system—the relational matrix—of foundational beliefs and values that instigate thought and action.

Unconscious assumptions also provide the context behind all partial beliefs, such as propositions. For example, the belief (statement) that unicorns do not exist is not solely dependent on the fact that no one has seen one, but on assumptions concerning plausibility, tense, and the nature of existence. The disbelief in unicorns could not arise without the implicit belief that self and world exist and are independent, that images are distinguishable from percepts, that psychic phenomena differ from external ones, that fantasy differs from perception, as myth from reality. Tense is relevant in the possibility that unicorns might exist in the future, or once existed in the past. Perhaps they might come into existence through mutation or genetic manipulation. Is it conceivable that a unicorn, or its fossilized remains, could be discovered in some part of the world, like an okapi in the jungles of the Congo? The belief about unicorns is not driven by a preponderance of fact, but by a knowledge base that excludes them as "real" animals and biases a proposition about their existence or history as mythic creatures. Fundamentally, a factual statement arises out of tacit knowledge (Polanyi, 1974) and assumptions that may have nothing to do, directly, with the conscious belief or proposition.

The content of a belief can be a category or concept that becomes a belief when it is accompanied by a disposition to believe it. The disposition is an aspect of its value. For example, the discovery in South Africa of *Australopithecus* by Professor Dart was ridiculed for years because the finding was inconsistent with the body of belief at the time. Conversely, the Piltdown hoax succeeded because the evidence was doctored to fit the expectations of an elite class. Just as a belief about unicorns arises in the distribution of animals in a category of horse-like creatures, the finding of an ape-like man must fit the category of man-like or pre-human creatures. In the gradual acceptance of novel fact, pre-suppositions guide belief, so for a change in belief one must change the pre-suppositions on which the belief depends.

What makes a belief true or false is the evidence for or against it, but the presumption of truth is, more fundamentally, an application of value to evidence, for example, what counts as evidence, what evidence can be accepted, what must be rejected? Minimally, value concerns the confidence placed in the evidence, in the instance of unicorns even the *absence* of evidence. Scientific belief would seem to be the clearest model of the relation of fact to truth, but science is not as open to new ideas as commonly supposed, especially when they run counter to prevailing paradigms. Scientific beliefs are assumed to be provisional and open to refutation, but this occurs primarily within a framework of related, shared assumptions. A truly original idea must challenge these assumptions: not only the explicit beliefs in the science, but the values and implicit beliefs submerged in the passage of tacit knowledge to proposition and fact.

At an early phase, categories that realize horses, unicorns, and centaurs are not clearly individuated; nor are the real and the imaginary, or the subjective and objective. In the actualization of a statement or question such as "do unicorns exist?" the context that prompts the judgment is trimmed away. The unconscious antecedents of the acquired knowledge that informs the belief contribute to hesitation, or to the acceptance of a fact-based truth. They account either for an emotional conviction or a lingering uncertainty that makes a judgment certain or provisional. Religious belief is the paradigm of the former, scientific belief of the latter. Science idealizes the provisional but conveys certainty. In an age of cloning, and the possibility, remote that it is, that even personality might be transplanted, what does it mean to say all men are mortal? Every concept, every object or fact has an undersurface of alternative possibilities that fail to materialize. The clarity we seek in thought conceals the ambiguity it seeks to resolve. In a footnote in the preface to his philosophical essay entitled "Love," Stendhal alluded to the feeling that underlies the most abstract propositions:, "I am continually beset by the fear that I may have expressed a sigh when I thought I was stating a truth."

It is often argued that a truth-judgment is the basis for action or that we decide what is true and then act on this decision. A truth-judgment that serves as the ground of further action would have motive force. I would argue that we are dealing with two actions, one the judgment, the other the behavior, the former providing justification for the latter, not a cause. From what source, then, do judgments and actions arise? How does deciding the truth differ from other conscious actions? Hume famously argued that reason can tell us what is true or false but not what to do; for that, an emotional push is needed. Feeling is in play when any truth is decided. I would amend Hume's argument to the effect that what is essential to an action based on truth, indeed, to the judgment of truth itself, is a feeling that gives the statement its force. This feeling is equivalent to value.

A false belief that is taken to be true is a sign of ignorance or delusion; a true belief that is taken to be false is a sign of confusion, denial, or resistance. The strongest conviction is often for false or untestable beliefs. Take Swedenborg's *Heaven and its Wonders and Hell,* in which the architecture of heaven is described in some detail. The account might be persuasive had he not begun by saying it was described to him by an angel.

Coherent arguments are often best refuted by attention to their foundational assumptions. This is the case for religious beliefs that depend on assumptions concerning the existence and nature of god. Certainty for a false belief or one without evidence, or even one that is readily disconfirmed, includes animistic, magical, and supernatural thought, as well as the belief in a personal god, in karma, or an after-life. To speak to god is prayer, to listen to god is hallucination. This illustrates the fuzzy boundary between a specific delusion, such as Swedenborg's conversation with an angel, and false beliefs that are widespread, well-tolerated, and held with conviction.

True beliefs may be denied because they are inconsistent with others that are more deeply held, such as those that owe to religious dogma, or those we deny to preserve sanity, of which illusory perception and the subjectivity of experience are examples. The belief in direct physical perception is deeply ingrained, for it evolved over millions of years as a means of coping and survival. There is no evidence that physical entities are directly perceived and much evidence they are not, to mention only the temporal lag in perception. Yet even if we accept the illusory nature of perceptual experience, we do not feel this "in our gut." There is a conflict between the explicit belief that the world is illusory and the implicit belief that it is real, yet one easily holds both at the same time. Feeling in the implicit belief is stronger than in the conscious belief.

Do we not sense that the passion in a conscious belief points to deeper motivations? One could say that the explicit belief in its derivation has become relatively affect-free. The affective tonality changes when there is withdrawal from the world, in psychosis or mystical contemplation, when the dominant phase in cognition approximates the sources of unconscious knowledge.

Some beliefs are ignored because they involve moral conflict, such as excusing an immoral act by someone who is admired and respected, accepting theft by a person attempting to do good, for example, the Robin Hood syndrome, justifying the lesser of two evils as in political choice, or blindness to infidelity to preserve a marriage. We avoid every-day truths such as the slaughter of animals when eating meat. We suppress truths that concern aging, the inevitability of death, absolute nothingness and the "view from nowhere," as Tom Nagel put it. We live as if life matters even when we accept the cosmic perspective in which life is without purpose or meaning and the earth is a speck in a universe that may be one of many. Into this void comes love as savior.

The account of true or false belief depends heavily on the authority of science, which in turn relies on the presumed objectivity of mathematical beliefs, their independence from the psyche and their extension to non-mathematical propositions. However, to assume that a truth-judgment for linguistic propositions such as "horses exist" corresponds to one for mathematical propositions, such as $2 + 2 = 4$, ignores the fact that horses are arbitrary members of a category that includes plough horses, zebras, and unicorns, that there is a diachronic passage from embryo to adult, and that, in evolution, small transitional horse-like animals preceded the modern version and probably deserve to be termed horses. Evolutionary gradualism is problematic for categories, not just of horses but of other organisms too, for it raises questions concerning the Rubicon, that is, boundary conditions, and the inclusion criteria. To say *"horses exist"* introduces all the complexities discussed in the case of unicorns, those of existence, mind, and object, similarities in genome across life-forms, tense, that is, once existed, now exists, will exist, and so on. These confounds are not resolved by a succession of truth-judgments on borderline instances; instead, they show that the truth of a simple statement on horses or unicorns is a valuation in search of the evidence that will turn it into certain knowledge or belief.

Microgeny of value and belief

Belief and value are intertwined: truth-judgments depend on valuations, and values engage beliefs. To common sense, value, which in German is *Wert*, is confused with object worth, which implies economic worth and the imposition of desire on objects that have intrinsic or commercial value, an account that entails a judgment like that in belief. But every value is an act of value-creation that is part of the process of act and percept-formation. Value takes a different form at each phase in this process: drive, desire, object. In a word, value is qualitative and dia-chronic, both evolutionary and microgenetic. It begins with trends in thought formation, inclinations, tendencies, early-instilled traits of character, and the categorical primitives of instinctual drive, passes through conceptual-feeling and eventuates in the worth of an object in the world. The ancestral origins of value are evident when an animal picks out its prey and displays primitive valuation in the category of hunger and food-selection, or a female bird shows valuation when she accepts a strutting male in the choice of a mate. The primitive belief is the category of the pre-object that is captured in predation or mat-ing, while the value is the direction that leads to that object. A prey might be perceived as an appropriate member of the category but its pursuit reveals a primitive value. That value might be first edible" and then "catchable," that is, out of the herd, the lion chooses the antelope it thinks it can catch, not the one it thinks will taste the best. Utilitarian value trumps esthetic value—but not always.

Over the course of evolution, or in the micro-temporal derivation of an act of cognition, unconscious drive develops to conscious desire, that is, to the explicit valuation of an idea or object. Conscious valua-tion is the valence applied to the aboutness of intentionality. To think about something is to value it. To form a proposition entails valuation in the choice of topic and form, in the defining features of the premiss and the inevitability of the conclusion. Value consolidates in objects as worth. The consolidation of belief in propositions as truth-judgments would seem to eliminate the subjectivity of value and belief, that is, their psychic quality, as concepts externalize into non-cognitive objects. We congratulate ourselves on this exclusion of anterior process in achieving an impersonality that from the psychological standpoint is artificial. To identify value with worth displaces it to a world of supply and demand, which corresponds to availability and desire. The subjective feeling that objectifies in the world often wavers between mind and object. Do I desire a diamond because it is valuable or does its value (worth) depend on my desire? Worth is the final tributary of drive in a progression to a sought-after object. If the objective is the subjective objectified, a continuous transition occurs from the roots of value in drive, through desire, to the feeling that relates to the quality or rarity of the object and seems independent of the observer.

A conscious belief is intentional in that it is about an object, while a conscious value has the intentionality of desire. Desire has greater specificity than the implicit value that precedes it. Implicit value is the disposition to a category of belief or action. When value and belief achieve a category, concepts and pre-objects in the category are accompanied by conceptual-feeling, that is, desire, fear, etc., which exhibit value in the pre-object. Implicit values are dispositions that become explicit as desires. The relation of desire to value is that desire refers to the inner feeling of wanting or needing the object or state of affairs, while value refers to the thing wanted. We desire what we value and value what we desire, but this merely points to the distribution of feeling in the actualization process, whether intentional and closer to the self (desire) or ingredient in the content (value) of what the intentional is about. As conceptual feeling undergoes further partition, the concept is derived to an object, and feeling develops into that object as worth. In sum, implicit value is disposition or explicit desire when it is "located" in the mind, and worth when it is "located" in an object.

Some beliefs, true or false, are relatively independent of value, such as the belief that Paris is a city in France; others, such as the belief that people should pay taxes, are also valuations. Generally, to believe is to presume, not to know. In one sense, to say "I believe" is to leave the door open to proof. In another sense, belief is closer to conviction than knowledge. Announcing a belief implies uncertainty, for a belief with conviction is deeper, like faith. In everyday language to say "I believe" is like saying "I think," though thinking implies a productivity and rationality that are inessential to belief. Belief has a substantive meaning.

We do not use the term believing as an activity in the sense of thinking. A thought is an idea, but thinking is the search for ideas, while believing is not a search but a state of belief. Beliefs consist of categories, concepts or objects and facts. In some respects, thinking is a transition from deeper beliefs—implicit categories, pre-suppositions—to partial concepts or ideas, that is, from generality to particularity, as the potential content in a belief is parsed or analyzed.

Some beliefs are unshakeable, but most can be altered by new facts or experiences. Even the belief god does not exist can change if one has a mystical experience in which the actuality of god's presence is deeply felt. The reverse can occur, when life becomes unbearable and the turn to god only brings more suffering. The story of Abraham and Isaac illustrates the limit to which a belief is tested to determine if it is truly felt. While a change in belief can have profound effects on the relational system that all beliefs subtend, most beliefs are modes of knowing that, when conscious, are adaptive and thus can be demonstrated or disconfirmed.

Contents in consciousness become objects of judgment merely in becoming conscious. The absence of options in the unconscious is one of the hallmarks of true faith. In contrast, the derivation to consciousness is accompanied by choice, deliberation and, usually, weakened conviction. The conviction in an explicit belief or value owes to the implicit faith that drives it. An implicit belief that becomes a conscious statement is open to question. That is why we think that the insistence on truth in a declaration of love vitiates the force of unconscious feeling. Superficial or *explicit* beliefs are malleable, such as the belief a politician means what he says, or that a lover will be faithful, or that it will rain next Tuesday. The belief that one is in love, or is loved, falls in this category. To say, I believe I am in love, casts doubt on the authenticity of feeling; an unconscious belief one loves or is loved is less corrupted by uncertainty. Lewis (1936) writes that cynicism and idealism about women are twin fruits of the same branch. At this point, however, one has passed from love to appraisal.

Values are similar in this respect. The core or implicit values that make up character are relatively immutable, for example, those that underlie honesty or courage, while the explicit values into which they discharge adapt to circumstance. As with belief, the authenticity of feeling in conscious thought is tested in decision and flexibility. An explicit belief informs a judgment; an explicit value provides the feeling that the judgment is correct. A belief with factual support passes to knowledge; fact becomes belief when it is infused with value. For example, the belief that my arguments are correct comes from the coherence and value assigned to them, while the facts or references cited in my writing are chosen according to the value they import to the beliefs I want to communicate. Value is the hidden factor in the certainty of belief. A belief without a value, like a concept without a feeling, is a naked idea or fact, while a value without a belief is a disposition without a justification. Belief is the "container" of value, which is its motive force. Unconscious beliefs and values define the person, for they are relatively constant over time. Explicit beliefs and values are adaptive and malleable, but serve as intermittent guides to the constancy of character.

Facts are more than neutral data. Facts begin as values and beliefs and detach as objects that are real or true. The value in the fact becomes apparent when its validity is threatened. The belief that the fact is true is charged with value, which is the energetic factor in belief. Belief and value—concept and feeling—combine at all phases from the inception of the mind/brain state to its outcome in (as) the world. Most beliefs and values are tacit or implicit. The belief, the fact and the knowledge that the pavement under my feet will not collapse when I walk on it is not in my present awareness. Were I conscious of this possibility or that at any moment a brick might fall on my head or I might have a stroke—the imminence of possible disaster—life would be terrifying. This occurs in some people. One thinks of the painter, Edvard Munch, as death-obsessed. We manage to cope by denial, distraction, and the replacement of grim thoughts by lighter diversions, immediate experience and future pleasures. Reason and distraction cannot allay the intrusion of a powerful belief, but the knowledge that, for example, a sudden collapse of the self or the pavement is statistically improbable, helps to offset a morbid fixation.

The belief in love, for god and a beloved

The mix of belief and value is critical in human relations. To believe one is in love is to have a special affection for someone; love is the value of that person to the lover. The hope contained in a belief is the trace of uncertainty that the love is genuine or reciprocated. One falls in love and hopes to be loved in return, but only when the belief is well-founded does conviction set in, often as much for love given as received. If one asks, am I in love, the answer to the question is probably no. Lovers who are uncertain if love is reciprocated search the eyes and gestures of the beloved for signs of love ... or its pretense. For the lover, feeling overpowers belief. Trust in the beloved, the belief one is loved, the wish to love and be loved—conscious hope or unconscious faith—is stronger than certain knowledge. Intuition plays a role when belief lacks conviction, as hope tries to interpret the beloved's intent. Belief and valuation; conviction and value, are inseparable. Love overcomes uncertainty and is the sincerest form of valuation, while a mitigation of value or belief opens the door to doubt.

The belief in love is unlike the belief that one could fall into a sinkhole, for love is immune to reason and not influenced by probabilities. Unlike travel on a plane, where one is reassured to know there is a one in a million chance of a crash, we do not say there is an 80% chance we love someone or a 60% probability we are loved. The value of the beloved makes the belief true irrespective of an "objective" judgment of the likelihood of genuine passion or lasting union. In fact, in true love, the longing to be together does not dwell on the future, but rather on loneliness in the present. Cracks in the union appear when future considerations replace immediacy of contact. True love is not true in the ordinary sense, for it is founded on false beliefs; it is true in the sense of certainty, the absence of doubt and the belief that what matters most is feeling in the now.

There are many who, for various reasons, say they do not believe in love and by implication that true love does not exist or has no value. The lack of belief in love is a bit like atheism, where a denial of god's existence forecloses the possibility of love for god, as well as god's love for the individual. The skeptic would say that a candid analysis based on reason and evidence suggests that the love for a person or god is an illusion, a neurosis or some other pathology, in any event, contrary to a rational, if dispiriting, even nihilistic view of nature. Is the lack of belief in romantic love like not believing in god, ghosts or fairies? The one is disbelief or cynicism for a feeling that goes against "selfish genes" and the grain of evolution, where judgment follows feeling, the other, where feeling follows judgment, concerns the existence of the object of the belief.

Even more than a beloved, god, ghosts, and fairies are entities for which faith is required to overcome doubt. What is a belief without an object? One can believe love exists yet doubt the existence of a personal object to love. One can give up the search, or believe one is incapable of loving, or think those who believe in love are deluded. A person who rejects the possibility of true love, or interprets love as dependency, a negotiation of power or a neurotic alliance, may deny the possibility of love for another and exhibit behavior that could be described as narcissism or self-love. Self-love can replace or deter true love, but it is more like the exertion of will in the service of self than a love of self as an actual or ideal object.

The similarity of the denial of romantic love to atheism in religious belief, *inter alia*, is a rejection of the possibility of a loving companion—the beloved, god—to share or mitigate life's joys and sorrows. The lover has an object to be loved, that is, the beloved, while love of god supposes a belief in god's existence. Lacking this belief, there is no entity to love. In human relations one says, my lover is not the person I thought him or her to be, which in a sense denies existence to love's original object. The beloved who is no longer the person once loved has ceased to exist as such in the mind of the lover, as has the belief that the person has great value. In religious feeling, however, god exists or not, but does not change if the devotee turns away. We do not think that if the concept of god changes, so too does god, except for a god of process or nature in continuous transformation.

A shift may occur from a personal to an impersonal god, or from a god with such human attributes as love, mercy, and forgiveness to a divine presence identified with natural process. This is not a god one loves. If the belief in a god outside nature shifts to a god identified with natural process, the feeling of oneness or personal union is no longer possible—there is no personal god—and the feeling likely shifts to one of awe and reverence. This is comparable to the shift of a beloved from a sacred ideal to an unholy other. One can believe in the existence of a personal god without loving god, but one cannot feel god's love without belief. One can believe in god and feel abandoned, as with a lover. One can believe in god yet doubt god's love or mercy, as one believes in the value of a beloved yet feels deserted or unloved. The capacity to love god is comparable to the capacity to love another person. Both involve the capacity to love, which implies the capacity to surrender one's will; and in both, true love is devout, unquestioning, and ideal.

Does a lack of belief in love apply only to romantic love or love of god, or to other forms of loving? A person may be passionate about food, clothing, jewelry, or other things, and have no desire to love or be loved. Such individuals, like those who love pets and shun people, the solitary or miserly, probably have a seed of regret for past misjudgments, low self-esteem or the reverse, an exaggerated sense of self worth, misanthropy, and/or disdain for others. In some people there may be an inability to form ideals, though idealization involves category-formation and should be universal, even if more pronounced in certain people. Perhaps in some a *negative* ideal of what is unappealing holds all qualities hostage to the negative ones. Ideal ugliness, evil or falsehood is no less conceivable than ideal beauty, goodness, or truth. This includes individuals who prefer the macabre or the outré, those who find pleasure in torment, and those for whom mendacity is more satisfying than truthfulness. For them, hate is as powerful and persistent an emotion as love. The negative value of a despised object is proportionate to the positive valuation of one that is loved.

Religious belief captures the tension between positive and negative ideals in the conflict of good and evil, or god and the devil. One can believe in god without believing in the devil, as one can believe in a force for good in the world without an opposing force, save ignorance. The devil provides a concrete image for misfortune and wickedness, for which a loving, idealized god cannot be responsible. A reasoned disbelief in god is more than an absence of need or faith; it reinforces isolation and the pride of certainty, and has consequences for the belief in all ideals as well as for intuition, the sense of mystery and the reverence for a complexity and beauty beyond understanding. For some, infinite complexity, order and beauty are equivalent to divinity; for others, these properties just exist and can be admired without religious feeling, though I would contend it is a small step from the grandeur and awe-inspiring complexity of the universe to an intuition of the divine.

Some people never believe in love, or never know love; others no longer believe in love, perhaps as the outcome of a judgment based on experience. They may see love as a fairy tale inconsistent with self-interest and evolution. Their mistrust is conditioned on disappointment, trauma, loss, or betrayal. When the conditions of life are unforgiving, daily struggle tends to infantilize love as foolishness. Others who suffer the same fate see love as their salvation, or a palliative for despair. In human relations, the incapacity or unwillingness to love can result from a loveless or injurious childhood, though abuse may be repeated or surmounted. What accounts for this difference? Does the fear of loss, of fragmentation or assimilation, restrain the person from the surrender that is essential to true love? Jung wrote, "where love reigns, there is no will to power; and where the will to power is paramount, love is lacking."

If love is ultimate valuation, does its negation imply an absence of all valuation save for objects that reinforce self-need or self-worth? If the love of others presupposes, as some believe, the love (valuation) of self, do those who deny or reject love no longer believe in their own worth? More likely, they care too little for the worth of others. The enemies of love are narcissism, arrogance, and pride. This is also the case for the ascetic—whether a Christian mystic, a yoga or Hinayana Buddhist—where self-absorption is notorious in spite of a reputation for humility. Only the selfish ignore others for a life of denial, penitence, and preparation for the hereafter.

Atheism in love—to coin a term, *aphilia, misophilia,* or *anerotica*—may not be the absence of need for the other but acquiescence to impersonal judgment. A person who relies too heavily on reason will invariably find fault with others and favor those who satisfy rational, not emotional, needs. A need for oneness with the other (or god) makes love possible, but there can also be a need for a self-sufficiency in which others are excluded. Personal necessity alone is the death knell of otherness; an excess of autonomy is an astringent to attachment that is not subordinate to personal gain. Perhaps a particular genetic configuration promotes bonding, like that in Bonobo chimpanzees. Time is relevant in that love is centered on present feeling and openness to future possibilities. The inability to give one's self to the present is a challenge to romantic (or religious) fusion. It endangers the immediacy of feeling that is essential to the richness and power of love, while doubt as to the future, hesitation, uncertainty, threaten the hope, trust, and receptiveness on which love depends. The story of the young man who asked Socrates if he should get married and was told, son, whatever you do you'll regret it, implies that love has slim chances to survive when the very question signals a doubt that is love's antidote.

Some say love favors the innocent or naïve, or that it is an intermittent and passing emotion initiated by physical attraction and stirred by sexual desire. Sexual attraction is often the foundation of romantic love, with sexual coupling the initial stage of loving and a fusion of the concrete that may precede the oneness of selves. The intimacy, unguarded openness and vulnerability of sexual union, the penetration and fusion of bodies, are surrogates for oneness. When the sexual is founded on self-pleasure it is easily mistaken for love. The individual gives what is necessary to seduce a lover or to have pleasure reciprocated. Physical fusion is part of normal mating. Psychic fusion is unique and transcends the carnality on which it is founded and with which it is often confused.

The vagaries and inconstancies of romantic love lead many to reject passion for friendship, but even friendship and filial love are inconstant and confounded by habit, familiarity, obligation, loneliness, and dependency. Many would say love for others or for things is a compensation that fills a void. The saying, if you want a friend get a dog, speaks to an endemic mistrust brought on less by disbelief in love than an inability to sustain it. There are as many reasons for not believing in love as for loving, and no doubt as many love as do not love, or cannot love, or for whom the feeling is rare or unknown.

Love is a fragile gift that can fade with too much or too little contact; conversely, love may grow in memory when the beloved is gone and the ideal remains. Daily chores, children, new encounters, desensitize lovers to original feeling, care, and nourishment. We know those for whom love grows over the years, when the ideal is not weakened by judgment, when love flourishes in spite of forgetting or experience, and the person could never fall in love again. But we also know those in whom a seemingly genuine love is questioned when a stronger love comes along. Even the most intense or resilient love can be obliterated by one that is more passionate.

Except for passion and value there is little uniformity among lovers. The capacity to love, its intensity and sincerity, are conditioned by the needs and character of a given individual. Even the fact that one does not believe in love does not prevent a revival of faith should the right partner come along, as when love emerges in a sudden encounter or the unexpected deepening or sexualizing of a friendship. We tend to think that skepticism or denial is a kind of resistance or self-protection against the distress of not finding true love, or the likelihood that love leads to heartbreak, as in the Tina Turner song, "who needs a heart when a heart can be broken." Judgment weighed against expectation often ends in despair, disappointment or indifference.

We hear many reasons for giving up on love, but reasons are justifications or excuses, so a deeper source of doubt or cynicism must exist, of which the individual is dimly if at all aware. Is love voluntary or involuntary? Do we decide to fall in love or not? Do we promote an incapacity or unwillingness to love, or the capacity to resist it? When we say love does not exist, do we really mean it? Is love a socially conditioned delusion, a false belief? Attachment to others may be real in parental bonding for it is part of our animal inheritance. But beyond attachment, would we say there is only self-interest, which may or may not include love?

Individuals give many reasons for not loving, some relating to the love object, some to the self; others to risks, rewards, and fears. They think of love as an investment of time and self, and choose a partner based on the economy of mutual advantage. Whether or not they believe in love, they forsake the search and settle for a safe harbor of companionship or material advantage over a storm of passionate uncertainty. Some choose a life alone, unencumbered by obligation, compromise, and self-restraint. Those unaccustomed to receiving love may remain detached and emotionally barren; the sociopath is the extreme. Reasons for an absence of love differ, but what is common is the character of the core self and whether the need for others is sufficient for sacrifice.

Commitment

The commitment to an object or activity, a beloved or any object, is based on the value of the object or activity and the belief that it is valuable. The commitment can arise from a sense of responsibility or duty, as well as passion and need, but all such reasons or justifications are intertwined with the value of the object and the needs of the individual. A person who is committed to a profession feels value in the work or in personal esteem or satisfaction. The degree of commitment ranges from duty to pleasure, from gratification to absorption, even obsession, yet all involve a valuation of the object to the exclusion of competing interests. One could suppose the lack of such interests accentuates the value of the one that remains, that is, that commitment is as much an absence of alternatives as a preference for the one or, at least after an initial stage of preference, options narrow down to habitual choices. As in other aspects of mental life, commitment is sculpted by the elimination of alternatives.

The belief that an object is valuable is an affirmation of its value. For others, the value of an object may appear independent of the belief. A person might feel obligation or engagement in a mindless, undemanding routine, or the work might be felt to be important and a source of pride and pleasure. The irrationality of commitment does not betray its lack of intrinsic or societal value. I am reminded of an acquaintance, an eighty-four-year-old proctologist, who was lamenting the lack of patients. I said to him, "Tell me, David, with all respect, have you not seen enough hemorrhoids in your life"? After reflecting for a moment, he replied, in all sincerity, "Well, yes, I suppose you are right. But now and then an anal fistula comes along." The charm of the remark was only equaled by its pathos. For many—for those "lives of quiet desperation"—it is not the felt value of work (marriage, etc.) but the absence of alternatives that plays a decisive role.

In sum

Value is feeling centered in an object or idea; belief expresses the concept out of which the object develops. Desire goes out to the object and is intentional. To desire or value a thing is to say the thing has (personal) value. In its dual meaning relating to desire and worth, value is closer to the object. We see this in the temporal aspect, with desire pointing to the future, and value to present feeling, in the verb-function of desire and the noun- or property-function of value. One *points to* something, the other *is in* something. Desire is a trajectory. Value also has a trajectory but the locus of worth is sought after in desire. In value, the self is in relation to objects, as when one says, I value that object or it is valuable to me. The feeling of value projected onto objects gives it an intentional quality. When value is a judgment as to worth, the act of judging, not the value, is intentional. The *aboutness* in value is a metapsychological inference. In this regard, being in love does not have the intentionality of the belief or declaration that one is in love.

Love is the greatest positive value we impart to objects or ideas. Love and passion for objects have a locus in mind. The passage of value from mind to world saps objects of feeling; their resorption into mind re-ignites emotions at a phase before they trickle outward to the world. The force of feeling in psyche is more pronounced at the proximal (intrapersonal or pre-object) than distal (extra-personal or object) segment. One can be as passionate for a political concept or idea as for the ideal of a beloved; in both, intensity of feeling points to an inner, psychic locus that diminishes, or turns to judgment, when a concept objectifies. Value is intra-personal in love, but when the dominant locus is in the world it shifts to *evaluation*. Feeling then turns to judgment and the affective quality of the object dissolves into appraisal.

An object actualizes a concept. The feeling in a concept becomes the value in an object partly in the world, partly in the mind; that is, the beloved *has* value and *is* valued. An object, a thing, a beloved, is an objectified concept, along with its externalized affect. The difference between concept and object owes, *inter alia*, to degree of externality, adaptation (by sensation), and individuation. Value—initially as existence, then as attention, then as worth—can expand or constrict with the field. When feeling is evenly distributed in the field, one believes (trusts, has conviction) in the existence (value) of all objects, that is, in the reality of the world. One feels and believes in the signification of a single object when attention sequesters in a beloved or other object of interest (fear, etc.). Since feeling is felt as intra-psychic and love grows in the imagination, and since images and ideas are, in some sense, less real than objects, the enhanced reality of the beloved gives the feeling of unreality like a dream, an hallucination or illusion.[1] The idealization of the beloved, the lack of objectivity, the resistance to the opinions of others, gives the impression of an illusion or misperception. At the same time, the heightened luminance of the beloved leads the lover to perceive reality with fresh eyes, as if for the first time, and the lover asks, is love real and reality an illusion, or is love (value) an illusion that is a screen from the real? In everyday terms, the lover asks, is this real or am I going crazy?

Love and madness

An illusion is a derailed perception; a delusion is a false belief. One can falsely believe that one loves or is loved, and misperceive the intentions of a lover. Lovers can be delusional, but is love itself an illusion or delusion, unlike other psychic phenomena? Children who believe in Santa Claus have uncertain knowledge of the world. Adults with such beliefs are delusional, even psychotic, if the belief persists and governs behavior. Some beliefs that are not open to reason, say the denial of evolution and the belief in intelligent design, or the belief by many that the planet has been visited, even populated, by aliens, we chalk off to ignorance or gullibility. This is also true for deeply held political beliefs and loyalties. Political ideologues who are rabid in their belief, closed to doubt and refractory to argument condemn adversaries as stupid, mendacious or victims of propaganda. The intolerance for rational dialogue, the certainty and resistance to confrontation, are characteristics of delusion and more often associated with false than true belief. That such ideation is near-universal exposes the roots of delusion in normal thought.

A strongly held belief, one with overriding conviction, points not to the truth or power of the belief alone but to underlying values or motivations that can, in principle, be dissociated from the belief itself. The belief can be deconstructed into what is believed and the (unconscious) motivation for holding the belief so strongly. A false belief can be justified as rational when its content is based in external reality, or it is a false interpretation of accepted observations. In the pseudo-science of astrology or fortune telling, or in the unproven ideas of a young science, a false belief taken as true becomes an *idée fixe* that is transitional to delusion.

It is easy to spot a delusion if someone believes he is persecuted by Martians, but not so simple when the belief is plausible, or when the belief is widespread in a culture, such as totemic or magical thinking. In a developed community, the distinction is still more difficult, whether it is harmless beliefs such as the value of health food supplements, or more pernicious ones, such as racism and prejudice. The unreality of the content, the encapsulation of the belief and how widely accepted it is in the culture are among the features that distinguish a person who is naïve, eccentric, muddled in thinking, "brain-washed," loony, deranged, or delusional. We don't say the belief in a personal god is a mass delusion, but even the religious would be suspicious if someone claimed to hear god's voice. The transition from a false or implausible belief to one that defies reason can be missed if other signs of delusion are wanting. There is nothing unusual about a person who believes that dreams predict the future or that people are reunited in heaven, but if the belief is so pervasive that it affects, even dominates, behavior, or is associated with flights of fantasy or other unsustainable ideas, the delusional quality becomes clear. In cases of confabulation or in the megalomania of tertiary syphilis one can be hard-pressed to distinguish an accurate account of personal events from pure fabrication. If a person says he hears noises in the attic and insists there are hundreds of rats, it may or may not be true, but if he claims the attic is filled with little green men the diagnosis is obvious. The amnesic who fabricates is closer to reality and the content can be manipulated by suggestion, while schizophrenic paramnesia is closer to fantasy or dream and the content is relatively resistant to suggestion.

Belief translates to action depending on the intensity of feeling (value) invested in it. Value gives conviction as a motivating force to action (or inaction). The psychotic or brain-damaged individual has a delusion that reflects individual trends in personality, while "normal" delusion occurs in a social context. In the absence of evidence, like-minded others reinforce the belief. Solitary individuals who believe in a conspiracy are often dismissed as erratic, paranoid or mad until a critical mass of believers gathers and the belief is taken seriously. This occurs in all areas of thought. Examples in science are phlogiston theory, the ether, alchemy, and geocentric astronomy. I would add to this list modern-day cognitivism. The way a false rumor spreads through a crowd, the violence of mobs acting without justification, are everyday examples. No wonder individuals are so ready to accept protestations of love and believe in what they hear and say. The belief one is in love can be manipulated. One can convince oneself it is true, as well as others. When the belief that one is loved is discovered to be false there is disappointment, but true love is not a false belief for those who believe it, even if others disagree and even if the passion conforms to some aspects of delusion. A political or religious ideology that drives behavior to an irrational extreme is labeled pathological or criminal. Similarly, the madness of lovers is a microcosm of the insanity of the mob. The belief that one is in love is intensified by the belief that one is loved in return. *Folie a deux* or shared delusion is probably a necessary condition of passionate love.

Lovers leave the ordinary world for a world of shared ideals. They live in a private universe of thought, dream or fantasy, not a public forum of discourse and common objects. In their ideal world, the boundaries of self are fluid. The beloved is incorporated into the core values and beliefs of the lover so that, truly, one can say lovers are of one mind, one self. The dissolution of self, its assimilation with the other, the breakdown of autonomy and individuality, the impress of the poetic, of magic and metaphor over the claims of reason and demonstration, the dream from which one is loath to awaken, the transport, the union, the *Liebestod*, life out of death, or the preference to death over separation, are features of passionate love as *folie a deux*. The storied madness of lovers, like the delusion of those who share a belief, true or false, can become a rationale for existence.

Delusion occurs with true as well as false beliefs, or rather, the truth of the belief is not essential to the delusion. The psychotic who believes the world is a dream is not irrational if he is a philosopher or a believer in Asian religion, only if there is action on the belief. Or one could say to have a conscious belief is one thing, to feel it deeply is another. The belief that we are meaningless dust in an indifferent universe on a scale beyond comprehension can lead to terror, alienation, even madness if not offset by the opposing belief in meaning, value, purpose, and love. The point of view from the standpoint of an outer reality is taken to be the foundation of truth, while the subjective point of view, to the extent it departs from objectivity, is taken as somewhere between opinion and delusion. A subjectivity that maps to the world is rational, but as much an illusion as that which is a symptom of psychosis. The unreal is a cure for the madness of thought stagnant in an objectivity irreconcilable with personal feeling.

In everyday life, a belief that is provisionally true and later found to be false—say, that chocolate is harmful or that having a child can save a failing marriage—can as easily serve as the basis of delusion as a belief thought to be false and later proven to be true. In science and in society, both outcomes occur, in science especially with novel ideas, in everyday life when a person "jumps to a conclusion" and later realizes the error. In science, a new idea is usually derided as false until it is accepted as true, while false beliefs are defended until they are bypassed or refuted. What is needed is an augmentation of the belief at the expense of competing or mitigating beliefs. A zealot who goes about arguing that the earth is round can be as crazy as one who argues that it is flat. A person who believes that people need to be convinced of an established fact must have a touch of madness. Still, to treat fact as belief is the beginning of productive thought, though it can lead to other outcomes, including delusion. A person who questions a scientific fact is often treated as a pariah.

Thought becomes pathological in the context of an irrationality that is maladaptive, that is, socially inappropriate, or injurious to self or others. A novel idea treated as delusion, that is, as a false belief before it is proven to be true, has been the death, and occasional re-birth, of many a professional career. A more or less rational belief can remain innocuous until inflamed by feeling (value) to irrational action. The lover who is a suicide or dies in a duel, or grieves for a lost or unrequited love, or discards a promising career in pursuit of a beloved, or submits to degradation and humiliation, or lives in hermetic isolation, in a word, goes beyond the limits in any sphere of conduct, exhibits delusional thinking regardless of the truth or authenticity of the belief. The risk and the lure of love is to leave *terra firma* and dive into the quicksand of possibility, even to the point of suffocation in blissful surrender. To define delusion as false belief misses the whole point of delusional thought, the uncertainties, the transitions, what is false and what is true, what is belief, and what is the role of feeling irrespective of the truth.

Certainty of belief is often a sign of wrong-headedness, but this does not mitigate the vivacity of the belief that one is in love. If love is madness, it is a madness many seek, for life is drab without it in one form or another: lover, family, work, hobby. False belief takes precedence in delusion when the content is bizarre, but falsehood has an appeal in arousing the process of truth-finding. A false belief that does not descend to the paralysis of dogma can propagate in the imagination. The absence of evidence allows fantasy to reign, and this can generate poetic or rational truths. A true belief leads to closure in fact and consensus. Shaw said that soldiers and lovers are irrational, for otherwise they would neither fight nor marry. A stirring act of courage lies in overcoming the rational fear of dying, one based on the *near* certainty of a true belief.

For creative activity, the truth of a belief must be held in abeyance for a novel truth to emerge. The hermeneutic of love brings individuality into relief against the dreary, the mundane, and uninspired. So what if love is an illusion? So what if one's beliefs are false? These are trivial objections compared to the new-found intensity, the thrill on seeing one's lover, the emptiness that is now overflowing, the rhapsodic excitement where before there was tedium and yes, the madness and the obsession. Like the descent of Orpheus into Hades, we risk sanity for passion in a regress to the chaos of the unconscious. Life in the living is measured by such moments, not only love but other beliefs—religious, military, political—where there is zeal, camaraderie and dedication to a purpose greater than oneself, even when belief and action are irrational. Such episodes survive in memory as peaks of lived experience.

In the course of life many mourn the passing of love and hope it will return, though at some point the desire to be in love will fade, perhaps also the need, with some even grateful to no longer be seized by passion. In consolation, we realize, often too late, that life is more than a succession of loves and lovers; it comprises of durations of felt experience—weddings, anniversaries, intimate moments, the birth of a child, accomplishments, travel—but in the actuality of living, love turns the boredom of routine into a life of existential immediacy.

Rupture

An intense love can vanish with a word, evaporate on a misunderstanding, or insensitive remark. How fragile is a love that cannot withstand a foolish jest, a jealous glance, a moment of detachment, a slight coolness, an oversight, or lack of ardor? The likely response is that it was never love at all, infatuation perhaps, for true love would not unravel so quickly and for so slight a cause. Perhaps this is the case for those who suddenly fall in love knowing little of each other, where there are seeds of uncertainty and distrust in all encounters. The rupture occurs because the misstep reveals an involuntary leakage of deeper sentiments concealed in the warblings of love-birds. This raises the question: are the truer signs of character the dependable continuities of speech and gesture or their disjunct in an episodic surprise?

Feeling can change and belief will follow, as a change in belief alters feeling. An intense love validates the belief that one is in love and supports the belief that one is loved in return. The lover must believe the reciprocity is genuine and that the beloved is worthy of the sacrifice. A belief that one's love is authentic is guaranteed by the feeling that inhabits the belief, but belief and feeling are hostage to life's conditions, events that deliver the lover to the moment, prior loss and disappointment. The belief that the feelings of the beloved are genuine and similar to one's own is more tenuous. This explains why lovers go to great lengths to convince a beloved of their love. It also explains the gravity of the slightest gesture, as the lover searches for signs that the love is genuine. The old song, "little things mean a lot," implies that small acts that point to character have a greater value than constant protestations.

The irony is that for belief to seek evidence of love in the acts of the beloved is in opposition to the subjectivity of personal feeling and belief. The object of love is in the world, but love begins in the imagination, as the conceptual sources of the object intensify. An inference as to whether the beliefs and feelings of the other are genuine signifies a passage to judgment based on objective criteria, that is, the actual evidence one is loved. In romantic love, as in the love of god, the power of love and the intensity of belief are blind to contradiction. The belief in love, like faith, does not rest on evidence. The idealization of the beloved—as with god—may include infallibility or perfection, while the motives of the beloved are equally inscrutable. In both, the power of love can overcome doubt and, again in both, the love given and the faith one is loved are decisive, not the final truth of what is believed. To say that one is foolish to love a person, or a god, who gives no evidence of love in return, ignores the fact that love is independent of truth. Love ignores objectivity to seek tacit approval in approximating the ideal in mind-external and in so doing elevates the spirit in life, art, literature, and music, even in science.

Note

1. In medieval verse, the lover is the Dreamer who converses with, combats and defeats the rival for his mistress, Reason. (Lewis, 1936)

CHAPTER TEN

Philosophy of romantic love

They declaim against the passions without bothering to think that it is from their flame philosophy lights its torch.

—Marquis de Sade

Introduction

The self becomes aware of the web of entanglement that underlies illusory autonomy when the luxury of choice is vexed by uncertainty and the gift of free will becomes the curse of indecision. The ideal will that is truly free is independent of opinions and coercions as well as personal bias, habit, and loyalties, a self so autonomous it is, in Kant's view, free even of time and history. The movement to autonomy that is the direction of process is unveiled by insight or unraveled by love. The starting point of philosophy should be the inception of thought in a ground of supposition and shared feeling guided by unconscious belief and valuation. A philosopher of originality knows that creative work is a descent to an imagination gravid with ideas that are for the most part discarded in the discovery of bare fact. Denuded of their contextual and micro-temporal history, facts alone are meaningless; their meaning is buried in the process of discovery. The shaping ideas that interpret the facts are hidden in the implicit beliefs and values of which facts are distal realizations. The unstated goal of discovery is to make history obsolete. This is why each wave of speculation repeats fragments of a past that is forgotten, or cannot be revived in its richness and with effort wasted in the debate about what is known rather than the process of fact-creation.

We sense the depth of a philosophy when it bypasses surface controversy for the undersurface of conscious thought. Discourse burrows into conceptual layers beneath what is illuminated. In the sphere of love, this means that the beloved is not waiting to be discovered, or that the other is appraised on being revealed, but is uncovered from within. The loved object begins as fact, like the givens of philosophy, or the techniques of an art form, or the scriptures of a religion. In each of these pursuits, a return to the breeding ground of fact delivers novelty out of an individual past into a communal present. The beloved, or a creative or mystical idea, or a proposition, all develop out of meaning and conceptual-feeling. The self arises each moment with minimal change, but there are times when it is transformed in acts of creativity, or in love and religious or mystical sensibility. The Christian who is "born again" by an acceptance of Christ in his heart undergoes a literal rebirth. The embodiment of self with god, or self with the beloved, or with an intuition or idea in artistic inspiration, can only occur when there is immersion with the object at a depth of engagement. This immersion rescues a solitary life, one that is no less fraudulent for its insularity than for its superficial contacts. The implication for philosophy is that a germinal idea, like a seed that sprouts beneath the soil, will propagate many shoots if it is well tended and encouraged with care.

Perhaps the most profound transformation occurs when the unconscious core assimilates to the beloved, who is first perceived indifferently, then with interest, and then, as a sudden event or in a gradual devolution, recedes to the shadows where anterior phases rekindle a self that is transfigured. This dual self of lover and beloved recurs in the constancy of genuine love as a fantasy, an apparition, or ideal transfixed in the imagination. The other can, of course, be left unloved in the world or later displaced to the world from the mind. But in conceptual embrace, the natural boundaries of individuality weaken, idealization is facilitated and the other does not fully objectify. Assimilation and idealization depend on inclusion of the other in an autonomous self. Absorbing the other is comparable to surrendering the self, which is also felt when the self does not possess an image or idea but is possessed by it. The rapture that accompanies an assimilation of self and idea has similarities with the oneness of genuine love.

Mystics understand the difference between faith/belief and knowledge/perception, the power of love, the limitation of fact, union versus attachment, inward descent and outward exploration, all relinquished in oneness with nature, with the beloved or a loving god. The makers of myths told of journeys as trials, a passage through the animal preconscious. The great soul seeks truth in dark places, creating the beloved as a prize of knowledge and the goal of conscious thought. In the shift from fantasy to reality, from myth to fact, from dream to perception, the interior voyage to and from the ground of being, where self and other begin, is a narrative of transfiguration. Yet it is reasonable to ask how far one can take this idea. After all, the other is not found in a hermit's cave, but is sought in the world. Is the other an external object for consciousness or a figural embodiment of unconscious longing? What part of love is objective, what part invention? Is the objectivity of choice incompatible with the spontaneity of genuine loving? Is the retreat to subjectivity a preparation for wonderment or an aftermath of deliberation?

Love and reason

A love that follows rational affirmation supposes a piecemeal disassembly and perusal of attributes: the physical features of shape, size, contour, motion of body parts, and the psychic attributes of sincerity, generosity, humor, wit, loyalty. Traits are assigned a certain, even numerical, value.[1] Judgment implies a metric of qualities. In this, it is quantitative, like a grade or score. Is love hostage to an aggregate of valuations? How fragile is a love that lives on an exchange of justifications?

The microgenetic formulation rejects appraisal in favor of revival and renewal. Reason is not the death of passion, but once it appears, love is on life-support. Better the neurotics of dependency than the nostrums of shared tenancy. The authenticity in need is unlike the allocation of responsibility. Two "half-hearted" efforts do not sum to a whole. Concession is not authentic giving. The effort shows subordination and lack of wholeness. The dream of irrational passion lives on in the need for disintegration that is the essence of love, even in an age where selecting a mate is like shopping for an apartment, sizing up a meal or reviewing a film, an age when relations are easily tattered and "trade-offs" are the rule. The innocence of the open soul can rapidly become the cynicism of the rational skeptic, as enchantment turns to deception. Reverence and sanctity have little signification in social or commercial transactions, to which love is not immune. Relations of power, as in the balance of domination and submission, may have the virtue of a love based on need. The wish for love recurs in fantasy, late into life, but most settle for what they can get. Why chase the blue bird of happiness when one has a chicken in the coop?

The central problem for judgment is that consciousness and reason do not instigate; consciousness of decision comes after the matter is decided. Acts are instigated and parsed to outcomes in which distal segments add, at best, a final veto to unconscious urge. Impulses are modified to finalities by a succession of constraints that weaken the force of drive (will). The partiality and detachment of conscious thought lessen the force and totality of unconscious need. The necessity of adaptation to the surround entails a loss of what is inessential, including that which the self needs but the world rejects. Judgment entertains options without the authenticity of need, which arises from below in the power of unreflecting urge. A scrutiny of options is judicious but reflexive, thus timid, heartless. Love *ab origine* is for the beloved, the all-in-all, the antidote to a life offered to many but given to few.

Can there be a philosophy of love that does not appeal to judgment or appraisal? The deeper question is what part reason plays in love. Is reason essential to the selection of the beloved, or inimical to passion? If reason is impersonal or dispassionate, how can it lead to love? If reason is swayed by emotion, how can we feel passion for those vetted by it? Obviously, we do not fall in love with just anyone, and when we are in love we may be at a loss to explain why, but the fact that one falls in love with A, not B, C, or D implies that choice is involved, albeit implicit or intuitive. In the pragmatic or adaptive sense, choice is rational depending on the ends to which it is directed, not necessarily the means by which those ends are achieved. Reason implies a process of reasoning, not an outcome of thought that appears rational. An animal might flee from a predator and we would count the response as rational, though reason does not play a role in the action. Human thought might lead to a logical conclusion reached by an "illogical" process. A dream might be taken as a premonition and, by chance, a catastrophe averted. What is adaptive is rational even if not arrived at by rational thought.

Moreover, reason can arrive at outcomes that, when tested in the world, were in retrospect irrational, say a life decision based on the statistical likelihood of an act of terrorism or a volcanic eruption, or the logical conclusion of a premiss that is false. This applies to human coupling, where there is a kind of logic in selection, even if the outcome is not reached by deliberation, or judged poorly by others, or proves later to be a misfortune.

On these grounds, it is logical that a masochist should choose and be chosen by a sadist, though the "choice" is motivated by needs that could be termed irrational, even pathological. To select a lover by unconscious need, not conscious desire, or to have desire driven by unconscious conflicts that are self-destructive or aberrant in spite of a satisfaction of the core, tends to be interpreted as an abnormal or unthinking act, with the self a victim of an egocentric partner or self-punitive wish, or an inadequate, that is, "needy," personality. The Stockholm syndrome in hostage taking or kidnapping, when the victim develops affection for her captors, illustrates the centrality of need (to survive, to avoid danger) over desire, when the fundamentals of desire in choice are blocked and the satisfaction of need, in survival, governs behavior. When need figures strongly in desire, the unconscious sources of desire become obvious. The match may seem to have logic, but it is nonetheless irrational, because it appeals to one facet of the personality or because it is one side of an oppositional tendency, as in submission and domination, while the person as a whole, that is, the full set of needs, remains unsatisfied.

This begs the question of what kind of wholeness is realized in union. If the coupling is based on sexual need, we assume a deprivation of needs that are non-sexual. For both sexual and non-sexual need, partial satisfaction is seen as deficiency and the union is considered to be a surrender to impulse or a compromise of character. An attraction that is purely sexual, even when for a time it is satisfying, ignores the greater psychology of the person, while a non-sexual love that is psychologically but not sexually fulfilling is more like friendship or familial affection. This is true not only of love that satisfies the psychological and not the sexual, but also of one that partly satisfies both in the faint hope—or its demise—that true love will come along. The assumption in traditional match-making was that a young couple would naturally come to love each other in the course of sharing a life (and a bed), or at least this was a desirable outcome. It would be hard to prove that relationships created in this way are less likely to produce an enduring emotional union than when young people first fall in love and then get married.

There are many forms of deprivation for which love is a panacea, but it is usually no cure for unhappiness. The root of unhappiness is the feeling of incompleteness or lack of wholeness, which can result from bad luck or poor choices, but is ultimately the inability to accept deprivation, which has as many faces as the dissatisfactions and failed expectations that are their cause. How one copes with a situation is a mark of character and implicit values. Every loss is an injury to the self. The imperfections of the individual can be assimilated in the other or become pronounced by their exclusion. For many, the void that is unhappiness is a garden where love can flower, but in the sphere of the affections, unless one is unhappy solely for the lack of love, love is more often a source of unhappiness than a cure.

Take the homosexual, in whom the absence of genital contact, or the inability or reluctance to satisfy a parental urge, or the recourse to psychological and legal fictions of various kinds, or the lack of gender complementarity even when there are compensations, can be felt as loss or incompleteness. In spite of "gay pride" and efforts to enhance self-esteem, many homosexuals are profoundly unhappy. This is not a condemnation. In heterosexual couples, after initial excitement has abated, the ideal, even in genuine love, often condenses to assessment, objectivity, and detachment. Areas of dissatisfaction or incompleteness find novel interests or coping strategies, or the love is not sustained.

Judgment

The objectivity of judgment or the aboutness of the intentional is antithetical to oneness, in that the other is distinct from the self and the beloved is no longer an ideal, if he or she ever was, but is perceived as a more or less impersonal object along with others in the field. Qualities compelled by reason are not those of an engaged love—absorption, obsession, fantasy, self-sacrifice—but are properties that pass from one interacting solid to another, as from an appraiser to the object being appraised, traits such as fairness, thoughtfulness, sharing, respect, and an assessment of strengths, weaknesses, the good and the bad, the quantitative inventory of likes and dislikes through which the lover navigates. These rational qualities are not the ingredients of love but its hoped-for accompaniments, at best, the evaluations of the reasonableness of a union. Reason desexualizes attraction and delegitimizes immersion. Like any dry concept, the rational is incompatible with extremes of emotion, while the marvel of true passion is its headstrong incaution and the involuntary rush of feeling.

It is doubtful whether the qualities of reason can be prerequisites for love, which has its own rules and obligations. Were it the case, absolute truthfulness between lovers—which to begin with is inconsistent with idealization and fantasy—would trump discretion and tact. The absurdity of the appraisal theory is that judgment, as a quantitative function, should assign a value to intensity or an appellation to couples, as to wine or cheese. A judgment theory should *predict* attraction and whether it will endure. Indeed, the appraisal of one partner by the other, if rational and objective, should be shared by impartial observers, or at least not widely disputed. Yet if the appraisal is specific to the lover, how can it be termed objective? How does reason apply when love develops on discontent and needs that are unsatisfied, of which the lover may not be fully aware.

Moreover, it is not clear what would ground a consensual opinion. We know couples who are inseparable and disconsolate with brief separations and others who thrive on partings, longings, and reunions. We know individuals with partners twice or half their age. We know some more strongly bound by argument than agreement. We know those who seek one sort of person and fall in love with another. Do opposites attract and similarities grow tiresome, or the reverse? Is like drawn to like, or must needs complement, not correspond? Can one predict an attraction, judge its success or forecast that a couple will fall in or out of love? Given the variation in need and personality, the idea that rational judgment can assess, determine, initiate, facilitate, or terminate a love is an example of a false premiss that, if followed to its conclusion, arrives at a judgment only by reframing or eliminating its topic.

Love dictated by reason may seem perfect "on paper," but if needs are ignored or deemed neurotic, and if a sexual union is subordinate to that of spirit, what is left to join lovers but intellect, which leaves little to distinguish romantic love from that for a fine book or pleasing oration? A good character can guide a couple to exemplify values that are equitable, but the couple will be in love only if the "fit" of core personality binds them together. Reason leads to truth, but the only truth in love is authenticity. True love is true not because it is realistic and rational, but because it is shared and genuine. This is its truth. So long as the qualities of lovers are idealized, so long as subjectivity and reciprocity prevail, so long as lovers are fulfilled in fantasy or actuality, the union is true to their needs. Reason must judge love to be true in this way irrespective of the substrates on which it develops, and regardless of whether the love flows from impulse or deliberation. This is not to deny that a loving friendship and tender feelings can develop on an appraisal of qualities, but rather to question the importance of conscious judgment in true love, where it is more often its antidote than its warrant.

How does judgment enter the process through which love develops? If *unconscious* judgment or appraisal determines the attraction to the other, one difference between conscious and unconscious decision is that of doubt. Hesitation, choice, and indecision are alien to the unconscious, where certainty prevails. This is the basis of the totality of a love that arises from need. Choice, uncertainty and doubt are attributes of consciousness and reflect the presence of options even if choices have not resolved with clarity. The unconscious does not so much choose A as eliminate B, C, and D. The elimination is an implicit failure in the evocation of a match, not a rejection, which is its conscious equivalent. The failure of evocation trickles into consciousness as rejection or disinterest. Reasons are given why those not chosen were unsuitable, but the fundamental reason, unlike the match to A, is that B, C, and D did not satisfy unconscious need.

Judgment is the rationalization for the giving of reasons, for love or its loss, as for all states of affairs. Judgment may be fair, but it is not an impartial weighing of the facts, as it is so often claimed. Apart from indifference to the outcome of a judgment or when nothing is at stake, some bias will inevitably creep into decision, whether it prevails or has to be overcome. The judgment isolates, and thus magnifies, the positive or negative qualities on which it depends; finally it will discredit, trivialize or deride arguments that are counter to its conclusions. This tactic conflicts with the concept of rational judgment as honest and impartial, but it is evident even in the arguments and opinions of the Supreme Court. In philosophy, where reason is the method and truth is the aim, we recall Whitehead's remark that philosophy is not—or at least should not be—a ferocious debate between irritable professors, but a dispassionate search for the truth. In philosophy, the fact, the theory, the alternatives, and the ideal are weighed together. Its gifts are insight and foresight, and a sense of importance which nerves all civilized effort (Whitehead, 1933, p. 21).

In love, when judgment intervenes, it may pass to a stage where negation (refutation, disapproval) outweighs approval, and the justification can no longer be maintained. The failure to satisfy foundational assumptions will surface and occasion a shift from unconscious predisposition to conscious choice. Uncertainty arises from the incompleteness of the unconscious match (assimilation), not indecision over whether or not the match is good. A betrayal of trust is one cause of the death of the ideal. When the person begins to wonder whether s/he is faithful, does s/he love me, faith turns to doubt, uncertainty sets in, feeling is withheld and love, if love is still alive, is no longer unconditional. We can think of choice as conscious or unconscious, but unconscious choice "informs" consciousness and deceives the self to think it chooses. An unconscious path becomes a conscious option, commitment becomes contingent and love is aborted to avoid further unhappiness. The uncertainty that is common at the onset of an encounter, say, when one meets a potential lover, is natural to gradually falling in love, but this uncertainty is for a belief that is waiting for confirmation, not a doubt the belief is true.

In the derivation of unconscious to conscious thought, conviction becomes provisional as the ideal objectifies in deliberation. Reason hesitates on the possibility of disconfirmation, whereas unconscious need is absolute. Need seeks reinforcement, judgment awaits assurance. The person must be convinced the other is worthy and that love will be reciprocated. Attributes are weighted according to needs, to adaptability, to openness and compromise. Once a lover is persuaded of the truth of a belief, hopes consolidate, conscious feeling withdraws to unconscious need and the bond is secured. There is a shift from what is possible in the unconscious to what is adaptive in consciousness. In unconscious belief, potential is not a sum of possibilities but a bias or proclivity. The shift can begin in need with an immediacy of closure and pass to feelings of affection and friendship, or it can begin with a conscious attraction, with love uncovered on a first impression. The beloved discloses the lover's need, or fulfills the lover's desire, much as when a skeptical believer has a divine revelation. The revelation is not "revaluation" or sudden awareness of something, but an uncovering of what was hidden. Intimacy allows a retreat to the unconscious where need inherits the choice that is relinquished in judgment.

The direction of thought is from unconscious drive to conscious reason, but when reason is suspended, in faith or in love, the shift from inner to outer, from totality to diversity, though uni-directional, can appear to go in the reverse direction. This descent of reason to its antecedents, that is, their incomplete revival, is not a true reversal. Ordinarily in the transition to desire, the consummation of need in the core passes to the definiteness of the object in consciousness. This allows the intensity of desire to focus on one object-ideal to the exclusion of others, but in the fractionation to the outer there is a diversity of explicit targets. For a largely conscious feeling, when desire is subdued or not all-consuming, the individual can go from one lover to another. In contrast, the unity of the unconscious rests on the effacement of what is displeasing by its immersion in the categorical.

A desire seems to begin in consciousness but invariably rests on an unconscious source. The intentionality of desire seems optional—one can act or not act on the desire—but whatever action is forthcoming, or vetoed, depends on sub-surface forces of which the individual is often unaware. The claims of childhood experience on decisions twenty or more years later, which for psa are the mummified remains of juvenile traumas, become the configural biases that drive the act. To emphasize the importance of conscious judgment in mate selection is to disregard the unconscious antecedents that condition the conscious outcomes. A judgment that appears to be rational and objective is little more than an explication of "decisions" to which the naïve self is predisposed. A clearer understanding of the mental state and the process through which it actualizes renders such ideas untenable no matter how plausible they appear.

Language and feeling

This argument should not be taken to imply a dissociation of reason and feeling. On the contrary, it implies the very opposite, that every feeling involves a judgment and every judgment entails a feeling. The feeling inside the judgment arises in the concepts out of which the judgment develops. It is ironic that judgment is used to evaluate feeling when judgment is an outcome of the feeling it purports to assess. The problem is clearer if we speak of concepts instead of judgment or reason, and if we first consider the relation of feeling to language. Concepts without emotion lack value and direction; emotions without concepts have no aims or objects. Feeling selects the objects that concepts carve out. The concept is an abstract frame embodied in feeling, while feeling is the formative energy of the concept. Concept and feeling are two limbs of the arc of intentionality—the desire and the object—with feeling giving the direction and concepts the aim.

The affective intensity of unconscious drive leads to conscious reason (words, language) by way of conceptual-feelings. Every utterance or act of thought resolves from drive categories that mitigate to desire and intentional feeling. While the path from drive to object is itself part of the object, an attenuation of feeling in the course of percept-development leads to thoughts that seem free of emotion, or to objects that seem independent of feeling. The object is not a product or target but a trajectory that begins with unconscious drive. The entire sequence, from drive through intentional feeling to the final idea or object, is a single act of cognition that embodies the content of its aim. Each recurrence from base to surface occurs over segments, which are treated as functions or components that interact. For example, we say that ideas are triggered by emotion or that reasons evaluate feelings or that thoughts are applied to objects. The affect-development is described independent of its objects; thinking is described independent of thought. The final outcome (object, thought) is cleaved from its actualization and treated in isolation. In truth, feeling evolves with objects and determines which ones are thought about, while ideas and words develop in the specification of conceptual-feeling.

An object-concept leads to objects, a lexical-concept to words; in both, there is a progression from the general to the particular. Reason involves the selection of words out of concepts and the partition or allocation of conceptual-feeling to a rational string of words as mental objects. The underlying coherence of lexical or verbal concepts leads to a pattern of words that makes sense, while the words seem to strive after the very concepts they discharge. The serial actualization of words in speech gives a collective realization of the potential and intensity of antecedent concepts. Some words, such as obscenities, are like objects, in that they embody the full intensity of background concepts, while most utterances or "mental statements" discharge concepts over time. Words as objects can have a strong affective tonality, especially in verbal rage or profanity, when the concept is compressed in words that are vehicles for the discharge of emotion. The derivation of concepts to words is comparable to that for objects, except that the serial order of speech transmits conceptual feeling over time, while objects discharge feeling directly. A string of words that unpacks a concept tends to dissipate feeling, though rhetorical skill and poetry can sustain feeling, even increase it, over an extended utterance.

The affective tone of concepts is most prominent intra-psychically and loses strength as concepts externalize in objects. Desire is *intra-psychic* but goes out with (into) an object as value, which is apprehended as *extra-personal*. The intra-psychic in language or perception is felt as a personal experience, while the extra-personal is perceived in the world. In sum, words and tones discharge concepts over time, objects satisfy them at once. The immediacy of meaning in the object contrasts with verbal or musical concepts that build up meanings and feelings over time. In music, in objects and in words, we are often uncertain whether feeling is in the mind or in the world, that is, is the beauty or feeling in the mind, or in the discourse, or in the melody?

The affective power of attenuated word-objects is reminiscent of animal sounds, barking, yelping, where vocalization is bound to feeling. The bark of a dog or the cry of a monkey is a signal of interest, hunger, danger, or anger. In the primitive state, vocalization and emotion are inseparable. In human speech, words seem liberated from the feelings behind them. We say the words describe or express feelings, not that they exhibit them, or that the expressive function of language gives way to the descriptive function. Feelings can be conveyed in words but also concealed or disguised. This gives the impression that language is extrinsic to feeling or that the relation is arbitrary. Words that deceive do not export the feelings they dissimulate, but that feeling is retained in the betrayal.

Words are "little objects," in which the affective tone is related to the background concept and the degree of partition. Words differ from objects in their dynamic of replacement and the constraints on recurrence. The constraints on speech are mostly internal, those in perception largely external. Musical concepts—in perception, song or composition—are similar to those in language, except for the relative lack of meaning in pure music. Tonal-objects that issue from musical concepts are affect-laden. Feeling is retained in the psychic locus of words and tones in contrast to auditory or visual objects. We are moved by hearing words and music, but only when they are felt "in the head," not in the world. The deep intrapsychic bond of language and feeling is seen in poetry, where few people can appreciate the beauty of poetry in a non-native language. This also applies, though to a lesser degree, to a musical idiom; apart from issues of personal taste, a melody in an unfamiliar idiom is unlikely to seem beautiful until the idiom is assimilated. The beauty of language, for example, in the compactness and imagery of poetry, has the most striking effect when the words are felt as intra-psychic. We often close our eyes to shut out the world and accentuate the feeling and the beauty. The emotive content of objects is less apparent, for they are driven outward by constraints on emergent form. Personal feeling is also reduced on detachment, while words and tones resonate in the psyche. What is left behind gives the object its emotive force. In object perception, affect is distributed in the relative stasis of external objects, while feeling in language and music is sustained in fluid transition.

In this respect it is useful to consider writing or composition. In my experience, feeling can be more pronounced in writing than spoken speech. In the latter, there is often an unspoken reservoir of feeling that is more fully enjoyed in writing. Spoken words, along with the feeling inside them, are ejected in the world where they perish, while written words are private until the thought is complete. Speech is constrained by the need to communicate to a listener; writing has a "freer hand." In some writers, the fear that creative energy will be lost once an idea is articulated makes them unwilling to discuss a work in progress. The conceptual-feeling that goes into writing is satisfied when the writing is over. This is no less the case for an email when the SEND button is pressed and the emotion is depleted. Is feeling expressed in creative poetry in a state of vivid emotion, or more likely, as Wordsworth wrote, does it come later in reverie and repose?

The series from concept to object leads to a stable world; that from concept to speech or verbal thought is in constant transformation. The two series are in parallel and rapidly iterated, with change or stability according to the objects replaced. The frequency of recurrence is identical for all "components" of cognition: action, perception, language. In altered states, a change in the frequency of replacement can affect object stability. A visual object such as a horse is replaced like words or tones except that the similarity of replications maintains a horse-like form and category even as the animal wanders about in a field. In speech, the antecedent concept gives coherence to what would otherwise be a succession of individual sounds. The process is the same, except that the object—in this case, the word—differs in each replication, so the background concept, its feeling and meaning, compensates for the lack of object similarity. This holds for music as well, where the musical theme is the glue of succession of individual words or sounds. When this is not readily accessible, as in atonal music, the sequence may seem random.

The behaviorist idea that one word calls up the next in causal linkage implies external relations. This idea survives in neural diagrams or circuit boards, though it was refuted by Chomsky, who argued that an utterance emanates from a core, or kernel, with parsing at successive levels. A series of visual objects assumed to be mind-independent does not so easily build up feeling, as is the case in film, where we sense that a mind is guiding the imagery. Film lacks the substantiality of objects and retains the affect that is lost in a transition to actuality. Unlike images or dream, the replacement of ordinary objects does not have a narrative other than its causal history, though some are tempted to infer meaning—fate, destiny, intelligent design—in the passage of events and physical nature. The less an object externalizes, the greater the feeling and meaning. Concepts and images are intra-psychic and thus felt more than objects, just as meaning is felt more than the words by which it is instantiated. Feeling as value in perceptual objects is less pronounced than in speech. Words, like actions, do not detach from the speaker, but occupy a space transitional from mind to world.

The fact that language does not just express feeling but evaluates and conceals it suggests to many that language and feeling are independent realms of cognition. When language conceals emotion, feeling remains undischarged. To have simultaneous thoughts is to have two concepts with differing affect-tone, perhaps derived from a state of conflict or ambiguity. Words are not autonomous instruments for the manipulation of thoughts, or the expression, description and concealment of feelings; they are mental objects serially generated out of affectively charged concepts. These concepts can accrue feeling, they can distribute into mental images (verbal, visual) of poetic imagination, they can go to immediate discharge, for example, anger, or they can undergo specification to abstract and relatively affect-free discourse. However, even the most elegant and reasoned elocution has, in its intentional character, an affect-laden source.

With this in mind, we can reconstruct the process through which conceptual-feeling passes into verbalization and thought. Antecedent and affectively charged object-concepts arise from core beliefs and values in relation to drive-energy. These pass to implicit beliefs and conceptual-feelings, then to lexical-concepts that, in overlapping tree-like patterns, partition a sequence of words or verbal images.

The coherence of the concept at each phase and the adaptation of the system of beliefs to actual conditions determine the rationality and utility of the thought. The partition is such as to diminish the feeling-tone in any single word. The feeling, which is most pronounced in the concept and its transition to imagery, is generated by the revival and satisfaction of the concept and the rapid replacement of speech sounds that dissipate affect in serial exposition. Like objects, the feeling in words can be concentrated in images, oaths or ejaculations or spread over sentences in serial discharge. In the former, the emotional content is obvious, in the latter, less so, and still less when the concept is abstract and relatively distant from the primary needs of the individual.

Meaning and feeling

Concepts are repositories of the implicit beliefs, values, and experiential memories that together give coloration to the affective tone that energizes them. These ingredients, which constitute the meaning or context of the concept, pass with increasing specificity to object and lexical concepts. At the base of the mental state, meaning is bound up with belief and value in relation to long-term memory; together, this makes up individual character. The qualities of the core are elicited at the onset of each act of cognition. To believe is to value, to value is to apply meaning, and to have meaning is to have value for the individual in conformity with implicit beliefs. The feeling for an object is bound up with its value, its value is bound up with its meaning, and its meaning realizes some aspect of the person's system of beliefs. This complex determines the bias, predisposition or proclivity to an outcome before the actual outcome is selected.

At the phase of object- or lexical-concepts, meaning takes on reference, or has an object as an incipient goal, that is, a figural contrast replete with meaning before the aim resolves. The cascade from meaning as potential to meaning as goal continues from one phase to the next, leading from generalized potential to definition and diversity. Finally, the image or object resolves and the aim is evident. Non-specific meaningfulness is non-intentional. This may develop to precision as connotation specifies to reference or subjective aim. Tacit context resolves to external reference, feeling becomes object value, and the emotive content of language achieves precise formulation in speech.

What can we say of value and belief apart from their contents? Usually, we speak of the value of an object or person, which is felt to be in the object or projected on it; but without an object, how can value be described? A core value such as courage is not apparent without exemplifications. Meaning is like value in this respect. It is the direction of feeling to a future outcome, including the contextual relations that guide the proclivity to that outcome. In language, meaning may become clear to the speaker only after the words have been spoken. Many discover what they think by talking about it. A person might exclaim, "yes, that is what I meant to say," or "what I really mean is that ...."

How is feeling related to meaning, belief and value? I would say, feeling is embedded in experiential context, which includes meaning, belief and value; value is related to desire and object worth; belief is related to truth and knowledge, meaning is the category of relations or interpretations in which a word or object appears. But these distinctions depend on conscious content, not phases prior to resolution. How can we describe the meaning of a word prior to its selection? The idea of markers, lexical features, semantic distance, fields of meaning-relations, category prototypes, employ contents to describe a process before it objectifies. We sense this in expectancy, anticipation, apprehension, uncertainty, pressure, tension, or the experience of knowing that we know but not exactly what is it that is known.

In sum, the transformation from potential to actual over micro-temporal phases in the passage from core category to act or object accompanies an affect-development intrinsic to each phase, elaborating a more or less identifiable feeling that reflects the dominant affect at a given segment, as well as feelings summoned up over the entire process. A state of apprehension, of desire or fear, of attraction or object-value, reveals which phase is dominant in the actualization. The more penetrating question, however, concerns the inner relation of affect and idea, which is a metaphysical problem that conceives feeling, process or change as becoming, and idea, substance, or stability as being (Brown, 2005, 2010a).

Objectivity and truth

If the truth of love is its authenticity, completeness or wholeness, what kind of truth is this, and how does it relate to the conventional account of truth in relation to statements of fact? The authentic is a kind of fact, but one that is more like beauty or aesthetics than truth reached by logic or demonstration. As long as love is subjective it will resist externalist interpretations; as soon as love becomes objective it relinquishes feeling and the inner life. This is the dilemma of those in love and those who write about it. To feel love is to be unable to describe it, at least while it is felt, while to describe it is not to feel it, at least not when it is described. Like love, mystical descent can be described but not the experience of union, which is invariably said to be ineffable. Fragments of the experience and phases in the descent can be retrieved that reinforce the genuineness of such claims. Such accounts confirm a different quality of feeling over phases in descent, and an inability to describe mentality prior to object-specification. The ineffable is the union of feeling, value, and belief at a phase that is inaccessible, that is, cannot be revived to consciousness. When a subjective point of view is replaced by an objective one, or feeling goes to third-party observation, the account loses its meaning and immediacy.

Fortunately for the chroniclers of love, objectivity has its day when love gravitates to evaluation or justification, as objectionable traits are rationalized or qualified. What remains as long as feeling endures is a mode of loving, perhaps a stage when *eros* ends and *philia* begins or romance goes to friendship. Friendship does not usually involve idealization, nor does mutuality require self-sacrifice. Friends come together out of wants, not needs, when conscious selection and appraisal have greater relevance. Friendship is closer to choice and shared interests; romantic love to unconscious need, often for the opposite in personality. We do not long for a friend as for a beloved, and partings are not as painful. The locus of friendship between love and acquaintance, necessity and choice, instinct and reason, makes it a valuable stepping stone from the thornier problem of passion to the tractable one of reason. It provides an alternative to the difficulties of emotion, and allows a cleavage of love from reason for a description in relation to judgment and language. The justification for this turn is discussed above, but it is facilitated by the absence of a vocabulary for emotivity, the instability of the dynamic of feeling, the distinction, since Plato, of reason and appetite, and current-day philosophy grounded in externalism, propositional attitudes and truth judgments.

The argument that love follows appraisal, rejected in the prior discussion, would still have to distinguish implicit (unconscious) and explicit (conscious) judgment, the former that of commitment and romantic fulfillment, the latter a frank assessment of the attributes of self and other, the qualities of the union and its rationale. The implicit judgment is the intuitive knowing that this is the right person and the selection of that person by way of attributes that may not be evident to consciousness. For an explicit judgment one should be as severe on the one who judges as on the one judged, for this will determine whether the compatibility of attributes and the harmony of fit or adaptation are authentic, delusional or a simulacrum. Yet the ability to judge one's own internal states, even less those of others, in love or other feelings or experiences, is severely limited. Love is not created by an inventory of qualities, no less than the taste of a meal is experienced on reading a recipe. The extension of this argument is that one cannot feel any emotion or any experience from a description of the underlying brain events. We cannot go from a third-person description to a first-person experience, though process theory does attempt to account for external events from a subjective point of view.

Evolution of love and language

There is much to be said of the relation of love to language, especially if we compare it to animals, where, in spite of maternal attachment, coupling and the appearance of grief on loss, it is doubtful they experience the equivalent of human love. We naturally assume that language makes the difference, so it is reasonable to think that language makes love possible, not just as a mode of expressing love but as a vehicle of thought essential to the arousal of love and its growth or decay over time. The question then arises: is love based on language and not possible without it, and not just language but a life-experience shaped, revived, and interpreted through language, as well as the beliefs and values that depend on language and many attributes of the self that are language-dependent, all of which go into the creation of the self and the selection of the beloved?

When children fall in love we speak of "puppy love," which alludes not only to immaturity but to a kind of animal bonding at a lower stage in evolution. If puppy love is not real or genuine love but a form of infatuation, a "crush," the maturity necessary for true love cannot be solely a result of language, since most children, by early adolescence, have reached an adult level of language acquisition. Rather, children do not have an adequate life experience, their emotions are coarse and they are selfish. This is why puppy love in childhood, though it may fully possess the child, is seen as shallow and transient, even if we describe it as honest, pure, and innocent. This is because lust is less a factor in young children than, say, curiosity, the senses are not jaded and feeling is sincere. There may be desire aplenty, and the child is closer to the inner life of imagination where love is born, even if the scope of fantasy is limited, and the still-forming self-concept assimilates more readily with the other; there is insufficient depth and refinement of emotion for the ferocity of commitment, the delicacy of intuition and the distinction of need and want within which the ideal is formed, qualities that are most essential for genuine loving. At later stages, infatuation differs from early childhood "puppy love" in that, so it is argued, it is generally short-lived and driven by lust.

It may be that love is not possible without language or some mode of communication, but what part in love does language play? Some language is probably needed to convey information between lovers, but the feeling of sincerity is in other forms of action, not words. When a lover hears the beloved and asks, does she really mean what she says, the lover is not searching for meaning but for truth and sincerity. We can say, "I love you with all my heart," but love is not in the heart. We can say, "I love you with all my soul," but the soul does not exist. Rarely, one says, "with all my mind," even if self-knowledge is limited and statements of feeling, if not deceptive, are often contradictory. It is common to hear a person enumerate all the reasons why the beloved is not right, yet the love—and who is to say it is not true love?—persists in spite of critical judgment. In sum, language and meaning make love possible by supporting the feeling of love and other desires. Without language, love might not develop, but it is not the conscious realization of words that is essential to love, but rather their precursors laid down in the formation and recurrence in every mental state.

Love: momentary and lasting

Proust wrote, "love, ever unsatisfied, lives always in the moment that is about to come." This is true of present experience. There is no bounded present, rather a now in continuous transformation, passing but not moving into the ensuing moment. The immediacy of feeling in love is more than oneness with the beloved; it is immersion in the ongoing, a sensibility to the exquisitely brief and the infinitely long, to time that "stands still" and time of extensive duration, a present suspended in time with a love that never dies, like Eliot's "music heard so deeply ... you are the music while the music lasts." In that moment, lovers feel an intimation of eternity. This feeling is depicted in art, as in the Ode of Keats', "she cannot fade, though thou hast not thy bliss, forever wilt thou love, and she be fair." In the timelessness of this moment, lovers vow their love *forever*!

What is it about the immediacy of love in all its fullness that usurps the totality of an instant as everlasting? Eternal love is not love that lasts for an eternal succession of instants, which even lovers know to be untrue, but in a felt oneness with the timeless duration of a point. The duration elaborated in a point is virtual, not incremented into an open-ended succession. The lack of incrementation and the indistinctness of boundaries allow for contraction to a point and expansion without limits. The feeling of *all-time* in the now is accompanied by the belief, at that moment, that the now is forever. The illusion of a love that transcends death and lasts for all future time has similarities to religious beliefs and the creative in art.

The fixation of real or imagined experience in an artwork transmutes into structure the transient and formless. This is the enduring gift of the imagination to the incessant perishing of the real. In the transformation of potential to actual, art shifts the internal and the dynamic to the external and enduring, recalling that moment of love when only now exists and, tenseless, exists forever. The finality of the artwork and the feeling that love is everlasting are not tokens of objectivity but types of a subjective ideal. The pattern in art is the reverse of love: from imagination to reality, from the non-temporal to the temporal, from an insubstantial image to an external solid, yet the aim of great art is an immortal work that lives on in the creative imagination, just as true love creates a timeless ideal out of a passing object.

Feeling is momentary, true belief is eternal. Feelings recur among individuals, but true beliefs—truths—are conceived as independent of those who believe them. Mystics know well that a true belief is always true, that is, is an eternal idea, when applied to love and in combination with intense feeling. This experience was beautifully described by Meister Eckert. The feeling of infinite duration that is the goal of meditation appears when the personal now expands to the limitless now of god's mind or, from a god's-eye perspective, to individual feeling. The now of the mystic spans or collapses all time in a oneness with nature or love-union with god. The trance of true love is union with the beloved. If personal or romantic love is prior to religious feeling, to participate in universal mind or all-consuming love would be a sublimation or extrapolation of feeling to religious or spiritual contact. Yet religious feeling may be founded on instinctual submission and the awe from which reverence for god is derived, with romantic love a secondary development. The more interesting possibility is that true love is an expression of—a path into—the deeper ground of religious awakening.

To become one with experience is the elusive aim of an impersonal reason that stands outside and engages. Reason is commentary. So too is art, but not life. To surrender to the moment is to be, not to mean. In relinquishing, one recaptures the before and after prior to the cleavage of a past that can be revived from a present that hovers over passage. Life lived in the present without knowing it is enlightened by the past without remembering it. Life directed to the future without detachment from what is ongoing is the aim of becoming. The oneness of true love has lovers clasped in nature's passage, as in the now of dream, when there is no agency, no past, no future, and a self passive to its own imagery. The experience of loving sexual union is not love replicated by sex. Coupling may be a heartfelt and mutual infiltration or an external contact that simulates union. External contact is not fusion, but even fusion is a misnomer for a coming-together that regains initial wholeness before the first duality.

What is common to these states is the collapse of past and future in the knife-edge of a now. This is not the specious present of ordinary wakefulness, not a stretch of virtual time that separates past and future, but an island of experience in an ocean of duration, the time of *Hua-Yen* Buddhism (Oden, 1982) with a now embedded in all-time past and future. In the mental state of such an occasion, object-formation does not carry the simultaneity of the unconscious into conscious temporal order. This gives the all-in-all of love, the rapture of artistic inspiration, a potential not yet partitioned to images and objects, the descent to mystical insight and religious intuition and a state of meaningfulness without meaning.

Note

1. The film "10" popularizes this idea in relation to the beauty of a woman, while the jokes that followed, for example, a 10 is a 3 with $7 million, merely reinforce the property/appraisal argument.

REFERENCES

Alberoni, F. (Ed.). (1981/1983). *Falling in Love*. New York: Random House.

Alexander, F. (1965). A note to the theory of perversions. In: S. Lorand & M. Balint (Eds.), *Perversions, Psychodynamics and Therapy* (pp. 3–15). New York: Random House.

Baudrillard, J. (1979). *Seduction* (B. Singer Trans.). New York: St. Martin's Press.

Bergmann, M. (1987). *The Anatomy of Loving*. New York: Columbia University Press.

Bradford, D. (2011). Brain and psyche in early Christian asceticism. *Psychological Reports, 2* (6): 461–520.

Brown, J. W. (1967). Physiology and phylogenesis of emotional expression. *Brain Research, 5*: 1–14.

Brown, J. W. (1986). Cingulate gyrus and supplementary motor correlates of vocalization in man. In: J. Newman (Ed.), *The Physiological Control of Mammalian Vocalization* (pp. 227–244). New York: Plenum.

Brown, J. W. (1996). *Time, Will and Mental Process*. New York: Plenum.

Brown, J. W. (1998). Psychoanalysis and process theory. In: R. Bilder & F. LeFever (Eds.), *Neuroscience of the Mind on the Centennial of Freud's Project for a Scientific Psychology. Annals of the New York Academy of Science, 843*: 91–106.

Brown, J. W. (2000). *Mind and Nature*. London: Whurr.

Brown, J. W. (2003). Value in mind and nature. In: F. Riffert & M. Weber (Eds.), *Searching for New Contrasts: Whiteheadian Contributions to Contemporary Challenges in Neurophysiology, Psychology, Psychotherapy and the Philosophy of Mind*. Vienna: Peter Lang.

Brown, J. W. (2005). *Process and the Authentic Life*. Heusenstamm: Ontos Verlag.

Brown, J. W. (2008). The inward path: Mysticism and creativity. *Creativity Research Journal, 20*: 365–375 [reprinted in J. W. Brown, 2010].

Brown, J. W. (2010a). *Neuropsychological Foundations of Conscious Experience*. Belgium: Chromatika.

Brown, J. W. (2010b). Simultaneity and serial order. *Journal of Consciousness Studies, 17*: 7–40.

Brown, J. W. (2011). The relation of embryology to linguistic and cognitive process. *Journal of Psycholinguistic Research, 40*: 189–194. Available at: http://www.springerlink.com/content/104271/

Buss, D. (1994). *The Evolution of Desire*. New York: Basic Books.

Denny-Brown, D. (1963). The physiological basis of perception and speech. In: L. Halpern, L. (Ed.), *Problems of Dynamic Neurology*. Jerusalem University Press: Jerusalem.

Dewan, E. (1976). Consciousness as an emergent causal agent in the context of control systems theory. In G. Globus, G. Maxwell & I. SAvodnik (Eds.), *Consciousness and the Brain*. New York: Basic Books.

Fisher, H. (2004). *Why We Love*. New York: Holt.

Freud, S. (1905). *Fragment of an Analysis of a Case of Hysteria*.

Friedman, P. (1959). Sexual deviation. In: S. Arieti (Ed.), *American Handbook of Psychiatry* (pp. 589–613). New York: Basic Books.

Gorer, G. (1966). *The Danger of Equality*. New York: Weybright & Talley.

Greenson, R. (1978). *Explorations in Psychoanalysis*. New York: IUP.

Hamlyn, D. (1978). The phenomena of love and hate. *Philosophy, 53* (5): 5–20.

Helm, B. (2005). Love. *Stanford Encyclopedia of Philosophy*.

Hofstadter, D. (1996). *The Love Affair as a Work of Art*. New York: Strauss and Giroux.

Hölderlin, F. (Ed.). (1969). *Hyperion*, English Transl. University of Pennsylvania Press.

Isaacson, R. & Spear, N. (Eds). (1982). *The Expression of Knowledge*. New York: Plenum.

Jaffe, J., Beebe, B., Feldstein, S., Crown, C. L. & Jasnow, M. D. (2001). Rhythms of dialogue in infancy. In: W. D. Overton (Ed.), Monographs of the Society for Research in Child Development, serial number 265, *66* (2).

James, W. (1884). What is an emotion? *Mind, 9*: 188–205.

Jung, C. G. (1961). *Memories, Dreams, Reflections*. New York: Random House.

Kaplan, L. (1991). *Female Perversions*. New York: Jason Aronson.

Kohut, H. (1971). *The Analysis of the Self*. New York: IUP.

Kolodny, N. (2003). Love as valuing a relationship. *The Philosophical Review*, 112: 135–189.

Krafft-Ebing, R. von (Ed.). (1965). *Psychopathia Sexualis*. (F. Klaf Trans.). New York: Stein and Day.

Leowald, H. (2000). *The Essential Leowald*. College Park, MD: University of Maryland Publishing.

Leuba, J. (1925). *The Psychology of Religious Mysticism*. London: Kegan Paul.

Lewin, K. & Zeigarnik, B. (1948). ... In: K. Lewin (Ed.), *Resolving Social Conflicts*. New York: Harper and Brothers.

Lévi-Strauss, C. (1964). *Le cru et le cuit*. Paris: Plon.

Lévi-Strauss, C. (1968/1978). *The Origin of Table Manners*. New York: Harper Colophan.

Lévy-Brühl, L. (1935/1983). *Primitive Mentality*. St. Lucia: University of Queensland Press.

Lewis, C. S. (1936). *The Allegory of Love*. London: Oxford University Press.

Linke, D. (2005). *Holderlin als Hirnforscher*. Frankfurt: Suhrkamp.

Lorenz, K. (1971). *Studies in Animal and Human Behavior*. Cambridge, MA: Harvard University Press.

MacLean, P. (1990). *The Triune Brain in Evolution*. New York: Plenum.

Mahler, M., Pine, F. & Bergmann, A. (Ed.). (2002). *The Psychological Birth of the Human Infant*. New York: Karnac.

McTaggart, J. M. (1901). *Studies in Hegelian Cosmology*. Cambridge: Cambridge University Press.

Nielsen, J. (1936). *Agnosia, Apraxia, Aphasia*. Los Angeles: Los Angeles Neurological Society.

Oden, S. (1982). *Process Metaphysics and Hua-Yen Buddhism*. Albany, NY: SUNY Press.

Pachalska, M., MacQueen, B. & Brown, J. W. (2012). Microgenetic theory: Brain and mind in time. In: R. Rieber (Ed.), *Encyclopedia of the History of Psychological Theories*. Springer.

Pascal, B. (Ed.). (1669/2006). *The Mind on Fire*. (Ed. J. Houston). Colorado: Victor.

Polanyi, M. (1974). *Personal Knowledge*. Chicago: University of Chicago Press.

Prinz, J. (2004). *Gut Reactions*. Oxford: Oxford University Press.

Rapaport, D. (1951). *Organization and Pathology of Thought*. New York: Columbia University Press.

Sander, F. (1928). *Ganzheitspsychologie*. Munich: Beck.

Santayana, G. (1923). *Skepticism and Animal Faith*. New York: Scribner.

Schachtel, E. (1947). Memory and childhood amnesia. *Psychiatry, 10*: 1–26.

Schilder, P. (1942). *Goals and Desires of Man*. New York: Columbia University Press.

Schilder, P. & Bender, L. (1964). *Contributions to Developmental Neuropsychology*. New York: International Universities Press.

Schneirla, T. (1966). Behavioural development and comparative psychology. *Quarterly Reviews in Biology, 41*: 283–302.

Schroeder, T. (2004). *Three Faces of Desire*. Oxford: Oxford University Press.

Silz, W. (1969). *Holderlin's Hyperion: A Critical Reading*. Philadelphia, PA: University of Pennsylvania Press.

Singer, I. (1994). *The Pursuit of Love*. Baltimore: Johns Hopkins University Press.

Smith, G. & Carkssin, I. (2001). *The Creative Functioning Test—Manual*. Lund, Sweden: Department of Psychology.

Steele, M. (2003). Attachment, actual experience and mental representations. In: V. Green (Ed.), *Emotional Development in Psychoanalysis, Attachment Theory and Neuroscience*. New York: Brunner-Routledge.

Valéry, P. (1943). *Mauvaises pensées et autres*. Paris: Gallimard.

Velleman, J. (1999). Love as a moral emotion. *Ethics, 109*: 338–337.

Von Domarus, E. (1944). The specific laws of logic in schizophrenia. In: J. Kassanin (Ed.), *Language and Thought in Schizophrenia* (pp. 104–114). Berkeley, CA: University of California Press.

Vygotsky, L. (1962). *Thought and Language*. Cambridge, MA: MIT Press.

Whitehead, A. N. (1933). *Adventure of Ideas*. New York: MacMillan.

Whitrow, G. (1972). *What is Time?* London: Thames and Hudson.